SAD MEN

Dave Roberts

BANTAM BOOKS

LONDON • TORONTO • SYDNEY • AUCKLAND • JOHANNESBURG

TRANSWORLD PUBLISHERS
61–63 Uxbridge Road, London W5 5SA
www.transworldbooks.co.uk

Transworld is part of the Penguin Random House group of companies
whose addresses can be found at global.penguinrandomhouse.com

First published in Great Britain in 2014 by Bantam Press
an imprint of Transworld Publishers
Bantam edition published 2015

A CIP catalogue record for this book
is available from the British Library.

ISBN
9780857501752

Typeset in Ehrhardt by Falcon Oast Graphic Art Ltd.
Printed and bound by Clays Ltd, St Ives plc

Penguin Random House is committed to a sustainable
future for our business, our readers and our planet. This book is
made from Forest Stewardship Council® certified paper.

1 3 5 7 9 10 8 6 4 2

Acclaim for *Sad Men*:

'Told with wit, warmth and an obsessive eye to detail that I have not seen since Nick Hornby was writing about pop music, *Sad Men* is both a brilliant memoir about a lifetime obsession with advertising and a heartfelt, curiously moving book that roams the world but always returns to the fantasies that were created by smart people trying to sell us stuff. Forget Don Draper – Dave Roberts is the world's favourite ad man.'
Tony Parsons

'Witty, wry and self-deprecating. Go buy!'
Freya North

'An insightful, eye-opening and often eye-wateringly funny tale.'
Sunday Sport

'If you wish to discover what kind of mad man becomes an ad man, the answers are to be found in *Sad Men*.'
Roger Lewis, *Daily Mail*, Book of the Week

'Genuinely enlightening . . . what is most surprising about the book, and the "obsession" detailed within, is just how moving and sympathetic it proves. There's a tendency to think of advertising as an intensely cynical industry, but what Roberts' story illustrates is that there is often an artistic impulse and integrity at play as well. More than this, *Sad Men* takes one of the bugbears of contemporary entertainment, product placement, and uses it in the most sincere and even heartfelt fashion.'
litro.co.uk

'A heart-warming memoir.'
thebookbag.co.uk

'Brilliant . . . always hilarious, and often wonderfully English. You'll love Dave . . . he's got real passion and drive. Funny and heartfelt.'
Book C**t

'Within the first few pages I was hooked . . . hard to put down.'
onemorepage.co.uk

Also by Dave Roberts

e-luv: an internet romance
The Bromley Boys
32 Programmes

This book is dedicated to Zac & Lila, Hazel & Ian, Billy & Frank, and Saatchi & Saatchi.

Prologue

By the time I was fourteen, my life was already planned out. I was going to marry the girl in the Flake advert (spoiler alert – that didn't happen) and become an award-winning copywriter for Saatchi & Saatchi, the world's finest advertising agency. The pursuit of the second and only marginally less ambitious part of this plan would take me halfway around the world before eventually ending up in America. Not in Madison Avenue and the glamorous, seductive world made famous by *Mad Men*, but in an average street a hundred miles from New York, in Hartford, Connecticut.

It was there, on a sweltering summer's day a few months ago, that I heard my wife Liz (who has never appeared in any chocolate ad) shout, 'Dave, the mailman's here with your package.'

'That's *post*man and *parcel*,' I mumbled, pushing myself away from the computer where I was writing an ad about frozen prawns, scheduled to appear in the October edition of *Sandwich and Snack News*. Even though we'd been living in her parents' attic for a couple of years, I had adapted to living in the US in typical British fashion – by not adapting at all.

As I leapt down the stairs, taking several at a time, I felt a mounting sense of excitement. I'd been tracking this parcel online for days, charting its progress across the Atlantic. It had been to Heathrow, East Midlands Airport, Cincinnati Sorting Facility, West Hartford Sorting Facility, and now, finally, it was here.

After signing for it with a flourish, I took the box into the kitchen, keen to see how many things on my wish-list Nick, my brother-in-law, had managed to send. The idea was that being surrounded by some of the things I missed most about England would help me get over my homesickness – things like Cadbury's chocolate which you just can't get in the US, unless you go to places with names like 'Ye Olde English Shoppe', which I could obviously never do.

I opened the parcel and let out an involuntary shriek of delight when I saw the treasures within. Even Liz looked impressed – a long way from the look on her face when she had seen the last piece of mail I got from England and completely failed to grasp (a) the sheer desirability of the 1949 Romford v. Bromley programme, (b) what a small price £24 was to pay for it on eBay, and (c) the fact that I only had thirty-two programmes and badly needed more.

I lifted out a box of Weetabix and instantly felt even more nostalgic for home than usual, sparked by memories of some of the brilliant adverts I'd seen over the years. While Liz saw nothing more than a yellow cereal box, in my mind I saw the cartoon bovver boys from the 1980s, starring parrot-voiced Brian. They didn't just want itchy breakfasts, they wanted Weetabix.

And so did I. Tomorrow morning, I would introduce Liz to my favourite first meal of the day: two Weetabix with a generous amount of butter and a layer of Marmite ('The growing-up spread you never grow out of') which Nick had thankfully also included. It would be, as they said in later commercials, 'unbeat-a-bix'.

Next out of the box was a Topic bar, which looked much smaller than I remembered, but the jingle asking 'What has a hazelnut in every bite?' was soon running through my head (as was the playground response 'Squirrel poo!').

A couple of packets of Smith's Crisps (he'd thoughtfully put in one for Liz too) brought back images of singing potatoes who, to the tune of 'Bobby's Girl', insisted that they 'wanna be Smith's Crisps' because 'if we were, what tasty light and golden crisps we'd be'. It was almost enough to make me burst open my bag there and then.

But I resisted, as I needed to leave enough room for a slice of cake and a cup of tea. Not just any cake, but an exceedingly good Mr Kipling cake. And not just any tea, either, but PG Tips, forever associated in my mind with the exchange between Shifter and Son, piano movers, which began with the son saying, 'Dad, do you know the piano's on my foot?' Whereupon his father sniffed and wiped his hand under his nose before replying 'You hum it, son, and I'll play it' as he started banging the piano keys.

As I waited for the kettle to boil, I realized that British advertising still had the same hold on me it had always had. My thoughts drifted back to the time when PG Tips put me on a path that would shape my life, where adverts would dictate much of what I did, and the desire to be a part of the world that created them would become an all-encompassing obsession.

I was three years old at the time.

Part One

One

My earliest memory is seeing a chimpanzee driving a van to a small shop on the high street. He then got a few boxes out of the back and delivered them to the shopkeeper, who was also a chimpanzee. If I had been old enough to know that I was watching an advert for PG Tips on TV and not real life, I'm sure I wouldn't have wasted much of my early childhood scouring Bromley High Street for a glimpse of van-driving chimps.

But the disappointment of not catching sight of them was soon overshadowed by the discovery of my new love. Advertising.

I learned to recognize the words 'End of Part One' when they appeared on screen, and stopped whatever I was doing (usually eating, or throwing things at my sister Miriam) to watch the adverts. From the outset they had a dramatic effect on my young life.

Whenever I dressed up as a cowboy, I borrowed my friend's NHS glasses so that I could look like the Milky Bar Kid, and instead of shouting things like 'Ride 'em cowboy!' I'd announce in a loud voice, 'The Milky Bars are on me!'

I took to following my mum around the house whenever she was about to go out, singing 'Don't forget my fruit gums,

Mum, I just love those fruit gums, Mum, don't forget my tube of fruit gums, those that last all day'. As she made a quicker than usual exit, I'd follow her down the front path repeating the words loudly. Although it worked for the boy in the advert, I was less successful: she usually came home having apparently forgotten my fruit gums. I'm sure she found my behaviour endearing and not in the least bit annoying.

A few years later, when my parents took me to the supermarket for the weekly shop, I followed them around, insisting that they replace the box of Persil washing powder in the trolley with Ariel. This was a product that had captured my imagination with its breakthrough use of hungry enzymes, which gobbled up dirt particles like prototype Pac-men. My mum, seemingly more convinced by Persil's 'whiter than white' argument, made me put the Ariel back on the shelf.

The battle over washing powder was forgotten a few months later when I was presented with a tube of Signal toothpaste. I had never wanted anything so much and had been so desperate to get it that I'd even promised to brush my teeth every night. As any TV viewer knew, Signal was different to every other toothpaste because it had a red stripe through it, which was made from hexachlorophene. This, the advert proudly proclaimed, sought out and destroyed millions of germs and apparently made your teeth really white. The results, in my case, were disappointing, but I convinced myself that I was finally free of germs that I didn't know existed.

While other kids lay awake at night thinking about dinosaurs and space travel, I pondered quandaries like 'If a million housewives every day pick up a tin of beans and say Beanz Meanz Heinz, how come I've never heard one single housewife say that?' and 'How *does* Mr Kipling manage to make so many exceedingly good cakes? He must never get any sleep.' I learned not to take slogans too literally after exploring the boundaries of Milky Way's claim to being 'the sweet you can eat between meals without ruining your appetite' by stuffing five down in quick succession.

Unlike most of my schoolmates, I didn't see Dusty Springfield as a panda-eyed, beehive-wearing permanent fixture in the Top Twenty, but as someone I desperately wanted to knock me up. This was inspired by her starring role in the Mother's Pride advert, in which she sang 'I'm a happy knocker upper, and I'm popular besides, 'cause I wake 'em with a cuppa and tasty Mother's Pride' while rapping on people's bedroom windows and offering a loaf of bread on a long-handled pole. Like you do.

Even my pre-pubescent fantasies were fuelled by what I'd seen on the flickering black and white screen in the breaks between programmes. I would often drift off to sleep imagining myself skiing down a rugged mountain, then adjusting my goggles, gazing with indifference at the sight of an avalanche that would have terrified lesser men, and calmly heading to a log cabin in the distance. My mission? To deliver a box of Milk Tray. The reason? All because the lady loved Milk Tray. (In my slightly confused version of events, the cabin door was opened not by the familiar Milk Tray-loving lady, but by the girl from the Flake commercial, whom I fancied more and desperately wanted to marry.)

When the time came to meet real live girls, I relied on adverts to give me the key to what they wanted. First of all, they wanted their men to smell of Old Spice; 'You'll become yourself, you'll find success' the ad promised, rather recklessly. I bought some. They also wanted someone who would take them to a Berni Inn for a romantic meal of prawn cocktail, steak and chips, and an Irish coffee to finish. As luck would have it, there was a Berni in Bromley High Street. The final piece of the puzzle was what drink they preferred, which seemed to be a toss-up between Martini ('Any time, any place, anywhere'), Babycham ('I'd love a Babycham'), and a Pony ('The little drink with the big kick').

The night before my first date, I could barely sleep. Even a mug of Horlicks ('The food drink of the night') failed to have the anticipated effect. For financial reasons, and because I was only fourteen, the whole Berni Inn/Martini/Babycham/Pony plan was replaced by going to see *Romeo and Juliet* at the Astor Cinema. The girl's name was Katie, and things got off to a good start when she seemed delighted to be given a box of Milk Tray. After that, nothing really happened. We saw the film, drank Kia-Ora orange juice (it was advertised in the intermission), then went our separate ways. Once again, I got the feeling that real life wasn't always going to be like the adverts.

This message was hammered home at the age of sixteen, when I bought myself a pipe. It wasn't an affectation but a genuine attempt to experience 'that Condor moment' – a sudden flash of clarity and understanding which apparently came when you filled your lungs with Condor smoke. That Condor moment, for me, turned out to be a spluttering cough and an attack of nausea. There was a similar result when I sought happiness in a cigar called Hamlet.

Undeterred, I began to plan for my future career in advertising, convinced now that it was my destiny. I even persuaded a piano-playing friend to help me write jingles; our best was one for Debenhams, the department store on Bromley High Street, which went 'Oh there's much more, much more at Debenhams, much more, much more to see' to the *Van der Valk* TV theme tune. And to think other teenage boys wasted their time writing songs about girls and the misery of their existence.

I'd also write newspaper adverts. One I was particularly proud of was for the Bradford & Bingley Building Society. It would, I felt confident, attract investors in their tens of thousands. The picture showed a flowerpot, shot in moody black and white. Inside the pot was a plant that had pound notes on its stalks. A hand, unseen, was pouring water over the plant from a watering can. The headline read 'Now there's an easier way to grow your money'. Inspired by the adverts in my already extensive collection of football programmes, there was very little body copy.

Too little, I realized later when I read it back – just a couple of lines which omitted certain details such as interest rates, contact details and, even more importantly, the name of the building society.

At school, the only subject I'd concentrated on was English. There didn't seem any point in studying anything that wouldn't help me become a copywriter – the job in advertising that most appealed to me – although my chemistry teacher was pleasantly surprised by the keen interest I showed in enzymes and hexachlorophene. When the time came for us all to join the workforce, my classmates became accountants and office managers (or in the case of my best friend, Dave, a milkman). I bided my time, waiting for the opportunity.

I had sixty-three jobs over the next few years, gaining valuable experience (as I saw it) in a variety of industries to prepare me for all the different products I'd soon be dreaming up ads for. Every Thursday I picked up my copy of *Campaign*, the weekly trade magazine, and applied for every junior copywriter position that appeared in it. Once, in the space of six days I hitched to Maidenhead for one interview, took a bus to Luton for another and a train to Edinburgh for a third. All without success. But not once did I even begin to question my destiny.

Thanks to *Campaign*, I no longer simply watched and admired adverts, I also knew the names of the creative behemoths responsible for them. I never tired of the 'Schhh . . . you know who' classic for Schweppes, in which the bottle of tonic water is switched on a train with an inferior brand called 'Starks' (copywriter, unsurprisingly: Jeff Stark), or the brilliant Dunlop ad which asked and answered the question 'Where would we be without Dunlop?' (copywriter: Andrew Rutherford). I was held spellbound by the footballing penguins of Penguin Biscuits fame (copywriter: Steve Sullivan) and the Kronenbourg ad in which Schubert was more concerned about his unfinished pint than his unfinished symphony (copywriter: Andrew Rutherford, again).

As well as being totally brilliant, these masterpieces had something else in common: they were created by Saatchi & Saatchi, probably the world's finest advertising agency. I was desperate to work for them.

And so it came to pass that on a chilly autumn day at the tail end of the 1970s I found myself heading to their office in Charlotte Street – for the fifth time that month. My friend Jon had got a job there as a junior art director. In my world, this was like having a friend who played for Manchester United. Or sang with Showaddywaddy. I would pop in to see him at work with the flimsiest of excuses. The number of times 'I happened to be passing' a building which was an hour's train ride and several stops on the tube away was astonishing. I think I was hoping to be plucked from the lobby as I waited for Jon, shoved into an office and told to write adverts all day.

As always, I felt a huge thrill as I walked up to the front step, which had the words NOTHING IS IMPOSSIBLE engraved on it. This was hugely inspirational but patently untrue. The likelihood of me being plucked from the lobby as I waited for

Jon, shoved into an office and told to write adverts all day? Impossible.

I sat and gazed, open-mouthed, at the receptionist, who was the most beautiful woman I had ever seen outside a Flake commercial. To avoid being caught staring, I closed my eyes and was soon picturing her stepping out of a Badedas bath and wrapping a white towel around her, her eyes catching mine as she let the towel drop to the floor. Because as everyone knows, things happen after a Badedas bath . . .

'Dave, Dave . . .'

Jon was standing in front of me, leather bomber jacket (the distinctive uniform of an adman) thrown casually over his shoulder. I fought to suppress a feeling of naked envy.

As I forced myself to leave the building with him, a young man dashed past, looking unbelievably cool in Elvis Costello glasses and skinny tie. He became even cooler in my eyes when I discovered he was merely a post-room junior who had been dispatched by his boss, Irish Mick, to feed ten-pence pieces into parking meters for the spaces occupied by expensive European cars. These vehicles, Jon explained, belonged to assorted copywriters, art directors, account directors, media planners and production executives who were far too busy to feed the meters themselves, especially when they were on lunch breaks that could last up to five hours.

As he was a junior art director, Jon's lunch break was slightly shorter, nearer half an hour, which was just enough time for a pint of Kronenbourg and a Bowyer's pork pie. It was also enough time to ask Jon for the most important favour I had ever asked of anyone: I wanted to borrow his bomber jacket for an interview for a job in Leeds. My latest theory for not being taken on by anyone was that I didn't look the part, especially with my faux sheepskin coat, which was made from some kind of acrylic blend. Not the sort of thing a proper adman would wear.

Jon readily agreed, and I showed him the advert which I'd torn from that week's *Campaign*. The headline read JUNIOR COPYWRITER WANTED and the copy, which I thought was a bit overlong, went on to say that Graham Poulter and Associates were 'The North's leading agency' (this was a claim that was made by at least three other northern agencies in the same edition of the magazine). I'd already phoned them before coming out and spoken to Fred, a belligerent American who asked me why I wanted to be a copywriter, then lost interest before I could complete my answer and told me to be there the following Monday at ten.

When I got home, I read and re-read *How to Get Your First Job in Advertising*, which had come free with a recent issue of *Campaign*. It was written by Dave Trott, creative director of BMP, an agency that was second only in my eyes to Saatchi & Saatchi. He was a genius, and I treated his booklet as my bible. Among the rules I committed to memory were 'If a product does not have at least one advantage, leave it alone' and 'Puns should be avoided'.

Armed with this knowledge and a leather bomber jacket, I felt I'd been given the keys to a career in advertising. I couldn't wait for my interview.

Two

The best way to get to Leeds from my flat near Abingdon was to take a train from Oxford and arrive refreshed and ready after a relaxing four-hour journey. Unfortunately I was broke so I had to hitch my way to the interview. This meant getting up at five a.m. and standing by the side of the M4 in the pouring rain, waiting for a lift, thinking, 'I bet Jeff Stark and Andrew Rutherford never had to go through this.'

My luck was in. A lorry transporting Chrysler Alpines ('The seven-days-a-week car') to Sheffield stopped and took me most of the way, then a sales rep in a Ford Capri ('The car you always promised yourself') picked me up and dropped me off in Leeds city centre.

I found the North's leading agency in plenty of time and was thankful for Jon's bomber jacket, which had probably saved me from getting pneumonia. It was stylish yet practical – a phrase I mentally filed away for possible use in an advert.

Like the Saatchi office, there were rows of European cars parked outside. Unlike Saatchi, these were all from Eastern Europe. There were Lada Nivas, Lada 1600s, Lada 1200s. It seemed that everyone in the agency drove a Lada. I was confused. Was this some kind of ironic northern cool? Would I have to work my way up the creative ladder just so that I could drive a Lada, a car so rubbish it didn't even have a slogan? I also noticed that several of them had a parking ticket; one of them had several parking tickets. Irish Mick would never have let that happen at Saatchi.

I walked up the steps, which had nothing inspirational written on them, and came face to face with the receptionist. As seemed to be compulsory in advertising agencies, she was pretty, although more like the mum from the Domestos advert than the Flake or Badedas women. She put a call through to Fred, telling him that I had arrived.

He came down to greet me, as belligerent in person as he had been on the phone. He was a big man in his mid-thirties, shaven-headed and dressed in a simple T-shirt and jeans combo. I presumed his bomber jacket was casually draped across the chair in his office. He glanced at his watch and then grudgingly gave me a guided tour of the agency. Fred explained, with a notable absence of enthusiasm, that what I was seeing was the UK's only integrated advertising agency, in that it had its own PR, sales promotion and photography companies in the same building. The impact of this was lessened by the fact that each of these companies appeared to have a staff of one.

The main thing I noticed during my whistle-stop tour was the people, whom Fred didn't bother to introduce me to. He was in too much of a hurry – we were almost running through the building. But everyone we passed seemed to have stepped out of a fashion magazine. They were exceptionally good-looking and perfectly groomed, the men wearing either Old Spice or the great smell of Brut, while most of the women seemed to favour Charlie perfume.

And then I entered the creative department. Looking around, I saw a dozen of the scruffiest, least attractive people

I'd ever seen in a professional setting. It was as though they'd been herded together and hidden in a dark room far from the rest of the agency. I immediately felt at home.

We moved on to Fred's office, which he shared with Clive, his co-creative director. It was modern and luxuriously appointed – a symphony of chrome, pine and plastic. On the wall were several framed posters of Ladas which, I soon learned, weren't there as a sign of their appreciation of Russian engineering: Lada was one of the agency's biggest accounts, and in order to demonstrate how much everyone believed in the product, they were used as company cars. After all, if the people who made the ads didn't drive them, how could they expect the public to want to?

This philosophy, I then discovered, didn't extend to the directors, including Fred and Clive, all of whom drove Porsches. Not because they wanted to, but because the agency also handled the Porsche account.

But it was Ladas that seemed to get Clive most animated. He had the look of a geography teacher who had recently come into some money. His immaculate suede jacket and perfectly ironed brown corduroy trousers were at odds with his floppy hair and rumpled appearance. He proudly told me that he and Fred would be flying out to Kenya in the New Year to film a series of Lada commercials. I was stunned and intrigued. What possible logic could there be for filming Ladas in Kenya? I couldn't wait to find out, but was told that they couldn't tell me any more as it was all highly confidential.

The only awkward moment came when Fred looked at my CV, for which I'd needed three pages to cover the sixty-three jobs I'd had since leaving school. I'd prepared for this and launched into my explanation of how it had given me the perfect background to work on pretty much any product. My time as a dish washer would be ideal for writing ads for, say, Fairy Liquid. My fortnight spent on the night shift in a biscuit factory was perfect preparation for persuading people to p-p-p-p-pick up a Penguin. While being an apprentice tyre-fitter for almost two days provided the necessary experience for involvement on Dunlop.

This was, in fact, the speech I'd prepared for my Saatchi & Saatchi interview, which I was convinced would be happening soon. The clients were all Saatchi and I'd been meaning to adapt it for the North's leading agency, but had forgotten.

Fred and Clive didn't seem to notice.

Then, to demonstrate my professionalism, I asked Clive what sort of portfolio they were looking for. Dave Trott, in *How to Get Your First Job in Advertising*, had insisted that this was an essential question to ask.

'Why don't you just show us what you've got?' said Fred impatiently.

I placed the Bradford & Bingley money-growing advert in front of them and sat back to receive the praise. Clive forced a smile and called it 'interesting'. I felt pleased and glowed in the warmth of the compliment. Or at least what I took as a compliment. It was only a few months later that I realized 'interesting' was advertising agency language for 'It's rubbish but I don't want to upset you and risk you having a tantrum'.

After I'd painstakingly gone through the other fifty of my home-made adverts, Clive asked his final question: 'Where do you see yourself in five years' time?'

I thought for a moment, then told him what I hoped he wanted to hear: 'Right here, winning awards for Lada and Porsche ads.'

With that, the interview came to a close. I felt confident that the job was mine. Fred promised I'd hear before Christmas.

Once outside, I saw Ladas in a whole new light. I enviously

peered inside a 1200S parked directly outside the agency and imagined myself behind the wheel. I was vaguely aware that Ladas were known for outdated technology, poor fuel economy and tank-like road-holding, but now all they represented was glamour and achievement.

Even as these thoughts were going through my mind, I knew they were flawed. Still, to me, the first tangible sign of success as a copywriter would be driving a Lada. And if I could convince someone – even if it was only myself – that a Lada was a car to aspire to, then surely I belonged in advertising.

As soon as I got home, I immersed myself in newspapers and magazines, studying the ads they carried, trying to discover what made them work. I was so eager to learn that I bought myself a notebook and started to make a note of anything I thought could be useful. Among these was the fact that most print adverts seemed to begin with the words 'When it comes to' and the penultimate paragraph always started with the word 'so'. Then there was the well-worn device that was used to sell any health-related item from painkillers to firm mattresses – dressing the model in a white coat. I also found an alarming number of headlines based on the phrase 'A Man for All Seasons', including 'A glass for all reasons', 'A shed for all seasons' and 'A town for all seasons'.

Advertising had completely taken over my life. I'd never wanted anything as much as I wanted that letter from Fred telling me that the job was mine. Every day I rushed home from work at the MG factory, and every day I felt crushed when I saw that it hadn't arrived.

It had been weeks since the interview. I was starting to get a bad feeling. It's been a general rule in my life that the more I want something, the less likely I am to get it. The last time I'd wanted something this badly was for Bromley to beat Sutton in an FA Cup match when I was eleven. They lost 9–0.

I decided to carry on as normal. And with Christmas fast approaching, this meant playing the pre-Christmas advert game with my flatmate and best friend Dave. Every 22 December we watched whatever was on ITV at 8.30 in the evening. In the first commercial break, he had to buy for my present the second product advertised; in the next break, I had to buy him the third product advertised. Even if it was a car. Or a pearl necklace. Or a Commercial Union insurance policy.

I was the more nervous as I had to go last, especially when I learned that all Dave had to buy me was some Campbell's Omelette Mate. But those nerves turned to relief when my gift to him was revealed to be a tub of Kerrygold Butter. We were both pleased with the outcome.

Then, on Christmas Eve, as I was wrapping the Kerrygold Butter, and just as I'd given up hope of hearing from the North's leading agency, a letter arrived. I didn't open it straight away. It was too important, too potentially life-changing. I made a cup of PG Tips, then sat down and slowly opened the envelope. As I took out the letter and nervously unfolded it a feeling of almost unbearable anticipation came over me. The letter was neatly typed, and with trembling hands I held it up to read.

Dear Dave,

Sorry to keep you hanging on tenterhooks for so long, but it was a tough decision.

It came down to two, yourself included. Unfortunately you were pipped at the post.

We would have liked to have taken both of you on, but at this point, impossible.

Best of luck in finding a position as a copywriter. Your

talent indicates that you should be in this industry.

Sincerely,

Fred.

I read it over and over, but it still ended up giving me the same message. I hadn't got my dream job. It felt like the lowest point in my life. Over the next few days I moved through the stages of disbelief and anger, before finding myself firmly in denial. It was then that I realized I had something to cling on to. 'We would have liked to have taken both of you on, but at this point, impossible' Fred had written. Over the most miserable Christmas I had ever known, I started reading things into those words that probably didn't exist. I took them to mean that there was a job for me in Leeds, it was just a matter of waiting for it to happen.

Rejuvenated by this realization, I took to ringing him a couple of times a week, to see if the agency was able to take me on yet. He was surprisingly amiable, though the answer was always the same. No.

Unaware that they weren't very good, I sent him ideas for Lada car adverts. Lots of them. The one I was most proud of featured a moody black and white shot of a Lada Niva, the top-of-the-range model (it cost over £2,000), with the headline 'A car for all reasons'. Every Saturday morning I'd walk up to the post office to send him my latest thoughts, which consisted of reams of paper covered in crudely drawn box-shaped cars and increasingly meaningless headlines.

Eventually, it proved too much for Fred. When I rang him in early March to see if I was any nearer to starting at the North's leading agency, he told me he'd had enough of being pestered by me. He could only see one way to stop it and that was to give me a job. I would be starting in early April. Until then, he added, could I please stop sending him ideas.

I managed to keep my part of the bargain and kept my Lada thoughts to myself as I prepared for my move up North. I gave a month's notice on my flat and then a week's notice at MG. My last act at the factory was to drive an MGB from the inspection bay to the car park, where it would be loaded on to a huge lorry. It was then that I made a promise to myself: I vowed that one day I would have an MGB of my own, parked outside whatever agency I happened to be working for. I then hauled myself out of the driver's seat and clocked off for the last time. I was now ready for the world of advertising.

But was the world of advertising ready for me?

A friend of a friend knew someone at Leeds University and had arranged for me to sleep on the floor at their place until I found somewhere to live. I treated myself to a coach ticket to Leeds and left the South behind, taking only a sleeping bag, a few clothes and a head full of headlines and slogans. I found my temporary home without difficulty and was shown my allocated piece of flooring. I laid out my sleeping bag on it and got inside, ready for a good night's sleep.

As I was drifting off, I suddenly saw my future with amazing clarity. I mentally fast-forwarded through the Leeds phase of my career, since this would only be a platform where I learned my craft and picked up a few awards along the way for my TV work on Lada and Porsche. Then Saatchi & Saatchi, the only agency I ever wanted to work for, would make a big-money offer. I'd be whisked off to Charlotte Street to take clients such as British Airways and the *Mail on Sunday* to new heights. Irish Mick would make sure my MGB was permanently free of parking tickets, and I'd spend lunchtimes in the pub drinking Kronenbourg with Jeff Stark and Andrew Rutherford, and eventually become creative director, which meant I would be Jon's boss.

I could feel myself smiling as sleep finally came.

Three

When I arrived at the creative department at 8.50, the sole occupant was drawing cartoons of monks on a huge drawing board. I approached him, carefully avoiding a large hole in the floor, and took a closer look. The monks were engaged in a variety of home improvement activities – one was carrying planks and a handful of nails; another, whose cowl disguised his face, was towing a large sink; a third struggled along behind, his arms filled to overflowing with drills, hammers, spanners and other tools of the trade.

The artist was an amiable, wavy-haired man who looked to be in his mid-twenties but dressed much older. I leaned forward over his shoulder while he continued to draw.

'Morning,' I said, willing my brain to come up with something interesting to say. 'So, what are you up to?'

'I'm doing a colouring-in book for a local DIY shop,' came the reply.

'What are they called?'

'Monks,' he said, peering over his glasses at me, as though the answer was obvious. 'The shop's called Monks.'

'Great.'

After several agonizing moments of waiting for another

nugget of information, and having no follow-up of my own, I decided to change the subject.

'So, is Fred around?'

'No, him and Clive are at the doctor's this morning. They're getting vaccinated for their trip to Kenya.'

'Oh,' I said. 'Well, I'm the new trainee copywriter. It's my first day.'

He shrugged, as if it were an everyday occurrence. 'I think that's your desk over there,' he said, helpfully.

'Anything I can do until Fred gets back?'

He looked around, and his gaze settled on a pile of books. 'You might want to have a look through some of those. It's where some of the people around here seem to get their inspiration from.'

I went over and picked my way through the pile. They were all books crammed with ads from around the world. There was the *Canada Advertising Yearbook 1975*, *The New York One Show Awards* books from the early seventies onwards, *D&AD* annuals (British Design & Art Direction – the best of British advertising) going back eight years and dozens of others. Bookmarks, made from torn paper, had been used to mark the car ads.

This was slightly disappointing. I'd been expecting to learn top-secret mind-manipulating techniques and instead discovered that ideas were stolen from old industry annuals.

I sat down and started to work my way through them as I ate my daily Mars bar. I considered this to be an essential superfood, with its ability to help me work, rest *and* play. It had become an important part of my day as I was convinced it improved my performance in all three key areas.

The first book I looked at was the most recent *D&AD*. There was an index at the back so I looked up all the Saatchi &

Saatchi work, despite knowing nearly every word of nearly every ad. With a quickening pulse, I turned the pages until I got to the poster Andrew Rutherford and Martyn Walsh had done for the Conservatives' 1979 general election campaign. Everything about it was perfect. The long, snaking queue of jobless people standing outside the Unemployment Office (although according to Jon, only about twenty extras had turned up for the shoot, so they photographed the same group over and over again, then stuck the pictures together). The simple yet powerful headline: 'Labour isn't working'. And the dream of a slogan: 'Britain's better off with the Conservatives'.

I thought it was the best piece of communication I had ever seen.

An hour later, as I was flicking through a recent Swedish awards book, I heard a commotion. I looked up to see a ruggedly handsome wild-haired man of around my age wearing what looked like a *Star Trek* sweatshirt storming out of the meeting room at the far end of the creative department.

'Rank amateurs!' he shouted in a broad Yorkshire accent, stretching the word 'amateurs' out over three long syllables. 'I refuse to work with such imbeciles!' (Three more long syllables.)

I watched, my mouth open with astonishment, as a small, dapper figure in a loud check suit, his bright orange hair parted down the middle, scurried after him. 'Mike, Mike,' he was saying in a pleading voice, 'please come back.'

'I will *not*,' replied the man I now knew to be Mike. And with that he disappeared from sight, leaving the orange-haired man standing in the middle of the room, just next to the giant hole in the floor, panic written all over his face. For a split second I feared he might jump.

Instead he turned to me.

'You're the new copywriter, aren't you?'

I nodded, not feeling the need to point out the absence of the word 'trainee' from my job title.

'I need an ad for WASS Used Cars. Big birthday bonanza. Massive savings on VWs and Audis. Absolutely massive. I'm talking streamers, balloons, champagne corks, the whole shebang. Capeesh?'

I nodded again.

He removed his round John Lennon-style glasses and mopped his brow in relief, using a linen handkerchief taken from the breast pocket of his suit. He then sat down on the corner of my desk to tell me more about WASS.

His eyes gleamed as he described the WASS experience, of how you went in there as a customer and left as a friend. He was positively evangelical about their wide range of quality used motors and unbeatable after-sales service. I couldn't help thinking he sounded – and looked – more like a used-cars salesman than an advertising account director.

His version of recent events was that Mike, the regular writer on the WASS Used Cars account, had been so offended by the client questioning the headline he'd presented and asking for alternatives that he had refused to do any more work for him until he apologized. Since Fred was away at the doctor's and Steve, the other writer, was busy, I was the only option available.

This was it. The moment I'd dreamt about. My first job. And since there were no ads for used cars in any of the awards books I would have to come up with something all by myself.

I sat down and turned to the cartoonist, who was smiling broadly, having clearly enjoyed the recent floorshow.

'Who was that?' I asked him.

'That?' he said. 'That, my friend, was Champagne Corks.'

I could work out how he'd earned his nickname.

I stared at the brief, which he'd handed to me. It basically repeated everything Champagne Corks had said, including his visual suggestions. I then spent the next couple of hours staring at my blank A4 pad, as if waiting for words to magically appear on the page. I was beginning to wonder if I'd been a little hasty in leaving MG.

The pressure increased when a slight, intense, unshaven man sat down at the next desk and introduced himself as Jacko. His evident liking for denim suggested a fondness for the kind of music that punks like me had little time for.

'We're supposed to be working together,' he announced, without a huge show of enthusiasm. 'I'm the art director. So, what have you got for me?'

'Well, I've got one idea.'

'Let's hear it then.'

I described a scenario of a long, snaking queue of people standing outside a WASS showroom. The headline would simply read 'Car not working?'

He thought about it for a few seconds.

'Got anything else?' was all he said.

I shook my head.

After an uncomfortable pause, he finally appeared to take pity on me.

'Fancy a pint?' he asked.

I readily agreed.

The nearest pub, which was called The Highlander, was across the road and down a small alley which wasn't visible from the road. Unless you knew where the pub was, you were unlikely to be able to find it. This probably explained why the only people there when we arrived were a couple I recognized from the office.

Jacko and I sat down and over a pint of Tetley's Bitter I found out how I'd managed to get a job at the agency when there hadn't been any vacancies. Apparently my predecessor, Carl, had been a bit of an enigmatic presence. He would drift in at least an hour later than everyone else, then sit at his desk writing away in longhand. At random times during the day he'd get up, put on his coat and slip out of the door, citing the need to get some fresh air and inspiration. On his return, anything up to a couple of hours later, he'd sit down and start writing furiously, seemingly inspired.

If it hadn't been for a piece of sheer bad luck, he would still be working there instead of me. What happened was that one of the art directors went for an interview at another agency a couple of hundred yards away in the next street. When he was being shown around, he saw a familiar figure scribbling copy on to an A4 notepad. It was Carl. It didn't take long for the full story to emerge. Carl worked full time for both agencies. At intervals throughout the day, he'd leave one agency and go to the other. He got away with this for nearly a year before being found out.

I also discovered why Champagne Corks looked like a used-cars salesman. A few months earlier he had been one. He'd worked for WASS and apparently fancied the world of advertising. Since no one at the agency wanted to risk upsetting one of their biggest clients, he was instantly given the job, despite no evidence of competence. I soon learned that every agency employed at least one friend, former employee or relative of a client.

As we were talking, the young man who had earlier been drawing monks came in and headed for our table.

'Ready for another one, chaps?'

Jacko immediately drained his glass and I followed suit, not

wishing to flout protocol. Our friend took the glasses to the bar
to be refilled.

'Who's that?' I asked Jacko.

'Failure.'

'Failure?' I said in disbelief. Not the nickname I would've
given him. He seemed really good at his job to me.

'Yup. You'll understand why after he's had a couple of pints.'

Failure returned with three pints of Tetley's, and conversation soon turned to Mike's outburst. Apparently, all the
account handlers were terrified of him, even though he was
only a trainee copywriter. The realization dawned that he
must have been the one who 'pipped me at the post'. I asked if
he was any good, and was slightly disappointed to hear that he
was 'brilliant'.

I got the next round in, eager to ingratiate myself with my
fellow admen. Once Failure had finished this second pint, as
predicted a change seemed to come over him. His shoulders
sagged a touch, and his face took on a morose air. By the time
he'd sunk the next pint his whole demeanour had transformed
and he was slumped on the table, mumbling something about
all of us being mere pebbles on the beach that we call Life. He
then started listing his various (and possibly non-existent) fail-
ings with girls, jobs and pretty much everything else. I finally
understood where his nickname had come from.

Jacko was ignoring him. It seemed that this sort of thing was
a regular occurrence, so, leaving Failure to his own mutterings,
we carried on our conversation. I told him how much I admired
Saatchi & Saatchi, hoping he felt the same way, but he didn't
seem that interested in advertising outside Leeds.

At least I found out why there was a giant hole in the middle
of the creative department – someone had decided that the
agency needed a fish pond there. And the *Star Trek* sweatshirts

half of my colleagues seemed to be wearing? They were free when you joined the company social club.

The conversation then turned to the WASS ad, and Failure took this as his cue to slope off home, presumably to lie down in a darkened room. Jacko told me that I couldn't go wrong with puns (which Dave Trott hated), streamers and, of course, champagne corks. His other tip? Just scribble everything down, no matter how bad – although I shouldn't bother with the 'Car not working?' line.

The next morning, I took Jacko's advice to heart. First on to the pad was the line 'The used cars dealer for all seasons', which I wrote down in huge letters, despite the fact that it didn't even mean anything. Of course car dealers were open for business all year round. It was hardly a selling point.

The second headline, again in massive letters, was even worse: 'If it wasn't for WASS, we'd all be riding round on bicycles'. The dubious logic behind this was that WASS had such good sales and service we'd all still be riding round on bicycles if they didn't exist.

The third headline was another that brought an early-morning blush to my face. 'WASS the best used cars dealer in Yorkshire?' it asked, nonsensically. It was a pretty poor pun; more importantly, it didn't work, because no one would ever say 'What's the best used cars dealer in Yorkshire?', they'd say 'Who's the best used cars dealer in Yorkshire?'

After that, my brain went blank.

Jacko's advice to write everything down was only serving to highlight my unsuitability for a career in advertising. This pitiful selection of headlines, accompanied by child-like illustrations of cars, had taken me the best part of the morning. It was too late to come up with any more ideas as the time had come to make my presentation.

I left my desk and shuffled into Champagne Corks' office, head bowed in shame.

'So, are you going to blow my socks off?' he asked, with an expectant smirk on his weasel-like face.

I shrugged and put the badly drawn layouts in front of him, tensing myself for the explosion.

He was expressionless as he looked through them, then suddenly burst into life. 'That one!' he said emphatically, jabbing his finger at 'WASS the best used cars dealer in Yorkshire?' 'It's bootiful, just bootiful!' (Champagne Corks was clearly a fan of the Bernard Matthews turkey ads.) 'Gets the client's name in the headline and lets the punters know we're the best. Good work, my son.'

Was he being sarcastic? I thought he probably was, but couldn't be sure.

No, he actually seemed to like it.

He then said something like 'Now let's sell the sizzle as well as the steak' and summonsed Jacko, whose job it was to design the ad around the brilliant headline. After Champagne Corks had given him a list of things he wanted to see in the design, such as balloons, streamers and champagne corks, Jacko and I were dismissed.

The fact that this headline was seen as fantastic only added to the growing feeling that advertising in West Yorkshire was a little different to advertising in Charlotte Street, London W1. But at least I was about to get my first exposure to the most glamorous part of the business.

The TV advert.

Four

The creative department were all crammed into the meeting room, where Fred and Clive were presenting the animatic (an animated storyboard) of their Lada commercial before setting off to Kenya to shoot it. It was an important technological breakthrough, as it allowed the client to see a rough version of what the finished product would look like before it was shot.

Until now, the whole project had been shrouded in secrecy, with wild rumours circulating as to the content. The most fanciful of these was that the leading character in the ad would be a kind of James Bond figure, taking on the baddies from behind the wheel of a Lada 1600 – which might have been stretching credibility a bit too far.

There was also much excitement as the agency had recently taken delivery of a state-of-the-art Betamax Video Recorder, a Sony SL-6200.

We all gathered around the TV screen to watch the crudely drawn animated version of the storyboard. The idea behind the Lada commercial soon became clear: various attributes of the cars would be linked with attributes of wild animals under the umbrella theme of 'Tough cars, tame prices'. So, when the voiceover talked of extra-thick skins, a rhinoceros was shown in its natural habitat. Then, to show that a Lada was unaffected by leaps and bounds (I think this referred to its suspension), the viewer would see gazelles leaping and bounding. I was full of admiration for how they'd managed to tie all the cars' qualities in with animals from the African plains. There was even a tortoise for the reinforced roof and underbody, as well as a toucan to demonstrate that the cars don't come with big bills.

After that, though, the idea seemed to run out of steam. A crocodile was used to demonstrate the fact that Ladas had Tectyl and underbody anti-corrosion protection as standard – which, as far as I knew, did not come as standard on crocodiles or any other creature. Finally, a polar bear was used to highlight extreme weather conditions and how 'Ladas just grin and bear them'. Despite not being an authority on the grasslands and jungles of Kenya, I was fairly certain that polar bears wouldn't be found there.

But these were minor quibbles. I was totally captivated by the sheer glamour of flying off to Kenya to shoot the ad and the excitement of being a part of something that was going to be on TV. As this was early in my career, I wasn't yet aware of the fact that most locations were chosen not by their relevance to the product, but more by where the creative team fancied going for a few weeks.

My desperation to be a part of the 'Tough cars, tame prices' campaign resulted in another career breakthrough – my first leaflet. It was a small part of a package launching the campaign, and would be handed out at 'selected' Lada dealers nationwide. On one side it would give a brief rundown on the Lada estate cars, before quoting various critics saying nice things about them on the other. I'd begged Fred to let me write it and he hadn't needed much persuading.

After a full morning during which I refused all temptation to get a coffee or a sandwich and ate nothing other than my daily Mars bar, I had written what I felt was a pretty good leaflet. Reading it back, it suddenly didn't seem quite so impressive. Although the headline felt right – 'Lada. More of what it takes to survive in today's motoring jungle' – I suspected the opening line might be a little tortuous. 'Contrary to popular belief,' I'd written, not actually knowing whether or not it was contrary to popular belief, 'not all full-size estate cars require the amount of pound notes you could get in their loadspace to buy them.'

What I was trying to do was cram two benefits into one sentence – something that would have horrified Dave Trott, who made it very clear in *How to Get Your First Job in Advertising* that a copywriter should lead off with one benefit and one benefit alone. He also wouldn't have approved of my overuse of the word 'rigorous'. 'Each Lada must go through a rigorous check at each stage before it leaves the factory in the Soviet Union,' I'd penned enthusiastically. 'Then, at the Lada Import Centre, each Lada must pass a rigorous 39-point inspection programme (including paint and bodywork).'

As if to make it up to him, I'd used a Dave Trott trick to finish. I'd noticed he liked to tie in the opening and closing paragraphs, so I'd ended with 'The Lada Estates. They'll leave you enough money to buy things to carry in them.' Despite a suspicion that it might be as clumsy as the opening, I proudly carried the handwritten copy to the creative department secretary and asked if she'd type it up for me.

I then returned to my desk, on which a large pile of newspapers and motoring magazines sat. It was my task to go through all the Lada reviews and pick out the best bits.

Three hours later, I struck gold. The *Greenock Telegraph*

had raved that 'performance was more than adequate'. I immediately wrote this out and, feeling rejuvenated, got back to work. It wasn't long before I found more usable material. The *Warrington Guardian* review contained high praise, as did the one in the *Reading Evening Post*. I was on a roll. The motoring magazines genuinely seemed to admire the cars and said so in glowing terms. I felt a sense of pride that wasn't entirely rational. Eventually, I collected eight quotes, which is what the brief had required me to do.

Now I just needed a headline. Something that would tie the whole package together. Something that would say how much every newspaper had fallen in love with vehicles that had previously been dismissed as dull and clunky. Suddenly, it came to me.

I leaned over to Jacko, almost too excited to speak. I took a deep breath and then, trying to sound casual but suspecting I'd written a brilliant line, said to him, 'That Lada brochure . . . I was thinking something like "The press are impressed".'

Before he said anything I knew he liked it, as I could see him nodding thoughtfully.

'Yeah,' he said, 'that'll do.'

This was cause for celebration. 'Pub?' I enquired. Even though it was only just opening time, I felt I deserved a Tetley's Bitter or two.

He answered me by standing up and slipping on his denim jacket.

As we walked over, he corrected me when I told him how much I liked the slogan 'Tough cars, tame prices'. 'It's a tagline, you southern jessie,' he explained. 'We *never* say slogan.'

In The Highlander we were joined by Champagne Corks, who bought the drinks. We talked about anything but work. I was pleased to discover that, despite his denim-dominated wardrobe, Jacko had the same taste in music as me – we were both big fans of the Buzzcocks, Blondie and Ian Dury. Champagne Corks was more of a Dr Hook man; he was also a 'huge, huge fan' of Meatloaf, Andy Gibb and the Three Degrees. His pet hate, much to our disgust, was Ian Dury's 'Hit Me With Your Rhythm Stick'. Luckily, after struggling to ingratiate himself for about half an hour, he gave up and went over to join a couple of fellow account execs at a nearby table.

It had been a good day, and it was to have a perfect ending. As we were leaving, Jacko asked me if I had any ten-pence pieces. I dug a few out of my pocket and gave them to him. He then put them in the jukebox, together with at least ten more, and selected G16, which he pressed over and over again. We then walked out, happy in the knowledge that Champagne Corks would be forced to listen to 'Hit Me With Your Rhythm Stick' about fifteen times in a row.

Jacko and I wouldn't be able to witness this as we were in too much of a hurry to get home by nine for our weekly appointment with another used cars dealer.

His name was Arthur Daley.

Five

Arthur Daley, the star of ITV's *Minder*, was a camel-coated trilby-wearing spiv who sold cars (or 'jam jars' as he called them) to unsuspecting punters when he wasn't being rescued from scrapes by his far less interesting bodyguard. Daley's habit of speaking in cockney rhyming slang was infectious and had swept the creative department.

As I was the only southerner there, it was assumed that I was an authentic cockney and, when at home, conversed entirely in rhyming slang. Never mind that I had grown up in a leafy suburb in Kent where I hadn't once heard anyone use language like 'have a butcher's' or 'up the apple and pears'. I was constantly bombarded with requests for rhyming-slang phrases, and since I was desperate to fit in, I did what anyone else would do in my situation. I started making them up.

And I probably would have got away with it had it not been for the pesky Trust Motors, another of Champagne Corks' seemingly endless car-dealer clients. He was briefing Jacko and me on a leaflet that would promote an 'unbelievable offer, a real cracker'. The offer wasn't actually that unbelievable: if the person reading the leaflet sent in the name of a friend who then bought a car from Trust, that person would be given £15.

As it was the morning after a particularly good *Minder* episode (Scotch Harry had nicked a suitcase full of forged banknotes), Jacko had the brilliant idea of doing the leaflet entirely in rhyming slang. I loved it. This was the kind of audacious thinking that was sure to get the attention of Jeremy Sinclair, creative director at Saatchi.

'How's this for a headline, old son?' I said to Jacko, really getting into the Arthur Daley part. '"We'll give you fifteen quid in your hand if your friend buys a jam jar from Trust".'

'It's OK,' said Jacko, looking unimpressed, 'but I think we could take it a bit further. What's rhyming slang for friend?'

This wasn't good. I had no idea, but couldn't let on. I took a sip of coffee.

'Brazilian blend,' I replied confidently.

'And what about the fifteen quid? We could say three fivers instead – what's fiver?'

I had a sinking feeling. If this ad went out and any real cockney saw it, I was in trouble.

'Fiver? That's, uh, deep-sea diver.'

'And hand?'

I was pretty sure there was no rhyming slang for hand. But that didn't stop me. 'German band,' I said, hoping he wouldn't catch the desperation in my voice.

'So that's "We'll give you three deep-sea divers in your German band if a Brazilian blend buys a jam jar from Trust"?'

I nodded.

While Jacko got on with designing the leaflet, I had the task of writing the copy. With a sense of deepening gloom, I came up with an opening line of 'Here's the plan', which, when translated into my version of authentic cockney rhyming slang, became 'Here's the frying pan'. This was followed by 'Give Trust the bonfire flames and Porgy and Besses of your

Brazilian blends who might be interested in blue-skying a jam jar or Desperate Dan from us', which, if you're not a proper cockney like me, translates to 'Give Trust the names and addresses of your friends who might be interested in buying a car or van from us'.

If it was possible, the rhyming slang became even more contrived and unconvincing after that. The sentence 'The guarantee is good for one year' became a totally unrecognizable 'The old oak tree is Norwegian wood for one Edward Lear'. This prompted Jacko to express his admiration. 'You southerners,' he said, 'you've got a language all of your own.'

He didn't know how close he was to the truth.

I was on the verge of coming clean and admitting that I was making the whole thing up when Mike came over to remind us that this was a Friday and it was lunchtime. Which meant it was Dangerous Pub time. This was a tradition started long before I joined Graham Poulter and Associates, which involved visiting a really rough pub in a generally unsafe part of Leeds. The point of this was never entirely clear.

Every week a different pub was chosen by Phil, our resident typographer, who seemingly had no sense of fear. Unlike me. I'd only been on one previous Dangerous Pub Friday outing, to The Gaiety in Harehills, well-known haunt of gangsters and drug dealers, where after just ten minutes I suddenly remembered I had to urgently get back to the office. Surely this couldn't be any worse?

Phil confirmed that it could when he announced that we'd be going to an Irish pub in Sheepscar known for favouring the cause of militant Irish nationalism. I wasn't sure I was appropriately dressed for the occasion, with my torn jeans and Sex Pistols 'God Save the Queen' T-shirt, but went along in spite of that. Anything to escape from the cockney nightmare I'd found myself stuck in.

It was a smaller than usual turnout for Dangerous Pub Friday, probably because the pub was considered a little too threatening, which meant that Fred, Phil, Jacko, Failure and I could all fit into one Lada. When we got there, the good news was that there were only half a dozen customers. The bad news was that they were half a dozen of the scariest-looking men I'd ever seen.

It was my round. It always seemed to be my round. As I approached the bar, I thought the best tactic would be to attempt to blend in by (a) getting myself a Guinness and (b) putting something Irish on the jukebox. The latter wasn't a problem, given that everything on the jukebox was Irish, but the Guinness was more challenging since I couldn't stand the stuff. I thought it was like drinking cough syrup. I didn't care if it was 'good for you', as the adverts had long proclaimed.

But recently another TV advert had begun to change my mind. During *Minder*, the latest Guinness one had been on. Written by Harry Shaw and John Knight at JWT, it showed the harp on the Guinness logo coming to life and playing an increasingly impressive rendition of 'Greensleeves'. The voiceover then compared learning to love Guinness to learning to play a musical instrument – all it takes is time and a little practice. That made sense to me, so I ordered a Guinness for myself and Tetley's Bitters for everyone else.

The place had fallen silent when we walked in, and apart from Christy Moore singing 'The Boys of Barre Na Sraide', it remained silent. The Guinness proved to be as unpalatable as ever, but I gulped it down. This time it wasn't just me who had to leave early. Apparently everyone had suddenly remembered some urgent business that needed taking care of.

Jacko and I got back to find Champagne Corks hovering. He'd been waiting for us and wanted to see what we'd managed to come up with. Jacko showed him the layout, complete with Failure's cartoons of deep-sea divers, a German band, a jam jar and a tin of Brazilian coffee.

As I read through the copy, I could feel my face reddening. There's nothing like reading something out loud to make you realize how rubbish it is. By the time I finished with the line 'It'll be the easiest bees-make-honey you've ever knelt-and-prayed', any confidence I might have had was drained out of me and I fully expected Champagne Corks to march into Fred's office demanding that I get sacked instantly.

Instead, he nodded enthusiastically. 'Bootiful, bootiful,' he said. 'Just one tiny thing.'

When he used that phrase, it generally meant he wanted to change everything. But not on this occasion.

'Can we just add something about Trust's fantastic parts department? What's "parts" in cockney?'

I didn't have to think long. I was getting good at this. 'That'll be their jack of hearts department.'

'Fantastic. And I want to say that it's always full of stock.'

'Always full of Brighton rock.'

He also wanted to add the following slightly implausible claim: 'Don't worry. Our salesmen won't, in any way, be pressuring your friend'. Which became 'Don't chicken curry. Our salesmen won't, in any ashtray, be pressuring your Brazilian blend'. This was to be followed by the reassurance that 'All we'll be doing is writing to them and pointing out the benefits of Trust Motors'. Or, as I put it, 'All we'll be doing is moonlighting to them and Sunday-jointing out the benefits of Trust Motors'.

I had a feeling that no one would possibly be able to make sense of this leaflet, especially if they were born within the sound of Bow bells. Luckily, Jacko had the magnificent idea of putting a translation on the other side, which we did. But even that didn't help. The response rate was zero. Of the 1,500 leaflets sent out, not one form was filled in and returned with the recipient's bonfire flame and Porgy and Bess.

Such a result was unlikely to excite Jeremy Sinclair, but since I was quite proud of the fact we'd tried something different, I sent him a copy, with a note saying that there was plenty more where this came from. It was only after posting it that I realized it sounded more like a creepy threat than a tantalizing glimpse of my massive potential.

There was only one consolation. I had saved Trust Motors from handing over a bunch of deep-sea divers.

The whole experience didn't seem to have much of a negative impact on Jacko and me. We continued to get plenty of small jobs, mainly overflow stuff from Fred and the other copy-writers, but what we really craved was an account of our own, one on which we would do all the creative work and even go to client meetings.

Our patience was rewarded a few months after the Trust Motors disaster. As Fred was passing my desk late one afternoon, he casually asked, 'What do you know about dressmaking?'

The answer should have been 'nothing', but I remembered hearing a story about actors at auditions who always claimed they could do things like ride horses, scuba-dive or fence if it meant getting the part, and who then quickly learned to do whatever activity was required. So I blurted out something I'd regret for the rest of my time at the agency.

'More than you'd think,' I said.

Six

The next day, I got into work to find a sulky-looking Jacko staring at a female torso, which was perched on a timber stand. I recognized it as a tailor's dummy, which was pretty much the extent of my fashion expertise.

'An ideal sewing companion,' said Jacko sarcastically, reading from a piece of paper headed 'Creative Brief', 'this fully adjustable dress form from A. E. Arthur allows for pattern adjustments before cutting, better fitting, and alterations.'

Admittedly, this was unlikely to be the kind of task to quicken the pulse of Jeff Stark or Andrew Rutherford either. But I was excited. Jacko was completely missing the award-winning potential in a quarter-page ad for a polystyrene dummy in an obscure sewing magazine. I immediately thought of Dave Trott's wise words: 'Before you even think of writing an ad, find out everything you can about the product'. This wasn't a problem I was facing, it was an opportunity.

Research was the key. That was how Charles Saatchi came up with his brilliant Health Education Council full-page ad, which told the reader exactly what happened when a fly landed on their food. Lines like 'Flies can't eat solid food, so to soften it up they vomit on it' and 'Then they stamp the vomit until it's a liquid, usually stamping in a few germs for good measure' only came about because Mr Saatchi waded through piles of government literature and old medical books. I wanted to apply the same kind of in-depth digging to A. E. Arthur.

I let my fingers do the walking and eventually found a dress-maker in the *Yellow Pages* who used an A. E. Arthur dress form ('The Venus model – I've got three of them') and was willing to talk to me about dressmaking. I then spent the next hour preparing a list of questions the answers to which would carry me and the readers of *Modern Sewing Monthly* way beneath the surface, to the heart of the subject.

After borrowing a voice-activated mini tape recorder, which Jacko seemed to find highly amusing, I walked the half mile or so to the dressmaker's studio and knocked on the door. It opened to reveal a lady who looked older than she'd sounded on the phone, probably in her mid-fifties. It also looked like her business was successful: there were dresses, and dress forms, everywhere.

After introducing myself and confirming that she had no objection to being taped, I put the recorder on the table and got straight down to business. After all, we were both busy professionals.

'Could you tell me a bit about what you do?' I began, confidently.

'Certainly,' she smiled. 'I'd say ninety per cent of my business is wedding dresses, bridesmaids' dresses, evening wear and day wear – that sort of thing. I do a few alterations as well.'

This was just surface stuff, designed to make her feel comfortable and develop a rapport. I then began to dig a little deeper.

'It's called a dress form, but can it be used for anything other than dresses?'

'Of course. Blouses, shirts, loads of things. I've even used it for nightshirts.'

I made a mental note. Versatile.

'Can you show me an example of a dress you've made using a Venus dress form?'

She indicated a torso with a half-sewn lime green dress pinned to it. I went over and studied the material, asking questions as I did so. 'What's the fabric?' 'Do you use a specific kind of pin?' 'How long does it take to get to this stage?' That kind of thing.

I was on a roll. My interviewing technique was proving to be both natural and remarkably effective.

Next I learned about the importance of positioning, whether it was collars and lapels, or lace, trims and ribbons. It was then time for a couple of questions I'd been saving up.

'And what's the most unusual use you've found for the Venus?'

'Good question,' she said.

I glowed at this unexpected praise.

'Actually, I sometimes use it to hang clothes on – keeps them in shape, stops creasing and so on.'

'And where do you see dress forms in five years' time?'

'I doubt they'll change much. Maybe made from a more advanced material?'

I noticed she hadn't said 'good question' to that one.

The fact I unearthed that I liked the most was that 'calico toile' was the name of a dress mock-up made of cheap material, to give an idea of what the finished design would look like. I was determined to use that phrase in my copy.

Advertising suddenly seemed very simple. Hard work, a single-minded determination to unlock the secrets of a product, and a voice-activated tape recorder created their own rewards. The only problem I was going to have would be what to leave out. I had enough information for dozens of ads. I felt, probably with some justification, that I was now the agency's leading authority on dressmaking. I even briefly considered a subscription to *Modern Sewing Monthly*, so I could keep up with the latest trends.

It was actually hard to tear myself away from my dressmaker friend, but I felt I'd taken up enough of her time. I thanked her and promised I'd send her a copy of the ad when it came out. She said there was no need as she was a *Modern Sewing Monthly* reader.

When I got back, Jacko was staring at another female torso. This belonged to one of the Squeaks, which was his name for a couple of extraordinarily beautiful girls whose job descriptions were vague. They could occasionally be found on reception, or sitting outside the chairman's office. But they were always together, and a visit to the creative department felt like a visit from royalty.

At first I thought 'Squeaks' was obscure rhyming slang, my best theory being 'squeaking pearls', which rhymed with 'girls' but otherwise made no sense whatsoever. Then, as soon as I heard the high-pitched squeals coming from them, I understood. It was a noise Jacko and Failure never tired of hearing, as they gazed lovingly at the Squeaks. Of course, they had no chance. The Squeaks only seemed interested in men with (a) Porsches, (b) expensive suits and (c) successful careers. Which pretty much counted Jacko and Failure out. That didn't stop them dreaming though, and each of them had drunkenly confided their feelings to me.

Knowing I'd get no sense out of Jacko while he was in this mood, I got to work. I played the tape back, taking notes as I went along. Then, using Charles Saatchi's ad about flies landing on food as my template, I wrote an audacious no-headline, copy-only ad. It went like this:

As dressmakers, we sometimes need a helping hand to take care of those fiddly tasks like checking placement of darts, pockets and buttonholes. Seeing how sleeves hang. And making sure there are no wonky hems, or that the ease of the lining is right.

The Venus and Diana dress forms from A. E. Arthur make the perfect assistant for the discerning dressmaker.

These versatile forms are fully adjustable and can do everything from fitting a tissue pattern straight from the pack to helping you make a calico toile.

Venus Model. Only £18.

Diana Deluxe Model. Only £27.35.

Admittedly, to those outside the dressmaking community it would probably make as much sense as the Trust Motors rhyming-slang leaflet did to, well, everyone who read it. But I was happy with it because it showed I'd not only taken the time to get to know the target market, I had also learned their language. The result was a piece of communication between equals. The copywriter as the representative of A. E. Arthur and the dressmaking professional. Building empathy. Understanding.

Jacko seemed happy to go along with me and produced a good-looking ad, with the words stylishly placed over a large photograph of the Venus and Diana dress forms. As soon as I saw it I felt an almost uncontrollable feeling of excitement. I knew I'd managed a few reasonably good ads in my first couple of months at the agency, but this one felt like the breakthrough. It was an ad that looked as though it had been written by a proper copywriter instead of a trainee copywriter.

Neville, the account director, seemed happy enough and told me he had a meeting with the client the following week, when he'd present it.

It was the longest six days I had ever known. When the day of the meeting finally arrived I was on edge the entire morning. As soon as Neville came back from the A. E. Arthur office, I pounced on him.

'Well, how did it go?'

He was smiling. This had to be a good sign.

'Went well, they approved it. Just a few small changes.'

He removed the sheet of copy from his briefcase, and I couldn't help but notice that a lot of the words had been crossed out. From what I could see, the good news was that they had at least wanted to keep some of my copy. Then it became clear which bit had been saved. The last bit. The ad, when it appeared in *Modern Sewing Monthly* a few months later, showed a large picture of both dress forms, with the A. E. Arthur logo in the right-hand corner. Underneath it simply read:

Venus Model. Only £18.

Diana Deluxe Model. Only £27.35.

That was all that remained of my in-depth, heavily researched and sharply focused dressmaking equivalent of Charles Saatchi's finest moment.

I was distraught. I'd never enjoyed rejection, but this felt far worse than that. I sat there, almost catatonic, as Jacko tried to console me. Even his reassurance of 'Well, it was rubbish anyway' failed to make me feel any better.

He went off to the pub and I said I'd join him when I felt up to it. After an hour of sitting in the office, reflecting on the unfairness of life, I wearily trudged across the road to The Highlander.

When I got there, Jacko and Failure were sitting with the Squeaks at our usual table by the jukebox. They were all laughing hysterically, as though they'd just heard the funniest thing in their entire lives. In the middle of the table was the voice-activated tape recorder, and I could hear my voice saying 'And what's the most unusual use you've found for the Venus?' That was enough to prompt everyone at the table once again to burst into tears of laughter. It appeared that my professional interest in dressmaking was amusing my colleagues.

I suspected it would also kill off any romantic chances I might have had with the Squeaks, which were probably non-existent in the first place.

But that didn't matter. There was someone else I'd been in love with since the day I started work at the North's leading agency.

Seven

I had developed a system for getting copy typed out. Whenever it was something I suspected might be rubbish, I took it to Kate, who was the creative department secretary. But if it was something I was really pleased with and it was on one of the bigger accounts like Lada, Porsche or Brentford Nylons, I'd head through to the production department and give it to Margaret, who was meant to handle any overflow from Kate.

I had a major crush on Margaret. She was like a buxom version of Siouxsie from Siouxsie and the Banshees, with cat-eye make-up and bright red lipstick. She dressed in eccentric fashion, even by advertising standards; her trademark was antique pince-nez glasses attached to a thin gold chain. The rest of her outfit would depend on her mood. One day she'd come in wearing a floaty kaftan, the next it would be a 1930s blouse teamed with PVC trousers. Her jet-black hair was usually worn in a Queen Victoria bun.

Margaret wasn't satisfied with merely typing out the words I gave her. My copy would often come back with grammar and spelling corrected, and on one occasion the words 'STOP SAYING THIS!' scribbled in red pen next to the admittedly overused 'And that's not all'. As well as usually being right, she was also quite intimidating, so I didn't raise any objections. Besides, I really wanted to ask her out. I fancied her, and we got on really well. Plus, we were the only punks at the agency and the only ones still upset about Sid Vicious having died.

She wasn't the sort of girl to give a box of Milk Tray to. A punk wouldn't do that anyway. She also wasn't the sort of girl to be impressed with my usual chat-up line of 'I'm in advertising', since her likely response would be 'So am I'. I was at a loss over what to do until the day I found myself looking through an old American awards book, searching for inspiration (in other words, something to steal) for a beer account we were pitching.

All the alcohol ads seemed to show a heavily moustached stud holding a glass of whatever was being advertised and a glossy-haired beauty draped over him, gazing adoringly into his eyes. Although the products were different, the message was always the same: drinking excessive amounts of beer/whisky/gin and having a bushy moustache will make you enormously attractive to women. A glance around the creative department comfortably disproved this, but it did give me an idea, one that anyone else would have thought of earlier. Instead of trying to find someone to play chess with at lunchtime (according to Jon, this is what Jeremy Sinclair and Charles Saatchi did most days), I would ask Margaret out for a drink.

Before I had a chance to talk myself out of it, I wandered through to the production department. After walking past Margaret's desk, I turned round, like Columbo did when he wanted to appear as though he'd just thought of something, and said in an offhand way, 'Um, do you fancy coming out for a drink?'

'What, now?' she replied. 'Is this that stupid dangerous pub thing?'

'No, I mean just you and me.'

'Sorry, got something on. Another time – maybe after work?'

'Tomorrow night? Thursday night? Friday night? Saturday night?'

'OK. Friday's good.'

I nodded, as though this was the expected outcome. I was a bit disappointed that she'd knocked me back initially, but a Friday date would give me time to clean and tidy my room. 'Every cloud has a silver lining,' I thought. I was even starting to think in clichés.

I didn't mention my Margaret news to Jacko, as it would have led to a mass outbreak of teasing. Instead I concentrated on the jobs at hand, the first of which was a new tagline for three small hotels in Liverpool, known as the Friendly Hotels group. The other task was to create a promotional leaflet for the same client.

We'd come up with the idea of a 'guess the price' competition, where we listed the menus for the wedding reception spread, Christmas dinner and 21st Birthday Special, and people had to say what they thought the price per head would be for each one. To give themselves the best chance of winning, they'd probably ring the hotels for the prices, find out how low they were and as a result insist on holding their next function at a Friendly Hotel. That was my theory, anyway.

And then I thought of something that would serve me brilliantly throughout my life as an adman. I decided that in the event of a tie the competition would be decided by which entrant had devised the best short slogan (I could hardly say 'tagline' could I?) for Friendly Hotels. Since the client couldn't be bothered going through all the entries to find the winner, he'd left it up to me and Jacko. All I had to do was delay coming up with the tagline for a couple of weeks, by which time competition entries would be flooding in. Then I'd read through them, pick the best one and present it as my own. What could possibly go wrong?

My heart was racing with the double excitement of this career breakthrough and my upcoming date. The sense of anticipation only grew as Friday approached. I took the day off and was waiting outside Spar supermarket when it opened at eight. Once inside, I rushed around the aisles, stocking up on heavily advertised cleaning products to get my room looking good for Margaret. I got some Shake 'n' Vac (the new carpet and room freshener from Glade), Airwick Air Freshener ('Fragrances that change your world'), Playtex Living Gloves ('The everyday beauty treatment for busy hands') and Windolene ('Wipe it on Windolene, wipe it off Windolene, that's how to get your windows clean').

I'd recently moved into a flat, after Fred had assured me that my job was safe ('for now'). It was in a large terraced house just around the corner from my favourite restaurant, the Flying Pizza. I shared with a scientist and a girl who worked in insurance. We all chipped in to rent a TV which we watched in the evenings, and to enhance my flatmates' viewing pleasure I gave a running commentary on many of the ads, telling them the names of the creative teams responsible. Every time the Lada ad came on, I let them know it was 'one of ours', hoping to leave the impression that I had had something to do with it.

After my usual lunch of Heinz tinned potato salad, I got to work. I even found myself doing the Shake 'n' Vac dance as I hoovered the carpet, singing quietly:

Do the Shake 'n' Vac

And put the freshness back.

When your carpet smells fresh
Your room does too.

Once everything was clean, I replaced the sleeping bag on the mattress with some brand-new Brentford Nylons poly-cotton sheets and blankets that I'd stolen from the photographic studio, and emptied each of the four ashtrays. I also briefly considered removing some of the ads from the wall, as they made me look slightly obsessed. Apart from a Heineken poster (written by Terry Lovelock at CDP), the others were all done by Saatchi & Saatchi. More specifically, Jeremy Sinclair. This included 'Labour's policy on arms' (soldier raising arms in surrender), as well as one of his first ever ads, the pregnant man ('Wouldn't you be more careful if it was you that got pregnant?'). In the end, I left them up, if only to cover some of the damp spots on the wallpaper.

I then showered and washed my hair with Head and Shoulders, a product I'd used for a couple of years now, ever since seeing their ad, which featured sultry brunette Gillian Benson from Shortlands, Kent – the part of Bromley where I went to primary school. According to Gillian, her beauty had been marred only by 'awful' dandruff, but Head and Shoulders had completely cleared the problem and she was going to use it from now on. As was I. For me, the excitement at seeing this local connection to a high-profile TV ad completely over-shadowed anything else that happened that year.

Once out of the shower, I got dressed in my best punk outfit and got the bus into town. I briefly wondered if Margaret would actually turn up, but she arrived at the Berni Inn opposite the Town Hall only minutes after me. It crossed my mind that the venue I'd chosen didn't exactly compare favourably with Jon's tales of champagne dinners at the rather more exclusive Embassy Club in Bond Street.

We went inside and, eager to prove my sophistication, I ordered a bottle of Mateus Rosé. As we waited for our prawn cocktails, conversation was slightly strained. At work it was much easier, since we were colleagues. The evening I'd imagined, where we were Leonard Rossiter and Joan Collins from the Cinzano ads, swapping flirtatious repartee as the air crackled with sexual tension, just wasn't materializing. Instead I was starting to get a sinking feeling, which turned to drowning when Margaret took a sip of wine and said, 'Look, you do know I'm not interested in being your girlfriend? I don't do that kind of relationship.'

I nodded, as though I was perfectly aware of this. More than that, as a fellow punk, I wasn't in the slightest bit bothered.

'Yeah, same here,' I lied, as my heart was crushed.

On the plus side, that seemed to remove the awkwardness from the evening and things picked up considerably. I discovered that she hated being a secretary and really wanted to be a copywriter. This revelation, plus the Mateus Rosé, prompted me to spill all about my Saatchi & Saatchi ambitions, how my sole goal in life was to work for them. The most recent *Campaign* had announced that they had just become Britain's biggest agency. It was front-page news. I wanted to be a part of Saatchi & Saatchi more than ever. Spurred on by their success, I'd redoubled my efforts and was now sending them packages of pretty much everything I'd written, despite absolutely no encouragement, not even a response. Margaret pointed out that ads like my latest half-page in the *Yorkshire Post* ('What's the four-letter word favoured by commercial vehicle owners? WASS') were unlikely to get Jeremy Sinclair reaching for the phone, and that quality might be a better tactic than quantity.

The best part of the evening was when she said how much she liked some of my work on Aladdin Thermos Flasks.

Actually, that wasn't quite the best part of the evening. That came after the Black Forest gateau, as I was slipping on my recently acquired flying jacket, and Margaret said something I really wasn't expecting: 'Let's go back to my place.'

And we did.

It was the start of a beautiful non-relationship. Even though she refused to 'go out' with me, she was perfectly happy to have me stay over, and once even stayed the night at my flat, which had long returned to its usual untidy state by then. I was particularly impressed that she recognized the Saatchi & Saatchi connection with the posters.

At work, we were just colleagues, although she now insisted on doing all my typing. This was great, apart from the time I handed her two sheets of A4 paper filled with some highly predictable taglines for Friendly Hotels, including the one they eventually went with: 'Stay with the Friendly people'.

'Must've taken you ages to come up with that,' was all she said, sarcastically.

She would have had a point if any of the taglines had actually been mine, instead of stolen from competition entry forms. Still, life was going well. My ads were appearing in the papers. I was going on long liquid lunches. And now I was sleeping with a secretary. For the first time, I was beginning to feel like a real adman. All I needed to complete the picture was a phone call from the creative director of Saatchi & Saatchi.

And that came four months later.

Eight

The phone rang as I was finishing my daily Mars bar and washing it down with a cup of PG Tips.

'Hello,' I said, my mouth stuffed with all the goodness of milk, sugar, glucose and thick, thick chocolate.

'Dave Roberts?'

'Speaking.'

'Dave, this is Arnold Middleton. I'm creative director of Saatchi & Saatchi and wondered if we could have a little chat?'

Despite the adrenalin that immediately flooded through me, my brain was quickly able to grasp one significant inconsistency: unless there had been a coup no one had told me about, Jeremy Sinclair was their creative director. I also had an internal phone list from Saatchi & Saatchi, which I'd stolen from Jon on one of my many visits to his office. There was no Arnold Middleton on it.

'Isn't Jeremy Sinclair creative director?' I asked hesitantly, afraid I might be shattering a fantasy world Arnold had carefully constructed.

'Jeremy? Oh yes, he's at the London office. We're in Manchester.'

That explained it. Bemusement turned to elation. I hadn't

even known they had a Manchester office. I knew they'd recently bought Hall's in Edinburgh and O'Kennedy-Brindley in Dublin, but these agencies had both kept their names. Finding out there was another Saatchi & Saatchi was like suddenly finding out I had a twin brother.

I asked him how he'd got my name, thinking that word might be getting around about some of my work on WASS, Trust Motors and even A. E. Arthur.

'Someone recommended you,' he said.

I hoped it hadn't been Fred or Clive.

Still, I didn't hesitate in agreeing to meet up for a chat. It wasn't London, but it was still Saatchi & Saatchi. Which meant that if I worked there, I would have a business card saying DAVE ROBERTS, COPYWRITER, SAATCHI & SAATCHI. More importantly, being part of the Saatchi empire would probably make a transfer to the London office much easier.

I arranged to meet Arnold when I was in Manchester the following Tuesday. I was going there to record my first ever radio commercial, which was for Trust Motors. Most of my fellow copywriters used Studio 169 in Bradford, which was quite a bit nearer, or one of the many perfectly good studios in Leeds. I chose Pluto, in Manchester, after hearing that it was run by someone who used to be in Herman's Hermits. That wasn't its only musical connection: Brian and Michael's catchy-but-unfashionable single 'Matchstalk Men and Matchstalk Cats and Dogs' (a song I secretly liked but didn't dare admit to Margaret) was recorded there.

I stayed late at the office the night before so I could get my portfolio together. Dave Trott recommended starting and finishing with your best work, which was why I decided to put ads from my Trust Motors 'Dad' campaign at both the front and back.

These ads were unique in my career thus far, in that they had worked. The idea was that a three-year-old boy, Jonathan (named after my Saatchi friend), was complaining about his dad being so busy selling cars that he didn't have time to write ads – so Jonathan had to step in. He was a pretty gifted three-year-old since not only could he write, he also used phrases like 'trade-in allowances' and 'part-exchange deals'. The words were accompanied by a brilliant cartoon by Failure showing Jonathan posing in his dungarees, his freckled face glowing with pride at the ad he'd allegedly written.

These had gone down so well that we were taking the same concept to a thirty-second radio commercial, in which Jonathan would be saying, in an unbearably cute voice, that his dad was so busy giving massive discounts that he'd had to leave the commercial in the hands of his young son. The studio seemed convinced that they'd lined up a perfect child actor to take the part of Jonathan and sounded as excited as I was. The client was delighted that I'd managed to cram so many benefits into the script, but slightly less delighted when Fred timed it out at eighty-three seconds, forcing me to make drastic cuts.

If the recording went well, I'd be able to slip the tape into my portfolio, and play it to Arnold. But my immediate problem was choosing the right ads to show him. The key here was originality. That was what it would take to impress Saatchi & Saatchi according to Jon, so I immediately discarded my Astral Caravans ad ('A caravan for all seasons'), all the work I'd done so far on A. E. Arthur, and, on Margaret's advice, the WASS 'four-letter word' ad.

I decided to lead off with 'My dad's got more Volkswagens and Audis than anybody else's dad', the strongest of the series. For the next spread I went with Margaret's favourite, a leaflet offering £100 off a holiday to anyone buying an Aladdin heater;

she felt I'd summed up the offer rather nicely with my line 'How to get a tan from Aladdin paraffin heaters'. Underneath that was the Lada 'press are impressed' leaflet. On the opposite page I put an ad for Friendly Hotels that said 'Next time you're in Liverpool, stay with friends'. This shared a page with another piece for Aladdin, the trade ad, which was designed to persuade shops and other retailers to stock up on paraffin heaters, as there was bound to be a huge demand. I was particularly pleased with my line 'Aladdin means business', and Jacko had given the ad a stylish look. Finally, on the last page was another one from the Jonathan series headlined 'My dad keeps giving people money'. In this ad, he decides to save up to buy a car from his dad 'so he'll give me lots of money too'.

And that was it. Four pages, four ads, two leaflets. Admittedly this wasn't much to show from half a year in advertising. But as Margaret insisted, quality was more important than quantity. These were fresh, original ideas and would hopefully be enough to get my foot in the Saatchi door.

The coach journey to Manchester was spent rearranging the portfolio. By the time I arrived, it was back where it had started.

First stop was Pluto, which was larger than the kind of studio I was used to; the doors alone were at least ten feet high. On the wall were half a dozen gold records. And in the producer's chair was a man I recognized from many *Top of the Pops* appearances, Keith from Herman's Hermits.

He greeted me with a firm handshake and asked if I wanted something to drink.

'Just a coffee, please,' I said, trying to suppress the excitement at having just clutched the hand that had strummed the guitar on 'Something Good'.

'Espresso? Nescafé? Bird's? Maxwell House?'

'Just Nescafé, thanks,' I replied, giving him the shaking-fist-full-of-coffee-beans gesture, like Gareth Hunt did in the advert.

He smiled and shouted to someone to get two cups of Nescafé. This was good. We were a couple of admen bonding over the business we loved. Things got even better when Keith (as I now felt comfortable calling him) introduced me to a petite blonde woman and her young son – the boy who was to provide the voice of Jonathan.

'Linda, Steven, this is Dave. He's the creative director from the agency.'

Creative director? Life was just getting better and better. A few hours earlier I'd been a trainee copywriter in a small provincial advertising agency who did the jobs nobody else wanted to do and had to make tea for everyone. Now people thought I was a creative director. I was mixing with celebrities and having people fetch coffee for me as I produced slick radio commercials that would be heard by millions (or, in this case, hundreds).

If only my old foreman at MG could see me now.

As we started recording, I suddenly felt a huge burst of joy hearing my words being read out, even if it was by a six-year-old child. To be honest, he looked more like the Milky Bar Kid than the cartoon version of Jonathan that Failure had drawn, but he sounded great. Cute, yet coherent. And when he delivered the line 'My dad works for Trust Motors and he keeps giving people money', the engineer, producer and the bloke who'd brought the coffee all burst out laughing. I allowed myself a modest smile, as if I fully understood their reaction.

It was only after I'd been to a few more recording sessions that I realized that laughing hysterically at anything remotely funny was something they always did. I think it was designed to make you want to give them any future radio jobs. If so, it certainly worked on me.

The process of making a radio commercial was far more straightforward than I'd imagined. Young Steven did a couple of readings, the engineer spliced together the best takes, put a piece of music in the background, and handed me a cassette.

I was so pleased with the way it had gone that I treated myself to a taxi to my other appointment in Manchester. This was how Jon always travelled when he was on business, so I thought I should start getting used to it.

The Saatchi & Saatchi office was on the first floor of a precinct and the only way to get to it was through a beautifully appointed roof garden. Once inside, the first thing that struck me was that it felt like a proper advertising agency. No gaping holes in the floor, no staff running around in *Star Trek* sweat-shirts. Everything was white and there were expensive-looking paintings on the walls and huge potted plants scattered throughout the building.

The receptionist, who exhibited near-Squeak standards of beauty, put a call through to Arnold while I sank into the luxurious leather visitors sofa.

Arnold kept me waiting less than a minute. He was a short white-haired man in his early fifties who bounded down the corridor and greeted me with an enthusiastic handshake.

Sitting down beside me, he told me all about the agency, about how quickly they had grown since being taken over by the Saatchi brothers in the early seventies. What he was look-ing for was a copywriter to take responsibility for overseeing every ad that came out of the place.

I suspected he thought I had a bit more experience than five months.

'Let me show you some of our work,' he said, taking me

through to a spacious white-walled boardroom where he proudly spread a bunch of ads over the giant oak table. 'This is our biggest client,' he announced, beaming, as he pointed to a couple of ads for Cold Shield replacement windows.

The one I looked at showed an idyllic family: a father and son building a model plane, while the mother watched her daughter through the window, playing on her new bike. The headline was 'Cold Shield windows. You simply have to admire them'. I looked for a hidden meaning, a double entendre, a laugh-out-loud punchline. After all, this was Saatchi & Saatchi.

There wasn't one.

The next one wasn't much better. It was from a Manchester United football programme and read:

Our choice!

United.

We are 100% behind the lads in their quest for victory.

Your choice!

Cold Shield.

Britain's number 1 replacement window company.

These were rubbish. I couldn't detect any Saatchi & Saatchi influence anywhere. None of Jeremy Sinclair's genius for condensing a complex thought into a few words. No sign of Jeff Stark's flair for the unexpected twist.

The rest were even worse. All the Moben Kitchens ads seemed to be announcing massive '50% off' sales, while a quarter-page effort for Edelson Furs sported the un-Saatchi-like headline 'A blue fox jacket at a price to fox your friends'.

This was a lot less intimidating than I'd imagined. I had to admit to myself that Saatchi & Saatchi (Manchester) weren't what I was expecting. But that was a good thing. I'd be able to come in, turn the place around with work worthy of the Saatchi name and then be taken down to London to work my magic there.

But just as I was starting to feel optimistic about my future, Arnold produced a piece of work that sent terror rushing through my body and drained the strength from my legs. It was a trade ad for Robertson's spark plugs. The headline read 'Robertson's means business'.

This was a disaster. The wording was identical to my Aladdin ad which made up one sixth of my entire portfolio. Would he accuse me of stealing his idea? Or would I just look as though I didn't have an original thought in my mind? Either way I was in trouble.

I reluctantly opened my portfolio. I still had a vague feeling that my work wasn't quite up to Saatchi & Saatchi standards, but I consoled myself with the thought that theirs wasn't either.

Arnold seemed to like the Jonathan ad – and that was when I lost my nerve. I held the next two pages together so that he wouldn't see 'Aladdin means business', and as a result turned straight to the last page and the other Jonathan ad. This meant that I showed him a portfolio consisting of just two ads, both of which were for the same client and which looked almost identical.

The interview came to a rapid end after that. Arnold seemed suddenly to remember another appointment and didn't have time to listen to the Jonathan radio ad. Perhaps he'd had enough of Jonathan.

As I was walking off, he thanked me for coming in and said,

'I'll give you a ring in a couple of days.'

He never did.

The next night, I went out with Bob, an art director from work, to try to get over the disappointment of having my dreams crushed. We decided to go and watch Leeds in a UEFA Cup game and go to a club afterwards.

It was at this club that I met a girl who couldn't have been more my type. She was a nurse called Caroline and looked a bit like the pretty young mum in the Horlicks 'helps you unwind' advert – apart from not having a giant key sticking out of her back, obviously. She was outgoing, interesting and funny. The evening passed in no time, and as we parted I asked if I could see her again. Maybe for a walk on Sunday.

'I'll give you a ring in a couple of days,' she said.

I'd heard those words before, so I didn't hold my breath.

Nine

Christmas was on its way. You could tell by the work we were doing.

Jacko was putting the finishing touches to our 'WASS super sensational seasonal savings' ad. The 'sensational' was at Champagne Corks' insistence, and it looked much like any other WASS ad, apart from a lone strand of tinsel among the familiar corks, streamers and cars. The 'Monks Merry Christmas crackers' quarter-pager was ready to go to the *Yorkshire Post* and showed a selection of DIY tool gift suggestions. The main attraction was a Black and Decker electric sander for 'an unbelievable £20.95'. To give the ad a festive flavour, Failure had provided a cartoon of a monk kissing a female monk (complete with cowl mini-dress) under the mistletoe. Brentford Nylons, meanwhile, were having an event called 'The great Christmas clearance sale', which I was trying to write about ('Acrylic blankets! Polyester pillows! Simulated brushed nylon sheet sets! All at an unbelievable HALF PRICE!') when Fred summonsed us into his office. We were desperately hoping it wasn't to brief us on yet another Christmas ad, as we were running seriously low on Yuletide inspiration.

It turned out that he had something far more important in

mind. Jacko and I, he announced, were going to be handling the next Lada campaign – the follow-up to the successful 'Tough cars, tame prices' advert. This was brilliant, and I immediately started thinking of location possibilities. We could shoot it in the Bahamas, or Tahiti. Or even Venezuela. I'd always wanted to go there.

As the reality of the news began to permeate into my brain and excitement began to build, Fred explained that he and Clive would be too busy on a top-secret project known only as 'Project R' to do it themselves. Although only a few of the agency's top people were in on 'Project R', we had a fairly good idea what it was, considering that (a) West Yorkshire Police had announced they would be running an advertising campaign to help them catch the Yorkshire Ripper, and (b) that uniformed officers were often seen in reception.

Fred then dismissed us and we went back to our desks, back to Christmas-related advertising.

When the brief arrived for the Lada campaign a few days later, I could barely stop shaking. My mouth was so dry that I was drinking can after can of Lilt, relying on the totally tropical taste to quench my nervous thirst. I reminded myself that the Lilt ads had been shot somewhere in the Caribbean. Perhaps that would be a good successor to Kenya for the next Lada campaign.

That idea was soon shot down with a look at the brief. After skipping past the usual stuff about the target market being 'unconventional thinkers prepared to show their independence by driving a challenger brand', I went straight to the important bit – the media list. And it was bad news: there wasn't going to be any TV. But the disappointment was short-lived and turned to joy when I saw the list of newspapers the ads would appear in. Lada would be taking full pages in several national papers, including the *Sunday Times*, *Daily Mail* and *Observer*. This really was the big time, a world away from a quarter-page in

Modern Sewing Monthly. Not only that, but Jacko and I were also going to present our work to the client. This was a first. It meant we were trusted.

It was turning into quite a couple of weeks. Firstly, the Trust Motors client had said that the Jonathan radio commercial 'couldn't be better' and asked Champagne Corks to say 'well done to the writer'. And as I was repeating those words over and over in my mind, Caroline rang me to say that she'd love to meet up again. That Sunday afternoon we went for a walk in Roundhay Park, and by the time we'd finished I knew she was the one. And just a few days after that, I was the copywriter on a major national advertising campaign.

I was starting to feel like the man in the Denim aftershave advert, who seemed to be a good-luck magnet; everything went his way. The line at the end simply said 'Denim. For men who don't have to try. Too hard'. At last I understood what Jim Phillips, the copywriter, was getting at.

Even Margaret informing me that she now had a boyfriend couldn't dampen my mood, even though this appeared inconsistent with her claim that she didn't do that kind of relationship. Besides, Caroline and I were far better suited and I had already formed a plan to play it cool for a few months and then surprise her with a romantic proposal.

I opened my writing pad and rolled up my sleeves. Literally. Jacko gazed out of the window, probably thinking about the brunette Squeak. That was all he ever thought about. He had no interest in helping me with headlines. Jacko was from the traditional school of art direction. It was the copywriter's job to come up with the words; he just did the pictures.

The first thing I asked myself was 'What would Charles Saatchi do?' That was an easy one. Research. OK, so it hadn't worked out with A. E. Arthur, but that was only because they lacked vision. I decided to start by looking at what other car manufacturers were doing before reading up on Russian engineering in a book I'd got from the library. It seemed more appealing that way round.

The media department kept copies of all our competitors' ads, so I wandered through and brought back a huge pile of old newspapers. I soon found what I considered to be the best car ad of the year, which, naturally, had been written by Jeremy Sinclair. It was for the Triumph Dolomite, and showed a driver getting a speeding ticket, with the headline 'The Dolomite Sprint takes you from 0 to the Magistrates Court in 11.4 seconds'; the copy then explained that 11.4 seconds is how long it took the Sprint to go from 0 to 'an illegal 71 mph'. This was not an idea I could steal, unfortunately, since the same acceleration in a Lada would take nearer 11.4 minutes.

A pattern soon emerged. The majority were using comparison advertising, which had only recently been allowed, to demonstrate that their car was better. The Austin Maxi, for example, was proud of having nearly two cubic feet more loadspace than a Talbot Alpine and almost twice the capacity of a Renault 16. The Volvo 244DL boasted of being less expensive than a raft of competitors, from the Ford Granada to the Mercedes 200. I already knew the Triumph Dolomite was quick, thanks to Jeremy Sinclair, but hadn't realized it was quicker than a BMW 320 or Alfetta 2000. Even Lada had got in on the act, by showing the new 1600 model and claiming, rather improbably, that it was so stylish you could easily mistake it for a £6,000 Mercedes, a £5,000 Audi or a £4,000 Volvo. Fred's copy was so persuasive that I almost believed it.

I couldn't help noticing that none of these ads, with the obvious exception of the Lada one, had bothered to include any of the Lada models. This wasn't really surprising since that would be like Barclays Bank comparing themselves to the Grimsby and Cleethorpes Mortgage and Investment Company.

That was when a thought came to me. I had never experienced this level of excitement before. It felt as though my heart was about to burst out of my chest.

'How about this for an idea?' I said to Jacko in a slightly hysterical voice. 'We tell people that other car makers are so scared of Lada, they won't mention them in their ads.'

He laughed. Then, realizing I was serious, asked me what I had in mind.

'Imagine a Lada 1200, shot from the side in moody black and white photography. Now imagine the headline "Come and see the car that nobody's talking about". Then you read on and it says that the reason other manufacturers won't mention Lada is because they're scared about coming second in economy, value, loadspace and stuff like that.'

Jacko didn't say anything. He just removed the cap from a black magic marker, releasing that familiar eye-watering odour, and started to come up with a design.

I could already see the finished ad in my mind. I leaned back in my chair and imagined Jeremy Sinclair reading the *Sunday Times* over breakfast, seeing the Lada ad, smiling, and nodding his head in recognition at a truly original idea. He'd then get out his voice-activated tape recorder (which I considered essential equipment for all copywriters) and say into it just eight words: 'Find out who wrote the new Lada campaign.'

I was determined that these would be the ads to land me my dream Saatchi job, and as a result I continued to scribble down headline and copy ideas on the bus, over dinner, even while watching TV at night. There was only one brief occasion when I put my pencil down and stopped thinking about Lada and that was on 22 December.

The time was approaching 8.30 p.m., meaning it was almost time for the annual ritual with my best friend and ex-flatmate Dave, where he had to buy me the second product advertised in the first break, and I had to buy him the third product advertised in the next break.

I had a nervy feeling in the pit of my stomach as a repeat of *The Jim Davidson Show* began (my flatmates were a bit grumpy as they wanted to watch Les Dawson on the other side). After what seemed like a never-ending ad for the caring, sharing Co-op, with kids singing carols, it was time to find out what Dave would be getting me.

I experienced a momentary jolt of excitement as I saw an opening shot of a jungle – he would have to get me a Lada! – but that turned to disappointment when the ad cut to a man lying in a hammock on the beach. I immediately recognized it as the latest Guinness ad. At least it would give me another chance to acquire a taste for the stuff, but I was crushed.

My only hope was that I'd have to buy him something just as cheap. Ten minutes later I leapt into the air in delight when I saw the welcome sight of the rather dumpy Mrs P. Fleischer of High Wycombe. She was talking about her love for Whiskas, finishing with the confusing line 'Love and Whiskas to pussy are two words that go together'. This was brilliant in two ways: it was cheap and, since Dave didn't have a cat, totally pointless. He'd recently moved in with his girlfriend Jill. I wondered what she'd make of him getting a gift-wrapped tin of catfood in the post.

I returned to writing about Ladas with all tension drained from my body. With the worry about a potentially expensive Christmas present gone, the lines flowed. By the time I went to sleep a little after three, I had some lines that gave me a thrill whenever I read them (which I did many times over). In the end,

Jacko and I chose three to present: 'Come and see the car that nobody's talking about', 'This is what Audi, Volvo and Ford are so afraid of' and 'Here's why nothing compares to the Lada 1600'.

Presenting to the client was easier than I'd imagined, despite the fact that I barely slept the night before. And this was when I learned that presenting work you believe in is far easier than trying to sell something you don't really like. All three ads were approved on the spot, which brought on a feeling of sheer heart-pounding elation. This must be how Charles Saatchi and Jeremy Sinclair felt after pretty much every presentation.

For once, it wasn't just me that was impressed with my work. Fred took me and Jacko out for a pork pie and mushy peas as a 'well done', and Mike, the writer who had pipped me to the post, thought the campaign was 'grand'.

When the first ad appeared, I got three copies of the *Sunday Times*. Jeremy Sinclair wasn't the only person I wanted to send a copy to. I also sent one to my parents, who hadn't been certain what I did for a living but thought it had something to do with copyrights. In fact I was so proud of the Lada campaign that I blu-tacked the whole set on to my wall, right next to the pregnant man and Labour's policy on arms. This, I felt, was a gallery of work representing two copywriters at the top of their game.

I wasn't quite so proud of some of my other work and felt my face redden with embarrassment every time I saw our WASS, Monks or Brentford Nylons seasonal efforts in the *Yorkshire Post*. Still, it could have been worse. I could have been in Manchester working on Cold Shield, who were running their own festive ad which had the longest headline I'd ever seen: 'Before Christmas you could be enjoying the benefits of our replacement windows and doors (but hurry, Christmas is coming)'.

Although I was still a bit down after not getting the Saatchi

(Manchester) job, I acknowledged that it would be better for my Saatchi (London) plans if I stayed where I was and took every opportunity to do high-profile work.

And that was my big mistake.

A week later, when Fred asked if there were any volunteers to write a low-budget TV commercial for WASS, I was surprised that everyone seemed to be avoiding his gaze. After waving frantically, trying to catch his attention, he finally looked in my direction. I couldn't believe my luck. It didn't really sink in that Jacko was shaking his head furiously.

Riding high on Lada-driven confidence, I decided that this was going to be the ideal opportunity to change the face of advertising by doing things differently. My big idea was to cast a 'real' person as the presenter, instead of the usual clone in a suit.

It was my first TV commercial, and it was going to be shot in London. Since it was the age of the train, I booked a ticket and managed to find a hotel within the means of the minuscule budget I'd been given. I couldn't wait to tell Caroline all about it and had decided to ask her to come down to the shoot.

When the time came, the words didn't quite come out as planned. Somewhere between my brain and my mouth the words 'Will you come down to London with me?' became 'Will you marry me?'

She seemed as surprised as I was by this unexpected proposal, especially since we'd only been going out for a month or so, but tearfully agreed.

I was now engaged to my dream woman and was about to make a commercial that would revolutionize advertising. And I was continuing to think in clichés, the latest one being 'Life doesn't get much better'.

Perhaps it should have been 'Pride comes before a fall'.

Ten

After getting back from London and witnessing the dismal reaction when I played the videotape of the WASS commercial to the entire agency staff, I spent the afternoon staring gloomily out of the window. There was a giant poster for the *Sunday Times* opposite the office that showed Adam and Eve gazing indifferently at a snake and asked the question 'Have you ever wished you were better informed?'

I found myself mouthing the word 'yes'.

I wish I'd been informed that a £2,000 budget wasn't nearly enough to produce a decent TV commercial, which was why no one else wanted to do it.

I wish I'd been informed that overruling the director to cast a mumbling, unshaved drunk to read my script was not a maverick, game-changing stroke of brilliance that would send me straight into the pages of *D&AD*, but a really, really bad idea.

And I also wish I'd been informed just how much it would hurt having your first TV commercial described by the chairman as 'an embarrassment to the agency'.

I could see his point, though. You couldn't really make out what the glassy-eyed presenter was saying, and since there hadn't been enough money for a voiceover, I'd had to say the words 'You can't go past WASS' at the end. I'd been so overawed when I did the recording; you could hear the fear in my voice. Everything about it was wrong, from the presenter's half-stumble at the fourteen-second mark to the pitiful couple of streamers and champagne corks in the final shot.

If the Lada campaign had been a ladder that took me to the top tier of copywriters at the agency, the WASS TV commercial was a long snake that sent me straight back to the bottom.

A phone call from Jon didn't help matters. He'd just heard that he was going to be in the next *D&AD*, after they'd chosen his admittedly brilliant trade ad for Daffodil toilet rolls. The concept was that a proof of an ad had been sent from the creative team to the Daffodil MD for his approval, and this took up the entire page. On it, the MD had handwritten his comments. He clearly wasn't happy with all the double entendres, which he'd crossed out and substituted with his preferred wording. So where the original read 'As the only branded 4-pack in this area of the market it will fill a vital gap', he'd deleted 'fill a vital gap' and replaced it with 'do very well'. Later, there was a line reading 'Your customers will get value with every penny they spend'. The irate MD had crossed out 'every penny they spend' and replaced it with 'every purchase'. At the end were the handwritten words 'See me before this is printed. MD'.

An appearance in *D&AD* was the ultimate achievement for art directors and copywriters, since it meant that their work was among the year's best. It also usually meant a big pay rise to stop other agencies poaching them. The Lada 'comparison' campaign had been my big hope to get into *D&AD*, but when I asked Clive if he'd heard anything yet, he looked confused and admitted that it hadn't been entered.

This was turning out to be one of the most depressing days

of my life, so I was relieved when Failure asked if I wanted to go for a lunchtime drink. Anything had to be better than staring out of the window at a poster that would undoubtedly also feature in *D&AD*, feeling sorry for myself.

I seriously considered having a Double Diamond, just in case it really did work wonders, but eventually settled for the usual Tetley's Bitter. But after a couple of pints it dawned on me that Failure might not be the best choice of companion to lift my spirits. He had started out positively, but the conversation was taking its predictable turn now that the requisite quantity of gloom-inducing alcohol had entered his bloodstream.

I'd made the mistake of telling Failure how lucky I felt about finding Caroline and that she was definitely the love of my life. This prompted him to reflect on his unrequited love for the blonde Squeak. He worshipped her, yet knew she was out of his league. 'I love her,' he mumbled into his beer, 'and she doesn't even know I exist.' I tried to console him, but he was beyond help and soon sloped off back to work. As a therapy session, it hadn't really worked for either of us.

I badly needed something else to take my mind off the WASS disaster and thought about cheering myself up by going to see a new band *NME* had been raving about. Unfortunately, Caroline had to work, so I dropped the idea. Besides, what kind of name was 'Depeche Mode' anyway?

Reading *Campaign* on the bus home (I liked my fellow passengers knowing about my glamorous career) reminded me of my mission in life. There was a double-page spread on Saatchi & Saatchi's success, and their plans to expand and create an international network. I needed to be part of this.

Much as I loved working with people like Jacko, Failure, Fred and Mike, WASS had been a serious setback to my plans. Advertising life was short, and Charlotte Street had never felt further away. As far as I was concerned, there were two routes open to me: I could either get a job in the Saatchi network, or at an agency that had plenty of high-profile TV clients, which would help me put together a portfolio that would force Jeremy Sinclair's hand.

When I got back to Caroline's flat, I rang Arnold at Saatchi Manchester in the vague hope that he'd somehow lost my number and had been trying to track me down so that he could offer me the job, but he told me that they had hired a senior (a word he stressed) creative team, who were already doing some great work.

In desperation, I flicked through the back pages of *Campaign*. This was where the jobs were. And this was where I saw an advert from BDH, an agency I had long admired. They were far more like a Manchester version of Saatchi & Saatchi than Saatchi & Saatchi (Manchester) were. And they were looking for a copywriter.

Manchester would be a great place to move to for several reasons. Caroline was keen to live there, I'd have far more Saturday afternoon football options, and, best of all, they had their own regional TV channel and newspaper. This was particularly exciting, despite the fact I'd always been unimpressed with regional TV. I hated having to watch teams like Rotherham United on a Sunday. But there was one huge advantage: a really embarrassing advert for, say, a used cars dealer in Leeds would only be seen locally and not across the Pennines in Manchester. The same principle applied to the *Yorkshire Post*, where most of my less memorable ads had appeared. Again, they would not have come to the attention of anyone living outside Yorkshire.

This gave me a slim chance of escaping the damage done to my reputation by WASS. Just to make sure, I removed all the WASS ads from the portfolio, so that there was nothing to link me with them. This still left enough work to take up eight pages, which felt about right.

I studied them closely, trying to see my work through the eyes of the creative director of one of the best agencies outside London. That was too depressing, so instead I concentrated on weeding out anything that wasn't up to scratch. That is the brilliant thing about portfolios. You get to include only the good stuff and leave out all the rubbish. A bit like advertising itself.

It was then that Charles Saatchi gave me a brilliant idea. I knew from my vast experience of interviews that one question that always came up at the end was 'Do you have any questions?' My plan was to research BDH thoroughly by going through my vast library of old copies of *Campaign* and memorizing every article that mentioned them so that I could ask intelligent-sounding questions. I didn't want to find myself wishing I'd been better informed. I'd learned my lesson from the WASS shoot.

It took hours and hours, but I managed to find quite a few relevant pieces. There was the announcement that they'd landed the Solvite account, and one of the founders had been interviewed about his plans for the 1980s. There were a few lines on the comings and goings at the agency, plus mentions of several prestigious awards they'd won. In all my years of reading *Campaign*, I'd never come across an award that wasn't described as 'prestigious'.

I was ready for my interview. And by the time I arrived at the BDH office overlooking the Old Trafford cricket ground I felt as though I was as well briefed as possible. It was just a shame I hadn't paid the same close attention to the coach timetable. If I had, I wouldn't have been twenty minutes late.

There was one other person waiting in reception, and he

looked every inch the adman. He was in his early twenties, with long curly hair, a leather bomber jacket (of course) and an expensive-looking portfolio. He was smoking a Marlboro, and he winked at me as I sat down.

If the idea was to intimidate me, it worked.

I noticed that his portfolio was bulging with work. Worse, it had a side panel which contained a VHS cassette. Which meant he had experience in making TV commercials that weren't so bad he was scared to show them.

I was about to slope off home when the kindly-looking middle-aged woman on reception asked if I was Dave. I nodded, and she asked me to follow her. We went through the creative department to an office at the end. A tall, slim man with fair hair and an eye-catching sleeveless Fairisle jumper extended his hand.

'Martin, creative director. Thanks for coming in. Take a seat.'

From that moment on, I couldn't have scripted a more perfect interview. The work went down well, we got on like old friends, and I showed genuine enthusiasm for the work they were doing. It was going brilliantly. Right up until the moment he asked something that was hardly unexpected.

'Any questions?'

This was the moment I'd been waiting for. A chance to show off the value of extensive research.

But my mind went blank. And the more I panicked, the harder it got to concentrate. Then it came to me. Something about Pritt Stick. They were launching a new product. Now what was it? The answer was tantalizingly close. Finally, I spoke.

'No, sorry.'

I don't know what caused me to go blank. Was it because he

hadn't asked where I saw myself in five years' time? Or was it my admiration for his jumper? Whatever the reason, Martin seemed relieved rather than disappointed.

'Well, I've just got one other candidate to see, but I'll definitely get something in the post to you this afternoon,' he said.

He shook my hand and smiled, but I wasn't sure whether it was an encouraging smile or a sorry-to-have-wasted-your-time smile. Watching the Marlboro-smoking adman strut towards the office I'd just vacated convinced me that it was the latter.

On the coach home I replayed and analysed every part of the interview and came to the conclusion that I'd completely blown it. My stomach churned as I imagined my rival pulling out his showreel to deliver the final coup de grâce to my hopes.

At least Martin stuck to his promise. The letter was waiting for me on the breakfast table the next morning, propped up against a jar of Marmite. I tore the envelope open, in a frenzied way that took me back to the last time I'd been desperate to land a job in advertising. This was starting to feel awfully familiar and I felt a cloud of doom envelop me.

I couldn't bring myself to read it, so I handed it to Caroline, telling her that if the phrase 'pipped at the post' appeared she should immediately set fire to it and we'd spend the day in the pub.

'Dear David,' she said, and then paused, as she saw me flinch in anticipation of the hammer-blow. 'Further to our meeting yesterday, I am writing to offer you the position of copywriter with this agency on a starting salary of six thousand . . .'

I jumped up and punched the air. A job in one of the best agencies outside London! Six grand a year! That was over a hundred quid a week, for doing something I loved. I'd never earned that much in my life.

'Working hours are nine to five-fifteen, blah blah blah . . . hour for lunch . . . compulsory contribution pension scheme, blah blah blah . . .'

It appeared that Caroline wasn't particularly interested in the minutiae of my working conditions, but she regained her enthusiasm when she reached the final paragraph.

'I was impressed by a lot of the work that you have done to date, and am quite sure you will be very successful with this agency.'

'Can you read it again?' I asked her.

She did. I sat still and let the feeling of sheer exhilaration wash over me.

'Looks like we're moving to Manchester,' she said, sounding excited at the prospect.

My leaving party took place in what Mike described on the invitation as 'the plush country and western atmosphere of The Eagle public house' and ended up at someone's flat, by which time everything had become a bit of a blur. The last thing I remember seeing was Failure dancing slowly with the blonde Squeak to 'I'm Not in Love' by 10CC. He had his arms around her and they were snogging passionately. Maybe neither of us was quite the failure we'd imagined.

It seemed a perfect moment to leave Leeds behind.

My fiancée and I found a tiny two-room flat in a crumbling detached Victorian house in the Manchester suburbs. What appeared to be a cupboard at first glance turned out to be the kitchen. The bedroom was so small that there was barely enough room on the wall for the two Jeremy Sinclair Conservative Party ads and my three Lada ads.

We moved in on a Sunday, and after a restless night's sleep I was dressed and ready for work by the time the alarm went off at 7.15.

End of Part One

Part Two

Eleven

Some things about my new surroundings at BDH were instantly familiar: the piles of well-thumbed advertising annuals from around the world (although the Norwegian one was a first); the secretaries who had apparently been supplied by a modelling agency; and the art director drumming his fingers while waiting for me to come up with a headline.

I had been paired with Danny, a nervy chain smoker, and even the job we were doing seemed oddly familiar. It was a trade ad for a TV advert that was set in a jungle. Yet another one. Jungles had enjoyed a burst of popularity among copywriters and art directors, with Lada, Guinness, Bird's Tropical Trifle and now Unger's Chipsteaks using the location to sell their products.

An Unger's Chipsteak was a meat product of uncertain provenance which was described in the brief as the 'market leader in the premium comminuted meat sector'. Comminuted? It sounded like a segment they'd invented just so they could say they led it. The advert showed Tarzan swinging home from the jungle pub via a series of vines, so that he could enjoy the Chipsteak being cooked by Mrs Tarzan (Jane, presumably). Although the jungle looked more like the woods in Longford

Park (which was just down the road) than the African wilderness, it was a high-profile advert and I enjoyed being a part of it. I felt a bit sorry for the creative team, though. They'd probably imagined an all-expenses-paid trip to Costa Rica, Cameroon or wherever else there were jungles, and instead ended up in a park in Stretford, just opposite B&Q.

I wrote down the words 'More of what it takes to survive in today's catering jungle', but quickly scribbled them out as I felt they bore more than a passing resemblance to my Lada line 'More of what it takes to survive in today's motoring jungle'. It was bad enough stealing ideas from old annuals; stealing ideas from myself was a new low. Instead I concentrated on jungle puns, recklessly ignoring the advice of Dave Trott, and it didn't take long before the inevitable words 'When you see our jungle commercial for Chipsteaks, prepare for a stampede' appeared on my A4 pad.

As Danny was putting pictures to my words, I saw a sight that made me feel as though I had finally made it. A tea lady. This meant no more having to make tea for everyone. And it wasn't just tea she supplied – her trolley carried a range of food, including Kit-Kats, crisps, Topic bars and Mars bars. No more having to go to the shops, either. This was life on the higher steps of the advertising ladder.

After my morning Mars bar, I concentrated hard on getting the words to the Chipsteaks advert right. Not just because it was my first job in a new agency, but because I'd recently started to see trade ads in a new light.

For most agencies, they were something to be passed on to the junior team, but I'd noticed that Saatchi & Saatchi held them in greater regard. In a recent copy of *The Grocer* I'd seen a couple of ads which bore unmistakable signs of having been created at 80 Charlotte Street. One in particular, for Purina dog food, was so good that I cut it out with a scalpel and blu-tacked it to the wall. It simply showed a 20kg bag with the line 'The fastest-moving dog food since postmen'. I immediately rang Jon and he confirmed that it was the work of recently joined copywriter Mick Petherick.

I knew from *Campaign* that there had been a few changes at Saatchi recently – Jeff Stark was working with a new art director, Paul Arden, while the new team of Fergus Fleming and John Turnbull were making plenty of headlines. They had done so much work I admired that they had their own section on the wall of my cubicle. This included trade ads, which I saw as conclusive proof that Saatchi & Saatchi took these seriously. And if they took them seriously, so did I. I wanted to demonstrate to Jeremy Sinclair that I understood the importance of this oft-neglected discipline.

As I was crafting the copy, I noticed that phrases like 'super beefy flavour and succulence' were making me crave a Chipsteak, which was good evidence that the ad was working. Especially as I had no idea what they tasted like.

'These Chipsteaks – are they any good?' I asked Danny.

'Yeah, they're OK actually. You know that we can buy 'em in bulk from the client?'

'How much?'

'Under half price, I think.'

This was exciting. The only time I'd been offered a special rate for a client's product was when the brunette Squeak asked if I wanted to own one of A. E. Arthur's Venus dress forms at the discounted price of £15.75. I declined, but suspected she might have had better luck with Jacko. Chipsteaks were a different matter, though. And that kind of price was too good to turn down.

Danny told me to go through to Annie in Media and she'd

sort it out. I found her and put my order in, perhaps getting a little carried away in the process.

When I got back to the flat after work, I broke the good news to Caroline. 'I bought a load of burgers and stuff from one of our clients today. Perks of the job.'

She didn't look as pleased as I'd imagined. 'What did you get?'

I took the list out of my pocket. If she wasn't impressed now, she would be by the time I'd finished. 'Eight boxes of Steakwiches, six to a box; six boxes of Escaloped Veal, four to a box; four boxes of Breaded Lamb Steakaways – new product, four to a box; same with Breaded Pork Steakaways; ten boxes of Chipsteaks – they're the bestseller – eight in a box; and a couple of boxes of Veal Cordon Bleu, only two in a box.'

'So you've ordered over thirty boxes of meat.'

'Comminuted meat. And it was a really good deal – less than a week's wages and should keep us going for months.'

She nodded. She was coming round.

'And where are you going to keep them?' she asked.

'What do you mean?'

'Well, we haven't got a freezer.'

A shudder ran through me. Shit. I hadn't thought of that.

'Well, I thought we'd get one tomorrow,' I countered.

This seemed to make her happier. I'd been avoiding buying practical things like household goods as I still had hopes of getting a jukebox (like Charles Saatchi), but now I had no choice. We arranged to meet outside the Arndale Centre at lunchtime.

As soon as I got in to work the next morning, I could see that Danny was looking flustered.

'We've got an urgent job, needed by twelve,' he told me.

I hoped it wasn't the Chipsteak trade ad needing a rewrite –

no, apparently we'd be going through that with the account director later. The urgent job was an ad that was going in Saturday's *Manchester Evening News*, and it was for Euro Exhausts, a new 'pop-in' garage where you could get your exhaust fitted on the spot, without having to make an appointment.

Sometimes an idea comes to you instantly. I experienced that feeling of raw excitement as I thought of a line that was truly original and groundbreaking. I scribbled it down before I had the chance to forget it and handed the piece of paper to Danny. It read 'Splutter splutter cough cough pop pop pop pop along to the Euro Exhausts grand opening'.

'What do you reckon?' I asked.

'Yeah, like it.'

I couldn't help noticing he was looking over my shoulder as he said this. Following his gaze, I saw what he was staring at – an advert showing a Unipart sparkplug:

Ours are made to start first time.

Our comp . . .

Our compompom . . .

Our compompompompet . . .

Our compompompompetitors . . .

It was part of my tribute to Saatchi superteam Fergus Fleming and John Turnbull.

My biggest disappointment wasn't that the idea had been done before – most ideas had. It was that I wouldn't be able to show it to Jeremy Sinclair and impress him with my originality, on the grounds that it wasn't really original, even though the theft had been subconscious. Still, it represented a decent morning's work and I felt that I'd got off to a good start with my career at BDH.

Buying a fridge/freezer was a race against the clock as both Caroline and I had only an hour for lunch, but after doing the rounds of city-centre electrical shops we found a Zanussi Z20/10 at Rumbelows which was within our £200 budget. By one penny. It felt like the right choice and I handed the salesman my Access card. Admittedly I had been swayed by the adverts which claimed that this machine was made on Planet Zanussi and, more credibly, was a product of the appliance of science. Crucially, it was on sale at the 'down-to-earth price of just £199.99', according to the poster in the window.

The 'appliance of science' line had been written by a young copywriter at Geers Gross called Adrian Press. Clearly a name to watch.

'Where are you planning on putting it?' Caroline asked as I quietly abandoned the idea of a last-minute lobbying attempt to get a Commodore Vic 20 Home computer instead. It was the same price, and you could write letters, play chess and keep home accounts on it. The only thing it couldn't do, unfortunately, was keep Chipsteaks frozen.

'In the kitch— Oh, I see what you mean.' The kitchen wasn't big enough. It would take up every inch of floorspace. And other options were limited. 'It'll have to go in the lounge.'

She nodded and said that she had to rush off; she'd just started a new job as a nurse at the BUPA hospital in Whalley Range. I was also in a hurry, and after arranging for the freezer to be delivered over the weekend, I splashed out on a taxi as I didn't want to be late either.

Ten minutes and £1.25 later, I ran up the stairs of the agency and made it with seconds to spare.

94

The creative department was empty. And when people started dribbling in over the next few hours I realized that the formal hours spelled out in my letter of appointment were more vague suggestions than hard and fast rules.

When Danny got back, we went to present the Chipsteak ad to Gordon, the account director. Gordon was a beefy, testosterone-fuelled man with intense eyes who looked as though he needed to shave several times a day. He grabbed a pen and immediately rewrote large segments of the ad while muttering under his breath. His changes, surprisingly, were good: he added a nicely judged line here and there, and wrapped it up with a cleverer ending than I had managed.

I wasn't used to account directors who knew what they were doing. As I read through the retyped copy afterwards, I had to admit that the advert was much improved. I was still a bit worried though and asked Danny if he thought the client would approve it. He pointed at Gordon and said that clients always approved things Gordon presented. Danny was right, and I couldn't wait to see the advert appear in *The Grocer*, alongside Jon's ad for Daffodil toilet rolls and John Turnbull's Purina ad.

The rest of the week passed quickly. I was having to work harder than ever, but the results made it all worthwhile. Danny and I were getting on well and he even chipped in with the occasional headline. I was beginning to think that we would be able to approach Saatchi & Saatchi as a team, but decided not to mention my plans this early on.

That Saturday morning, our new Zanussi Z20/10 fridge/freezer was delivered.

'Where do you want it, mate?' asked the middle-aged man in a brown linen overcoat with a big Rumbelows logo embroidered on the breast pocket.

I showed him through to the living room and pointed to a space next to the rented TV. He acted as though he'd never had to install a fridge/freezer in someone's living area before, but I was already seeing the benefits. To start with, it made getting a can of Heineken while watching football much easier.

I was soon in love with our fridge/freezer. I'd never had one before. It was the first time since leaving home that I hadn't had to write DAVE on every carton of Ski Yoghurt in the fridge just to make sure no one nicked them. Caroline and I often sat on the sofa admiring the sleek, clean Italian lines of our Zanussi Z20/10. I might not have been so impressed had I known that it would almost destroy my advertising career.

Twelve

Over a Bank Holiday weekend we had Ungers comminuted meat products for nine meals in a row. Chipsteaks for breakfast, Breaded Lamb Steakaways for lunch, Veal Cordon Bleu for dinner. We had no choice – even the spacious Zanussi Z20/10 with its 3.5-cubic-feet freezer capacity couldn't hold the thirty-four boxes I'd bought, so we had to get through as many as we could as quickly as we could. I'd reached the point of sprinkling curry powder and pouring HP sauce or Heinz Ketchup on whichever comminuted meat product I was eating, just to try and persuade my taste buds that they were getting something different. But Caroline and I had already gone way beyond the point of ever wanting to see another Chipsteak or variant thereof again.

My diet may have been a bit limited, but work was a lot more interesting. It was all going well, largely thanks to Gordon, who had taken on Margaret's role of correcting my copy and expanding on it by rewriting anything he didn't like. Which was plenty. But as the weeks rolled by I became increasingly assured that I was able to act like a real adman, even if my place of work wasn't quite Saatchi, or anywhere near Charlotte Street.

Gordon had just brought a major new account into the

agency, which Danny and I would be working on. It was a chain of electrical stores, dotted around the north of England, called Vallances. I was familiar with the Leeds branch as I had spent an entire £95 tax rebate there, on a space-age Sinclair Microvision pocket TV, so I could watch cricket at work. The tiny two-inch screen and fuzzy picture quality made this virtually impossible, however, and I tried, unsuccessfully, to take it back.

My first thought for Vallances was to get a celebrity. This was inspired by Saatchi's brilliant use of JR Ewing from *Dallas* in their Dunlop campaign. JR was synonymous with oil, and he'd heard about Dunlop's tyres 'that save petrol'. In the adverts, he did his best to make sure people didn't try them. In fact, his mission seemed to be to suppress the news that they even existed.

I thought this was brilliant, and it was also the inspiration behind my only previous attempt to use a celebrity, when I wrote a WASS script for comedian Frank Carson, whose catch-phrase was 'It's the way I tell 'em'. In it, he would be standing in front of a selection of cars, finishing his pitch with the words 'It's the way I sell 'em'. No one really liked the idea.

Gordon, unsurprisingly, was keen on a more aggressive approach. His thought was that since Vallances had the cheapest prices, we should come out and say just that. He wanted to use the headline 'Vallances – you can't buy cheaper', which wasn't a million miles away from an advert I'd seen in the *Bromley Advertiser* on my last visit home that went 'Comet. Lowest prices – that's a promise'. The good news was that Gordon liked my tagline 'At Vallances prices you don't need to shop around'. Which at the time I thought was true.

Then we got the brief for the first ad, and way down the list of products featured was the Zanussi Z20/10 fridge/freezer, which was priced at £202.99. I immediately pointed out to Gordon that this wasn't the cheapest, as I'd just bought one for three pounds less. He shrugged his massive shoulders and wandered off.

Once he'd gone, I checked the details, just to make sure it was the same fridge/freezer. Model number Z20/10? Check. Gross capacity 6.7 cubic feet for the fridge, 3.5 cubic feet for the freezer? Check. Auto defrost and reversible doors? Check. There was no doubt about it. This was exactly the same model. The only difference was that it cost £202.99 at Vallances. I even dug out the Rumbelows receipt from the sea of bus tickets in my pocket to make absolutely sure I'd got it for £199.99.

I felt a deep sense of moral outrage, which is rare for a copywriter. But in the end I did exactly what the client wanted. Which isn't rare for a copywriter.

When the ad appeared in the *Manchester Evening News* a couple of weeks later, it stirred up my feelings all over again. As I made my way to the pub, all I could think of was how wrong Vallances had been to make such an outrageous claim.

Our lunchtime pub of choice was The White Lion, the main attraction for my colleagues being the Webster's Bitter on tap. The main attraction for me was the Space Invaders machine, which I headed for as soon as I had that first pint in my hand.

It was hard to believe that technology had advanced so much in the few years since Pong, an electronic tennis game, was at the cutting edge. So much so that it had been used in a Heineken advert by Collett Dickenson Pearce (copywriter John Kelley, art director John O'Driscoll) in which a glass of Heineken refreshed the losing paddle, turning it into an easy winner. That game looked positively primitive compared to Space Invaders, a machine that allowed you to destroy aliens before they got a chance to destroy you. These weren't cuddly aliens like the ones in the Smash advert, who found the idea of peeling potatoes instead of getting them from a packet so amusing. These were aliens who wanted to wipe you out, along with the rest of humanity.

Following a satisfactory session – I was just short of my high score when I lost the last of my three lives – I sat down next to Bruce, a fellow copywriter. After several pints, the feelings of injustice over the Vallances fridge/freezer claim once again bubbled to the surface.

'I just don't get how they can say they're the cheapest when they're clearly not,' I said. 'Look!' I reached into my pocket for the receipt. 'Three quid cheaper at Rumbelows.'

'Don't let them get away with it, mate,' said Bruce.

'Oh, I won't, don't worry about that,' I responded.

'I can't believe they'd expect you to lie just so they could flog a few more fridges.'

He was clearly goading me, intending to fuel my genuine sense of outrage with his faked sense of outrage, but I was too drunk to notice.

'Yeah,' I said. 'This is *wrong*. You know what I'm going to do?'

'Do tell.'

'I'm going to put in a formal complaint to the Advertising Standards Authority.'

Bruce nodded. 'It's the only way to stop this kind of thing happening again.'

I sat back, my anger finally coming under control. The decision was made. I couldn't back down now even if I wanted to. I had somehow managed to get myself into a position where I would be complaining about one of my own ads.

When I got back to the office, I drafted a letter, which Bruce helpfully offered to type out using the typewriter of a secretary who fancied him. When he brought it back, I signed it and he hurried off to the postbox outside the office to post it.

I felt satisfied that I'd taken a stand and was confident that I'd done the right thing. A feeling that lasted until I started to sober up.

There comes a time after every heavy drinking session when the question 'What have I done?' invariably surfaces. For me, it came later that night when I was getting stuck into my Veal Cordon Bleu.

Put simply, if Gordon found out what I'd done, he would probably kill me; if Martin found out, he'd just sack me. The potential repercussions were enormous. Vallances would almost certainly shop around for a new agency if they discovered that the copywriter on their account was responsible for them having to scrap an expensive ad. And BDH would end up losing commission from the ad worth thousands of pounds, on top of a client they'd only recently landed. News of both outcomes would spread rapidly throughout the industry. Possibly all the way to Charlotte Street.

This cloud continued to hang over me the next morning as I worked on a series of small-space ads for Vallances, pretending to concentrate really hard so that Gordon and Martin wouldn't come and talk to me. Gordon had already briefed me on these ads, and his idea was that since the prices were so good (and I made a conscious decision not to check them against Rumbelows') the headline should be nothing more than the price.

Before this, I'd only ever used two ways to give prices, and that was to preface them with the words 'just' or 'only'. Now I was exploring a third way. So the Philips 4139 Toaster was shown with a huge £13.95 above it and a line underneath saying 'It's not often that a Philips Toaster pops up at a price like this, but it has at Vallances'. I had seriously considered incorporating the subhead 'unbelievable value' as a covert way of alerting the public to the truth, but decided that might just inflame the situation. I was glad to have something so undemanding to work on, but still I felt a slight twinge of guilt every time I wrote the line 'At Vallances prices you don't need to shop around'.

The letter arrived just as I was beginning to think the advertising gods were taking care of me and my complaint had somehow got lost in the post. The ASA logo on the envelope caused a gnawing sensation in my stomach and I suddenly couldn't face my breakfast of toast and MaMade marmalade. Predictably, I couldn't bring myself to open the letter and handed it to Caroline. She was used to this by now and did what I wanted her to do without asking.

'Dear Mr Roberts,' she read out loud, and I could see from the panic in her eyes that it wasn't good news. 'The ASA Council has now adjudicated on your complaint and agreed with our recommendation that the ad breached their code. We ask you to treat the attached report as confidential. It will be made available to journalists under embargo, from the Monday before publication. Vallances will also receive a copy of the adjudication today. Thank you for bringing the matter to our attention, L. Parker (Miss), Investigations Executive.'

Caroline looked up from the letter and saw that I was slumped over the kitchen table.

'This isn't good, is it?' she asked.

I shook my head.

I was on edge the whole of the next morning at work, knowing that news of my complaint would be out by now. The only hope I clung to was that the ASA hadn't named the complainant, but I didn't really believe that.

It was almost a relief when I looked up and saw Gordon storming towards my desk. He was not looking pleased; even more alarmingly, he was holding the ad in his right hand. I mentally scanned the room for an escape route, but it was too late. He slapped the ad down on the desk in front of me, and I braced myself.

'Some tit has complained about this ad,' he shouted, with typical fury.

'Oh, you're kidding me.'

'Nope. Standards Authority says we have to pull it, so you're going to have to do a new one. You've got twenty minutes.'

And with that he stormed off.

I could hear Bruce giggling on the other side of the partition.

I had never been happier to rewrite an ad. This time they could make whatever claim they wanted. I wouldn't complain.

It took several months before the fear of being found out gradually faded, to be replaced by the excitement of my and Caroline's forthcoming wedding. And as the day approached, there was yet another life-altering event to embark upon.

A shopping trip to the Co-op.

Thirteen

Normally we went to Sainsbury's for our weekly shop because, as everyone knew, good food costs less at Sainsbury's. But these were exceptional circumstances. What with the cost of hiring suits, going on a honeymoon and saving up for the deposit on a house, we were just about broke.

After carrying out a bit of price comparison research I came to the ghastly conclusion that we had to think the unthinkable. We had to sacrifice getting our usual brands from Sainsbury's to stock up on the Co-op's own-brand products instead. 'Look after the pennies,' I thought to myself, making my regular journey into cliché territory, 'and the pounds will look after themselves.'

The very idea of going without our usual heavily advertised products prompted a sinking feeling. A life without Hovis bread, Signal toothpaste and Ribena felt like a life without hope. And no Yeoman Instant Potato, Heinz Rice Pudding or McVities United Biscuits? Insupportable. Yet it had to be done.

It was traumatic to pass the display of beautifully arranged bottles of Corona, whose every bubble had passed its fizzical, and place a one-and-a-half-litre bottle of Co-op Lemonade, with its dull, uninspired label, into the shopping trolley. Equally difficult was ignoring my favourite margarine, Flora – even though I could hear Terry Wogan's voice in my head, whispering that it was 'high in polyunsaturates' which made it 'the margarine for men' – and picking up a tub of Co-op's clearly inferior 'Silver Soft' margarine. It just felt wrong, somehow.

The most crushing disappointment of all came when it was time for tea. More than twenty years of enjoying the PG Tips chimps shifting pianos, riding in the Tour de France and living the good life in a stately home counted for nothing as I found myself having to choose Co-op '99' Tea Bags, on the grounds that they were just 57p for eighty as opposed to 73p.

The only occasion this new-found discipline failed me was when I simply couldn't bring myself to choose Co-op Creamed Tomato Soup over Heinz Cream of Tomato Soup. The latest ad for the latter, promising 'red waterfalls tumbling into a tomatoey ocean', proved too strong to resist and Caroline agreed that we would be justified in paying the extra twelve pence for four tins.

Still, the detour to the Co-op had served its purpose. As we loaded the 'Your caring sharing Co-op' bags into the car, I felt sure we'd done the right thing. The £3.74 we'd saved could go towards the cost of the honeymoon.

Despite my initial excitement at the riches on offer at BDH, I had discovered with time that our combined salaries didn't stretch as far as we'd imagined, mainly due to my lifelong ability to live beyond my means. Being this poor was demoralizing, and yet another reason for me to start working for Saatchi & Saatchi as soon as possible. Famously, they paid huge money. In fact they had recently taken on Geoff Seymour, a copywriter, at a salary so enormous that it had been named after him. The £100,000 a year it had taken to persuade him to move to Charlotte Street became known universally in the trade as 'a Seymour'.

If I'd been on a Seymour, or even half a Seymour, we could have shopped where we liked. Not only that, my planned surprise honeymoon, beginning at the Hotel Odinsve in Reykjavik and ending up at the Hotel Skeppsholmen in Stockholm, would have comfortably gone ahead. But with my annual income of slightly more than a twentieth of a Seymour, we had to make do with a tour of Cornwall B&Bs, culminating in three nights in St Ives with Mr and Mrs Brookbank.

The wedding would be taking place in a church in the small Devon village where Caroline's parents ran the post office. But before we could drive down there, I had one last job to do for Gordon. He'd been chasing the Indesit electrical goods account for ages and they had finally relented and given us a one-off project, a six-week national press campaign for the Indesit 101 automatic washing machine. If we did well, it had been hinted that plenty more business could follow.

As I stared at the brief, I was faced with conflicting instincts – the desire to produce award-winning portfolio-boosting work in the national press versus fear of what Gordon might do to me if the campaign didn't work.

I scribbled the word Indesit on my pad a few times, hoping that something would leap out, and as I was staring at it for about the fiftieth time, an idea suddenly came to me. With adrenalin pumping through me, I wrote down the word 'Indesitscribable'. This was brilliant – one word that combined 'Indesit' and 'indescribable'.

The feeling of elation vanished as quickly as it had appeared, when it dawned on me that I'd subconsciously stolen Aero's

'Indescribabubble' line, which had been the work of Salman Rushdie, a copywriter at Ogilvy & Mather.

I was badly missing Danny, who could be relied on to come up with a few original thoughts, which then often sparked something off in me. But he was away on a shoot for Chipsteaks and I would be working with Andy, a junior art director, on this. We quickly decided on a comparison campaign, mainly because that was what Gordon told us to do.

Once again, Gordon's instincts were spot on. The more I found out about how well the Indesit 101 compared to its competitors, the better it sounded. By the time I'd ploughed through everyone's brochures and covered the wall with torn-out photos as well as close-up illustrations of features, it was obvious that the Indesit 101 was the finest automatic washer on the market. I felt totally confident that when consumers saw my headline 'Can any machine match the incredible Indesit 101?', they would shake their heads and say to themselves, 'Absolutely not.'

As I looked at the comparison table Gordon had given us, I felt genuinely sorry for anyone who had recently bought a Hotpoint 18331. Despite paying over thirty quid more, they would be missing out on two-spin speed, separate temperature control, a three-part soap dispenser and a no-spin button.

The Indesit 101 was so clearly superior that I felt a sense of pride when I wrote things like 'Indesit are one of the world's largest producers of domestic appliances' and 'Unlike many companies who simply assemble machines from bought-out parts, we manufacture most components ourselves'. I could actually feel my chest swelling as I added the words 'To our own standards'.

As I moved on to the trade ad, the copy took on a tone of desperation as it sank in what was at stake. When I described the comparison campaign, it somehow went from being fairly routine to 'Probably the most aggressive washing machine advertising ever' where 'as you can imagine, the effect will be shattering'. A simple phone number became 'a specially installed Action Line to deal with the anticipated rush of orders'. And the fact that someone might be interested after reading the comparison ad became 'The customer is virtually sold on the idea of an Indesit 101 before she has even set foot in the shop'. I'd done everything but plead with them to put in a large order for Indesit 101s.

I told Andy that since we needed to communicate our message in a no-frills businesslike manner, the headline I'd come up with was simply 'The comparison campaign starts on 7 October'. 'It doesn't need anything else,' I explained. 'This isn't the time to try anything clever.'

The real reason for that headline was, of course, that I couldn't think of anything clever.

Instead of going to the pub with Andy at lunchtime, I stayed in the office and enjoyed a couple of sandwiches (ingredients: Co-op Long Loaf sliced bread, Co-op 'Silver Soft' margarine and Co-op Lemon Curd). It was painful missing out on my usual Webster's Bitter, pub lunch and Space Invaders, but sacrifices had to be made.

When Andy got back, he finished the layout, which looked great. He was happy, since his work would be appearing in the national papers. Gordon was happy, probably because of the line about this being the most aggressive campaign ever. And I was happy, since I could now go off and get married.

On the morning of our departure, due to a stocktaking miscalculation Caroline and I were already out of food and had to have Co-op Creamed Rice Pudding for breakfast. At least it had the bonus of a 'win a Metro' competition on the label, which I entered instead of reading the *Guardian*.

This was prompted by the thought that pretty much any car would have been a far smoother ride down to Devon than our Vauxhall Viva. We'd got it cheap because (a) it had been painted in bright blue emulsion paint and (b) it was a left-hand-drive. It was the sort of car that even a Lada owner looked down on, but it somehow managed to get us to Cheriton Fitzpaine, where the wedding would be taking place.

The first thing I thought when we arrived was that the location was straight out of Geoff Seymour's Hovis advert (Collett Dickenson Pearce). It was an idyllic country village with stone cottages and narrow cobbled streets; the only thing missing was a small boy pushing his bike up the hill with a basket full of brown bread, accompanied by the sound of a brass band playing the New World Symphony.

And everything about the day itself was just as perfect. Jacko and Mike had come down from Leeds, Andy from Manchester and Jon from London. Jon was the official wedding photographer, on the slightly irrational grounds that he had an Olympus Trip, which was the same camera used by David Bailey to photograph a wedding in a recent D&AD Silver Award-winning advert. For a present, Jon had got us a small plastic jukebox, which would have to do until I could afford a real one (apparently Charles Saatchi now had several). Mike, for reasons best known to himself, gave us a plastic model of the Vatican, which lit up at night. Andy's contribution was a Tower Royale non-stick saucepan. Apparently he too had been influenced by a classic advert, the one showing a doctor easily removing a pan that a little boy had wedged on to his head, thus demonstrating its non-stickability.

As I and my best friend (and best man) Dave pulled up to the church in a Bentley, courtesy of Western Limousines Ltd, my thoughts naturally turned to Geoff Seymour and the fact that he wouldn't have needed to hire a Bentley since he already owned one.

The wedding went brilliantly. I even managed to avoid thinking about advertising for the entire ceremony, although the vicar did look a bit like the one in the Ben Sherman shirts advert who sang 'It's a Ben Sher-man'. I was so caught up in the occasion that I didn't even tell Jon I'd spent the week working on a major national campaign or ask him whether any copywriter vacancies had come up at Saatchi & Saatchi (not until the reception, anyway). He was also on his best behaviour, not mentioning the fact that he'd got into *D&AD* until the same time. When he did get around to it, he also hinted that he was art-directing some charity ads which could well make next year's edition.

After that, thanks mainly to an excessive amount of the 'reassuringly expensive' Stella Artois (coincidentally, one of Geoff Seymour's taglines), things became a bit of a blur, but it had been a fantastic couple of days, topped off by dancing to John Lennon's 'Imagine' with my new bride. It was the Indesit 101 of weddings. Nothing I'd ever done compared to it.

When Caroline and I got back to Manchester after our honeymoon, our first major decision as a married couple was to abandon the Co-op experiment and get back to normal shopping. I was hoping for a pay rise – perhaps taking me up to a fifteenth of a Seymour – since the Indesit ad had gone down well and they'd given the agency a couple more projects.

The second major decision was to use the money her parents had given us as a wedding present to buy a washing machine with a no-spin button and electronic speed control. Since no machine could possibly match the incredible Indesit 101, we bought one from Comet, which had recently won the prestigious 'Retailer of the Year' award. As a major bonus, it came with twenty-one free packs of Bold Automatic.

The third major decision was to take our first steps on the property ladder, buying a mid-terrace house in the quiet, peaceful suburb of Chorlton-cum-Hardy, known – ironically as it turned out – as Nothing-Ever-Happens. Within weeks of moving in, the Manchester riots, which had started in Moss Side, were spreading and getting uncomfortably close. Cars were burning in nearby streets, the sky was lit up like Fireworks Night, and we entered married life to the distant sound of windows being smashed.

We never really felt in any danger, though. Besides, Caroline had her crossword puzzles to take her mind off things. And I had beer.

Fourteen

Beer seemed to be taking over my life. The Heineken poster from my old flat now dominated the living room, with its message 'Heineken refreshes the parts other beers cannot reach', while the fridge had as many cans of Heineken as the freezer had boxes of Chipsteaks. But more importantly, Danny and I had been handed the chance to become BDH's Beer Men.

Beer Men were the glory boys of an agency. They were the centre-forward, lead singer and opening bowler all rolled into one. Beer Men lived by a different set of rules. They could wander off to the pub at any time, without question, and get reimbursed for every pint they sank while there. They could sit in their cubicles, drinking glasses of beer all day, while everyone else had to make do with cups of coffee. And if they needed a few cans to take home, these would be instantly provided. They could basically justify any of these things and more in the name of product research.

And all because they worked on the agency's beer account.

Every big agency had its Beer Men. At Saatchi it was Jeff Stark and Jeremy Sinclair, whose campaign for John Bull Bitter always made me laugh with its glorification of Romford. At BMP it was John Webster, who was spoken about in hushed tones for his Yorkshire Bitter adverts, while Dave Trott proved there was more to him than writing career advice booklets by combining with John Webster to create the greatest beer advert I'd ever seen – the 'Gertcha' one for Courage Best, with its superb soundtrack, featuring Chas and Dave, which amazingly worked despite containing no cockney rhyming slang whatsoever.

Earlier that afternoon, Gordon had told us that he wanted a name for a new beer, brewed by the agency's biggest account, Webster's. I'd often wondered who came up with product names like Ry-King crispbread, Vapona fly killer, Hai Karate aftershave and Batchelor's Marrowfat Peas. Now I knew. It was people like us. This was my chance to be solely responsible for the name of a beer that would be seen in pubs (not to mention off-licences) throughout the country. Hopefully this would include The Pregnant Man, Saatchi & Saatchi's private pub in the mews behind their office, named after Jeremy Sinclair's classic poster.

After work, Danny and I decided to carry on at my place, and as I ran through the names I'd come up with so far it was apparent that the beer wasn't refreshing my brain. Some of the ideas made little sense, and there was a hint of desperation towards the end, with suggestions ranging from 'Beerschot' (I bet nobody else had thought of naming a beer after a Belgian second division football team, even if it was one with a pub in each corner of their ground) to, simply, 'GoodBeer'.

Before Danny could run through his suggestions, I noticed our glasses were empty. The only regret I had about the new house was that we no longer had a fridge in the living room. This meant a trek through to the kitchen every time we needed a refill.

'Another beer?' I asked Danny.

'Cheers.'

'Chipsteak?'

'No, I'll pass, thanks.'

When I got back with the beers, he read out the names he'd come up with. 'Top Brass' was his favourite, and he had plenty more on the same brass band theme, including 'Trombone', 'Black Dyke' and 'Floral Dance'. They all made the shortlist, alongside a few of my uninspired efforts. We were desperate to do a really good job because there had been rumours of a big-budget TV commercial for Great Northern Bitter, a local brew, in the pipeline – and it wasn't too far-fetched to think that Gordon was looking to see if we had what it took to become Beer Men.

The fact that I didn't have any good names didn't turn out to be a barrier to success, as Gordon absolutely loved the name 'Top Brass', and so did the client.

We had passed the test, but there was more. The next step was a poster for Great Northern Bitter party cans. Once again I worked at home on it – or, more accurately, I was watching *News at Ten* when the idea came to me. There was footage of rioters looting an off-licence in Rusholme and the line 'Carry out and carry on' suddenly popped up in my mind.

Gordon liked it. We knew this because he then handed us the brief for the Great Northern Bitter TV advert, which was by far the biggest job I'd been given. It had a budget that was huge, even by London standards. The task was to launch the beer into the southern market, where it would compete with a couple of other northern brews – Trophy Bitter, whose advert featured wry northerners in cloth caps, and John Smith's Bitter, whose advert also featured wry northerners in cloth caps.

We had somehow to reach the same heights.

For once, the Charles Saatchi 'immersing yourself in the

product' strategy was enjoyable. We started drinking cans of Great Northern Bitter at around ten in the morning, and only stopped to go to the pub at lunchtime, where we drank pints of Great Northern Bitter. When we got back around three, the drinking continued. Or as I called it, research.

Occasionally my subconscious drew me towards a classic Saatchi poster blu-tacked on to our cubicle wall, which showed the male symbol of a circle topped by an arrow pointing upwards, followed by the same picture, but with the arrow now drooping. The line, written by James Lowther, said 'If you drink too much, there's one part that every beer can reach'. I managed to ignore its warning. My work was more important. And right now, three weeks after being briefed, we'd reached a stage where Gordon was getting impatient for ideas.

Most of our scripts featured northerners in cloth caps, and most of them had whippets by their feet as they supped ale and said things like 'ee by gum'. I'm sure if we'd been advertising French Bitter we would have had beret-wearing onion-sellers on bicycles, and if it had been Scottish Bitter there would have been tartan-clad redheaded giants tossing cabers while eating porridge.

Despite this unimaginative portrayal of northern folk, there was one idea we quite liked. The trouble was, I had a feeling that while Gordon had demanded something that stood out from our competitors' ads, this merely blended in.

It was set in an evening class somewhere in London. The packed classroom was full of men wearing, you guessed it, cloth caps. They had whippets at their feet. I'd lived in the North for more than two years and still hadn't seen anyone who looked like that, in the same way that I'd never heard a Londoner speak in rhyming slang. Perhaps these things existed only in ad world. Anyway, the teacher was showing them how to look and talk like northerners, so that they could go up North and drink Great Northern Bitter. The concept of the ad was that you no longer had to go to these lengths to get your hands on Great Northern Bitter, because it was now available in the South. This was going to have to be our big idea because we didn't have time to come up with anything else. Gordon had summonsed us.

When we got to his office, he seemed on edge, drumming his desk with his fingers. Gordon was a man in a hurry, which made me want to draw out the last few precious moments of peace as long as possible. I'd been worried about how he was going to react all morning. The previous Beer Men had been kicked off the account with a very public bollocking. All they'd done wrong was present an idea that Gordon didn't like.

As I read our script through to Gordon, doubts suddenly flooded into my brain. Why couldn't I have portrayed northerners as something other than cloth-cap-wearing whippet owners? And besides, why would any pub turn down customers just because they were from a few hundred miles away? My mouth was so dry with nerves that I had to keep stopping for a sip of water. Once I'd finished, I was shocked to see a look of excitement on his face.

'Yeah, yeah,' he said, 'but how about this for an idea? We open on a giant cannon or catapult-type machine in Manchester, where a brewery foreman is making sure it's aimed at London. Then launching a barrel of Great Northern Bitter from it, fizzing through the air . . .'

He sat back in his chair, relishing the scenario he was describing. I felt the first stirrings of doom, as I realized this was a truly original idea that didn't rely on cloth caps or whippets.

'So you then cut to a pub in London. Phone rings. Landlord answers it, says "Yup, great", puts it down. "That was

Manchester," he announces to everyone in the pub. "The Great
Northern Bitter is on its way!" They all cheer and move outside, where a bunch of them form a circle, holding a blanket.'

The pain and humiliation increased as he got to the climax.
I was sitting listening to an account director's idea that was
better than anything I had been able to come up with.

'They can now see the barrel speeding towards them through
the sky . . . the manager's telling them where to stand – left a
little, right a little . . . and then the barrel lands perfectly in the
middle of the blanket. Not wanting to waste a second's drinking time, they carry it inside, to a round of applause.'

This was catastrophic. It was really, really good. Worst of all,
he hadn't finished yet.

'Then we cut to the landlord, looking as though he's just
remembered something. "Hang on," he says, "didn't we order
an extra barrel this week?"'

I knew what was coming, and my heart sank.

'And at that moment a barrel crashes through the ceiling,
bounces on the wooden floor and smashes through the window.
Of course, everyone just carries on drinking.'

That was it. The official end to my career as a Beer Man.
When an account director is credited with writing a script,
there's no coming back. It was back to working on shit accounts
for me. Back to doing ads for Chipsteaks.

'Then you show a pint of Great Northern Bitter on the
counter, surrounded by debris, with a payoff line,' Gordon
finished triumphantly, apparently unaware of my inner
turmoil.

'How about "Great Northern Bitter. Specially imported
from Manchester"?' I offered, desperate to play at least a tiny
role in this.

'That'll do,' he said. 'Now why don't you go and write it up?'

I felt a small glimmer of hope.

'Me?'

'Well, you're the copywriter, aren't you?'

This was a last-minute reprieve that changed everything. My heart was beating faster and faster as the full repercussions became clear. Gordon was telling me he wasn't interested in getting any credit. A warm feeling spread through my chest as I read through the notes I'd made while he was talking. This was really great. This was Dave Roberts in *D&AD* great. Whenever Beer Men gathered, presumably in a pub, my name would now be spoken.

I then went through the bizarre process of getting Gordon's script typed out and presenting it to him, for once confident that he would love it. He did, and only changed a few lines of dialogue. 'Great work,' he said, managing to look as though he wasn't being sarcastic. It was as though he'd already forgotten that it was entirely his idea.

In my mind, I was already picturing myself filling out the *D&AD* entry form for this, with the name Dave Roberts alongside the space reserved for 'copywriter'. Well, I'd written out the copy, hadn't I? And I'd added the line at the end. So technically this had been a collaborative effort.

I then excitedly started thinking about the shoot. Who would direct it? I'd had a look through *Campaign* and my preference was Hugh Hudson, who had directed both the Trophy Bitter campaign and *Chariots of Fire*. Danny had also come up with a shortlist, headed by Paul Weiland, a Dave Trott favourite.

We both knew that this would be an advert people would discuss in pubs and factories, boardrooms and living rooms, as well as creative directors' offices in Charlotte Street. And it was all mine. Well, mine and Danny's. Gordon's part in the creative process was already forgotten. I was sure that this advert was going to take me places. London, perhaps, where my career could start in earnest. And also Cannes, where it had every chance of picking up a Gold Lion, the ultimate accolade.

Where I didn't expect it to take me was Stockport.

Fifteen

When I got into work one wet and windy spring day, Danny was deep in conversation with a man who looked older than anyone I'd ever seen in the creative department. He must have been at least thirty-five.

'Dave, this is Jerry. He lectures on advertising at Stockport Tech.'

Danny was already putting on his trench coat and edging towards the door.

'Sorry, must dash, got a shoot. See you on Thursday.'

And with that he was gone, leaving me to look after Jerry. Apparently Martin was letting him spend a fortnight with us, as he wanted to get some hands-on experience in the day-to-day workings of a large agency.

He looked surprised when I took a can of Great Northern Bitter from my stash under the table and started drinking it. I offered him one but he declined, looking pointedly at his watch. He wasn't a Beer Man. I couldn't really expect him to understand.

When he asked what I was currently working on, I took him through the Great Northern Bitter script, even acting out the part where the regulars catch the barrel in the blanket. Jerry looked suitably impressed.

'What a great idea,' he exclaimed. 'How did you manage to come up with that?'

I carefully considered my reply, suspecting it might be fed back to his students as gospel. 'Who knows where any ideas come from?' I said philosophically. 'I always think it's just a combination of hard work and luck.'

A simpler answer might have been 'Gordon'.

'And I take it that these are ads you really like?' he said, indicating my gallery on the cubicle wall.

I nodded, grateful that he'd changed the subject.

'So you're a bit of a Saatchi & Saatchi fan, then?' he asked. 'A lot of Jeff Stark's work there.'

I raised my left eyebrow in wry Roger Moore fashion, something I'd practised in front of the mirror. 'You like his stuff?'

'I do. You know his Schweppes Tonic advert, where the man and woman switch bottles?'

'Of course. The other bottle has "Starks" on the label.'

Jerry nodded, as though this was basic knowledge in the world of advertising. He then leaned towards me and said, 'But did you know that the woman's voice had to be dubbed afterwards because she couldn't get it right on the day?'

This was news to me. I was suddenly resentful he knew something about Jeff Stark that I didn't.

'Yes, I'd heard that. It was shot on a private railway in Kent, you know,' I added triumphantly.

Jerry's face froze for a second, before breaking into a smile. He was clearly satisfied that we were on the same wavelength. He then reached into his portfolio and spread it open.

'These are some of the ads I use on the course.'

I leafed through them, and most were familiar, including three of Jeff Stark's: the *Daily Mail* launch ad 'When will someone produce a Sunday that isn't overwritten or underdressed?', the 'peaches and cream' magazine ad for Nivea, and his brilliant Youth Opportunities Programme newspaper ad 'Are we trying to lower the retirement age to 16?'

And then I came to one I'd never seen before. It stopped me in my tracks, because it was a press ad for MG. I didn't even know they advertised. But this had apparently been in the *Sunday Times*, and showed a car that was made at the time I worked there. The headline read 'Why a brand new MGB is already a collector's item'. I liked to think that the answer was because Dave Roberts had helped build it, but the copywriter had an alternative explanation: MGs were considered such a gilt-edged investment, they often increased in value over time.

'Nice. I used to work at the MG factory, probably put the doors on that car there. I've never seen an ad from them before – what was the agency?'

Jerry looked at me sideways before giving me an answer that sent shockwaves through me: 'Saatchi & Saatchi.'

I was stunned. If this wasn't a message from the advertising gods, what was? It was now beyond any doubt that my destiny was to work for them. After all, who better to write ads for MG than someone who had sweated on that very production line? Although 'sweated' is perhaps too strong a word.

This revelation prompted a heartfelt discussion, and we chatted about everything from Jeff Stark to Jeremy Sinclair. My passion seemed to give Jerry an idea.

'I've got a proposition for you,' he said.

Before he could elaborate, the phone rang. It was Caroline, who was just finishing her shift at the hospital.

'Guess who I was nursing last night?' she said, almost breathless with excitement.

'No idea.'

'It's someone really famous.'

My heart began to beat faster. There were few things I enjoyed more than brushes with fame, even if this one was via my wife.

'Give me a clue.'

'He's quite old and really nice.'

'No, no idea,' I said, desperate to find out. 'Who is it?'

She could barely contain herself. 'It's Samat,' she exclaimed triumphantly.

'Who?'

'Samat.' She sounded deflated at my lack of recognition. 'The others were sure you'd know him.'

'Sorry, doesn't ring any bells. What's he famous for?'

'Dunno. I'll find out tomorrow.'

And with that, she put the phone down.

I turned back to Jerry. 'Any idea who Samat is?'

He shook his head.

'Me neither. Anyway, you were saying . . .'

'Yes. I was wondering if you might be interested in lecturing on copywriting to our Third Year students for a couple of nights every week. Say, two hours a time? We'd pay you, of course. Ten pounds a session.'

I sat back and tried to look thoughtful, as if this approach wasn't totally unexpected.

'Thanks for the offer, Jerry, I'll definitely think about it.'

'OK, well, why don't you sleep on it?' he said, putting on his grey trench coat. 'I'm back in the morning so let's talk again then.'

I couldn't help noticing that his working day had lasted around half an hour. He was clearly going for authenticity in his creative department experience.

Of course, I didn't have to think about his offer. My ego had already made the decision. I felt hugely flattered at the thought of imparting knowledge gathered from years of experience to what I already thought of as 'my' students. I needed the money, too. The fact that they were Third Year students was a plus. It meant that I didn't have to start from scratch and talk about the basics; I could get straight into discussing the finer points of copywriting. I was already picturing myself in the pub after one of my lectures, surrounded by a group of eager young followers, hanging on to my every word. It would transform me into an authority on advertising, a guru. I might even get one of those tweed jackets with leather elbows. And what about a pipe?

Yes, I felt it was my moral obligation to give something back to advertising. To pass on my wisdom to the next generation.

When Jerry came back the next morning, I was ready with an answer.

'When do you want me to start?' I said.

'Well, the new term starts next week. Do you think you'd be ready for Tuesday?'

What did he mean, ready? All I had to do was talk about copywriting to a bunch of kids who shared my passion.

'No problem,' I said.

To show I was taking my new career seriously, I sat by myself in the pub on the day of my debut lecture, making notes on the back of a Benson and Hedges packet about the subjects my lectures would cover. I'd start by talking about the industry greats: Jeff Stark, Jeremy Sinclair, Dave Trott and David Abbott. That'd be the first four sessions taken care of. I'd work out how to use the remaining hours at my disposal later.

When I got home, I felt ready. There was just enough time to grab something to eat before driving to Stockport.

Just as I'd sat down to my Chipsteak and chips, the phone rang. It was Caroline, wanting to wish me luck, which she did before returning to the subject of the mysterious Samat.

'I can't believe you didn't know who Samat is,' she said.

'Why not?'

'He used to be manager of Manchester United.'

'No he didn't.'

'Yes. Samat Busby. Have you really never heard of him?'

That's when the penny dropped, and I blurted out a plea for her to get me his autograph.

'This probably isn't a good time, given that he's just had surgery,' she pointed out.

I had to accept that I would probably have to do without Sir Matt Busby's autograph, said 'Well, say hello from me, then', and put the phone down.

It was only afterwards that I realized what a ridiculous thing that was to say. Was I really expecting her to go up to one of Britain's greatest post-war football managers while he was recuperating from surgery and say 'My husband Dave says hello'? That'd be a great comfort to him, wouldn't it?

Luckily, there wasn't time to wallow in my embarrassment. I had a lecture to deliver. My students would be waiting for me.

I was in a state of high excitement when I arrived at Stockport College of Technology that night. After consulting Jerry's hand-drawn map, I soon found the classroom and was surprised by how full it was. There must have been at least twenty-five students there, most of whom were male, had long straggly hair and wore leather jackets. A few of the ones who didn't already looked bored and resentful. They all had their notepads opened in front of them. As if that's what they'd been told to do.

'Show of hands, please, for those who consider Jeff Stark's work on Schweppes Tonic to be the peak of his career?' I began dramatically.

No hands were raised.

'Well, how about Jeremy Sinclair's work for the Conservative Party? Has he ever bettered that?'

Again, there was no response, apart from vaguely quizzical expressions.

It was then that I realized they had no idea what I was talking about. They'd never heard of Jeff Stark, Jeremy Sinclair or even Dave Trott. I had badly overestimated their knowledge of copywriting. These were meant to be senior advertising students. What had Jerry been teaching them? A feeling of panic suddenly gripped me. What was I going to talk about? There was only one thing for it. I had to go back to basics.

'Let's get back to basics,' I said, which apparently was the right thing to say, judging by the relieved look on Jerry's face. 'Copywriting,' I continued, 'is an incredibly varied life, where you write copy for a variety of clients.'

As soon as I'd started going down this road, I knew it was a mistake. I hadn't prepared for this or given any thought to where I was going with it.

'One day you could be writing copy for Great Northern Bitter, next day it could be for Avis Rent-a-Car, Sainsbury's or Heinz Cream of Tomato soup.'

My confidence was draining away by the second. What else was there to say about copywriting? I wrote copy for ads. That was it, wasn't it? To buy myself a bit of time, I decided to carry on with my list until something else came to mind.

'Or Fairy Liquid,' I added, in a voice that was sounding increasingly desperate. 'Or Mars bars, or St Ivel Prize Yoghurt, or even the Halifax Building Society.'

Was I really going to try and fill the next hour and fifty-five minutes by listing companies that advertised? And then what? I did a quick mental calculation. Four hours a week for thirty-six weeks meant I'd have to fill 144 hours talking about copywriting. I couldn't even manage five minutes.

'Or *Yellow Pages*,' I continued. 'Or McVities Homewheat Biscuits, or Castrol GTX, or, um, Walker's Crisps.'

Already a few of the students were looking bemused. One young man caught my eye. I was sure he had noticed the sweat dripping down my forehead. I then looked to Jerry, pleadingly. He was biting his lower lip. He didn't look happy. He looked as though he'd kill me if I listed one more advertiser.

I couldn't help myself.

'Or Radox Bath Salts, or Mr Kipling Cakes, or Lyons Quick Brew Tea or Bird's Custard, to name just a few.'

My students were getting restless. Those who had been making notes had put their pens down. There was a lot of shuffling around in chairs and I had the distinct feeling that a chorus of boos and a mass walkout couldn't be far away. I had to do something.

It was then that inspiration finally struck.

'If you could excuse me for a few seconds, I have to fetch something from the car.'

I rushed out of the door, sprinted to the car park, climbed into my car and sped off with tyres squealing. I even checked the rear-view mirror several times on the way home to make sure Jerry wasn't following me.

My career as a lecturer was over. So it was just as well that my career as a copywriter was about to finally take off.

Sixteen

In an outlandish twist, the actor playing the foreman at the Great Northern Bitter factory was wearing a stereotype-busting bowler hat, and there wasn't a whippet in sight. He was gazing through a telescope, issuing instructions to his cloth-cap-wearing minions as they prepared to launch the barrel from a massive cannon.

'Left a little, right a bit, and a bit more. Stop! That's perfect. Fire!'

The barrel soared into the air at great speed before rapidly running out of steam and thudding into the ground about five yards from where it had started.

'Cut!' screamed the director, looking satisfied. 'That's a take.' He'd got what he wanted, which was the barrel beginning its journey.

The director walked over to me, smiling. 'This is going to look great. Nice script.'

I looked down modestly, like Princess Diana always did, and managed to avert his gaze. 'I hate how the copywriter always gets the credit,' I lied. 'It was a team effort.'

Wanting to avoid any further discussion on the ad's creation, I asked him what he'd be shooting next.

'We'll be doing the scene outside the pub, where the regulars are catching the barrel.'

'Great.'

He then had what seemed to be an afterthought.

'Do you want to be in it?'

Had he detected some acting ability in me? Did I look like a London pub regular? Or was he just sucking up to the client? Whatever the reason, this was a seriously brilliant turn of events, as it would comfortably avert any suspicions people might have about my part in writing it.

'Yeah, why not?' I was suddenly desperate for the shoot to restart. It surely couldn't be more than half an hour away. 'How long before you need me?'

He looked at his watch, then over at where the set construction was taking place. 'By the time the camera's set up, lighting done, set ready – maybe three hours?'

Three hours? *Three hours?* What was I supposed to do for three hours? Then it struck me. Saatchi & Saatchi was only two stops away on the tube. I'd go and pay Jon a surprise visit and drag him out for a lunchtime pint, during which I could tell him all about my upcoming Hitchcockesque cameo. And one pint only: despite being a seasoned Beer Man, I needed to be sober for my acting debut. Who knew where this could lead? Ridley Scott, who'd directed the Hovis advert, was now a big-time Hollywood director.

It was all I could think about as I walked the familiar route from Goodge Street Station, a station I'd always had a soft spot for (more stations should have lifts, in my opinion). My fantasies were further fuelled by the sight of those words NOTHING IS IMPOSSIBLE carved on to the top step at the Saatchi office.

The receptionist didn't look surprised to see me and had

started dialling Jon's number almost before I'd had a chance to ask for him.

He came down straight away and sat down next to me.

'What are you doing here?' he asked, which was precisely what I was hoping he'd ask.

'Oh, just doing a shoot over in Soho. Beer advert. Taking a break while they set up the next shot. Fancy going to the pub?'

'What, now? It's only just gone eleven.'

I forgot. Jon wasn't a Beer Man. He was restrained by conventional drinking hours.

Just as I was about to launch a compelling argument for why he should accompany me, I caught sight of a vaguely familiar figure at the top of the stairs. Someone I'd seen in *Campaign*, I thought. He was slim and clean-shaven, smartly dressed, with expensive-looking shoes. His dark hair was swept back and there was an unmistakable air of self-assurance about him.

'Is that . . . ?'

'That's Jeremy, my boss.'

'Jeremy Sinclair?'

'Yes.'

My heart was thudding against my ribcage and I felt dizzy. My mouth went dry as I stared at him, walking down the stairs deep in conversation with a woman who was carrying a clipboard.

Jon was looking concerned.

'Dave, are you all right?'

I nodded, but had temporarily lost the power of speech. There was only one thought in my mind: I was in the same room as Jeremy Sinclair, breathing the same air.

When I finally managed to say something, it wasn't in reply to Jon, but a question: 'Do you think he'd look at my portfolio some time?'

'I dunno. Ask him.'

That was easy for Jon to say, but Jeremy Sinclair was getting nearer and nearer and I knew I had to do something. He was twenty yards away, fifteen yards away, ten yards away . . .

I suddenly found myself shakily getting to my feet.

'Excuse me, Mr Sinclair,' I heard myself saying in a voice that sounded nothing like my voice. 'I'm a copywriter with BDH in Manchester and I'm wondering if I could maybe show you my portfolio some time?' I then realized I would be in a much stronger position once the Great Northern Bitter commercial was on air. 'Maybe in the New Year?'

Jeremy Sinclair looked at me distractedly, as though he wasn't expecting to be pounced on in his own reception area. But seeing I was with Jon seemed to be enough to satisfy him. 'Sure, give me a ring,' he said in an offhand manner, and continued on his journey.

'See? That wasn't so hard, was it?' said Jon.

I was keen to discuss the hidden meanings in that short sentence uttered by the greatest living copywriter, but Jon was adamant that he wouldn't be able to come for a drink, although we did arrange to meet up after work.

As I walked back to the tube station, all I could hear echoing through my mind were Jeremy Sinclair's words: 'Sure, give me a ring . . . Sure, give me a ring . . . Sure, give me a ring . . .' To try and calm myself down I took the scenic route, which involved walking past The Pregnant Man and surreptitiously glancing through the windows.

I got back just in time for lunch. At my previous shoot, this meant sharing the engineer's cheese and pickle sandwich. This time there were proper caterers and I got to choose from Thai chicken curry, lasagne and some vegetarian option made out of puff pastry and mushrooms. I had all of them.

While I ate, I noticed that there was plenty of activity on the set, with carpenters constructing the outside of a pub and a cameraman (who preferred to be known as 'director of photography') holding a light meter, looking at his watch and scowling in the direction of the director, who had just turned up.

My fellow barrel catchers and I were summonsed. I was surprised by how much detail went into our instructions. Each of us was told exactly where to stand, and when we caught the barrel (which would be dropped from a small tower of scaffolding) we were to celebrate.

After standing in our positions for around half an hour, we were finally ready. The director shouted 'Action!' and the barrel was dropped from above, landing slap in the middle of the blanket. We cheered, as instructed, and carried it to the door of the fake pub. I didn't have to fake my excitement: not only was I taking part in the filming of a TV commercial, I'd just spoken to Jeremy Sinclair, in person.

The director seemed pleased, but wanted to try it again. He wanted us to show more enthusiasm. It was at this stage that I decided to make my part a little more prominent, by giving myself a few lines. As the scriptwriter, I felt I could do this, and the next take gave me the opportunity to try them out.

'Here it comes!' I shouted. 'Look, the barrel!' I gesticulated wildly into the distance, looking maniacal and playing shamelessly to the camera. 'Let's catch it!' I shrieked, in an unscripted ad lib. 'Ready lads?'

There was no response from the lads because I hadn't given them any lines. But the director looked a lot happier than they did. 'Thanks everyone, that's a wrap for today,' he announced, and the long process of dismantling this set and setting up the next one in readiness for tomorrow's work began.

After a quick couple of pints with Jon – who in reply to my

questioning told me that Jeremy Sinclair hadn't said anything about me – I went straight back to the hotel where I spent a quiet evening in front of the TV, comparing every advert unfavourably with the one I was shooting.

Sleep was particularly difficult that night due to the combination of meeting Jeremy Sinclair, starring in a potentially award-winning advert, and getting carried away with room service and eating far too much. But an unexpected thrill the next morning revitalized me: the director invited me to look at the rushes with him. This was raw, unedited footage from the previous day, without sound, from which he could pick out takes that he liked. Although I was more focused on critiquing my own performance, and was disappointed by the lack of close-ups, I could sense that this was going to become a really good finished product.

The scenes shot later that day merely confirmed this. When the landlord realized that he'd ordered another barrel, his expression was genuinely funny. And the barrel bursting through the ceiling and bouncing out of the window was so spectacular, the cast and crew broke into spontaneous applause once the director had yelled 'Cut!'

The shoot had taken two days, and editing would take place over the next few days. Once that was done, and voiceovers added, a tape would be dispatched to Manchester via Red Star Parcels – tellingly, a Saatchi & Saatchi client.

Intoxicated by my first proper shoot (I'd finally managed to convince myself that the WASS one didn't count), I'd forgotten a job I'd promised to do before getting back to the office. I had to come up with an ad for *The Grocer*, telling the trade all about Great Northern Bitter coming to the South.

Just as the train was passing through Potters Bar Station, it came to me. We would use a photo of the cannon, with the barrel flying out, and the headline 'Great Northern Bitter. Launching this autumn'. It felt as though the genius of Jeremy Sinclair had rubbed off on me.

This feeling was confirmed when the U Matic cassette arrived with the finished version of the advert. I watched nervously with Gordon, awaiting his reaction, but I needn't have worried. He loved it. And so did I, especially since my ad lib made the final cut. Not that you'd know unless you stood a few inches from the screen and constantly replayed the scene in slow motion, turning up the sound really loud. Which I did. If you didn't do this, all you saw was a slightly podgy figure in a brown mohair jumper leaping around as though he'd just scored the winning goal in a Cup Final.

Or just met Jeremy Sinclair.

Gordon looked almost as happy, so much so that he was going to enter it for the Cannes Festival, the pinnacle of the advertising world. If we managed to win, it would be even more prestigious than getting into *D&AD*. This was thrilling news. The closest I'd got to Cannes was at my Leeds agency when I wrote a sales promotion leaflet for Girling-Butcher spark plugs, offering the chance to win a ten-day break in Cannes. Naturally, I used the headline 'Yes you Cannes!'

The first London showing of the advert was during a *Coronation Street* episode in September. Jon managed to catch it and thought it had a great chance of getting into *D&AD*. For the next few months I felt as though I had truly arrived as a Beer Man. I even started thinking about new ideas for John Smith's Bitter, which I could well end up working for at Saatchi & Saatchi, while banking a Seymour. Obviously I'd continue with the same campaign theme they already had – you don't mess with another Beer Man's work.

The Great Northern Bitter work was obviously the high point of my career so far. By now I'd completely rewritten its history and wiped out the fact that it was all Gordon's idea. I felt that unlike my presentation to Saatchi & Saatchi (Manchester), I finally had enough decent work to fill more than two pages of my portfolio, and couldn't wait to take it down to Saatchi & Saatchi (London). When I rang Jeremy Sinclair a week before Christmas, having spent days trying to pluck up the courage, I didn't get to speak to him but managed to set up an appointment for January through Jilly, his secretary.

All in all, life was looking better than it had at any time since I first started in advertising. At last I felt confident about the future. Everything was going my way.

And then my lifelong best friend, best man and former flatmate Dave came to stay for a few days.

Seventeen

From the moment he arrived I'd been waiting for Dave to ask me about my brand-new Philips VR 20/20, which I rented for £15.95 a month. Finally, he did.

'That's one of those video recorders, isn't it? What's it like?'

'It's amazing – look.'

I picked up a cassette that happened to be sitting on top of it and put it in. I then sat back down, holding the remote control, which was costing me an extra £1.95 a month.

'This is an advert I did recently,' I said, trying to give the impression that I was about to give an unplanned, spontaneous demonstration.

I pressed the play button, 'Great Northern Bitter' appeared on screen, and for the next thirty seconds I watched spellbound, though wishing I'd toned down my performance a little. 'Understated' was not a word that sprang to mind.

I glanced at Dave. He looked impressed, which was the general idea. And the demonstration was far from over.

'But now, say you want to see something in slow motion, you just do this.'

I pressed the slow-motion button, and Dave (for the first time) and Caroline (for about the thirtieth time) watched four men slowly catch a slow-moving barrel with a blanket.

And that wasn't the last of the capabilities of the Philips VR 20/20.

'You can even freeze the picture,' I announced.

Clearly, the best way to demonstrate this would be to stop on the frame that showed me celebrating wildly.

'That's you, isn't it?' said Dave, peering closely at the screen.

I pretended also to take a close look.

'It is, too. I'd forgotten about that. It was the director's idea ...'

Satisfied that I'd managed to let my lifelong best friend know that I had not only written but starred in a potentially award-winning advert without actually telling him, it was time for the main event. I put the tape back into my portfolio, ready for Jeremy Sinclair, and we sat down to see what we'd be buying each other for Christmas.

I had a gnawing, sickly feeling in the pit of my stomach. I initially put this down to the Chipsteaks, which I'd cooked in Bisto gravy, but then realized it was more likely to be nerves. The first ad break during *Brideshead Revisited* would reveal the present I'd be getting from Dave; I, as usual, would be buying him the third product advertised in the second break.

There were nine words I desperately wanted to hear coming from the TV: 'Tremble, Earth creatures. You face a terrible new threat.' That would mean we were watching the advert for the Galaxy Invader 1000, a hand-held, just-different-enough-to-avoid-legal-action version of Space Invaders. This was the present I wanted more than anything, and as an added bonus it would cost Dave an eye-watering £23.95 in Earth pounds. But as soon as the second advert started, my heart sank with disappointment. The opening scene was instantly familiar – a group of lads in a pub (no cloth caps or whippets, so I knew they had to be southerners), some drinking from wobbly glasses that appeared to be made from see-through rubber. 'Do some lagers taste soft around the edges?' a wry southern voiceover enquired. I couldn't take any more. Using the remote control, I turned the sound off. I didn't need it to know that my Christmas gift from Dave would be a can of Hemeling Lager ('There's a harder edge to Hemeling'), which would set him back about thirty pence at Asda.

He looked smug, and for the next ten minutes we tried to concentrate on Lord Marchmain's emotional return home to Brideshead, but were really just waiting for the adverts.

The third ad in the next break began with a rising sun against a pastel background. I initially didn't recognize it, but it certainly didn't look good, and a feeling of dread rose in my chest.

A voice then cut in to announce, 'Only our prices are like other holidays.'

I let out a strangled shriek as a graphic slowly appeared on screen:

Majorca from £140.

Thomas Cook Holidays.

From good travel agents everywhere.

I spent the next minute trying to avoid Caroline's glare and ignore Dave dancing around the room singing, 'And now I'm off to sunny Spain, y viva España!'

Out of a mix of guilt and desperation, I immediately got to work thinking of ways to raise £140. An idea came from an advert in a break towards the end of *Brideshead Revisited*. I was still in a state of shock, but it just about registered because I was already familiar with the 'Solvite win a striker competition', where the lucky winner got to pick a striker and every time he scored a goal for the rest of the season, the winner would receive £100 cash. I was familiar with it because it had been written by Bruce and Neil in the next cubicle to mine. Bruce and Neil were known as the Solvite Men.

The Solvite Men were the only people with more prestige at BDH than the Beer Men. Solvite was a huge client and, more importantly, did spectacular adverts. The most famous featured a stuntman in white overalls pasted to a board and taken hundreds of feet into the air by helicopter.

It was no surprise that Solvite's latest competition had a football theme. Bruce was obsessed with it. He was a lifelong Chelsea fan, and when he brought his baby son into the office, he didn't just introduce him as 'Pete' but as 'Pete, who's going to play for England one day'.

There was a pile of entry forms for the 'Solvite win a striker competition' on their desk, and when I next got a chance to leaf through them and saw some of the tie-break answers, I felt the first stirrings of hope. All the entrants had had to do was complete the sentence 'Solvite solves it because . . .' And some of the answers were terrible. Mr A. K. Lyon of Dewsbury felt that 'Solvite solves it because Solvite's a superstar', while J. Robson from Glamorgan came up with 'Solvite solves it because it really works'.

Unfortunately, I couldn't enter. All competitions have a line in the small print about 'not being open to advertising agencies or their employees'. This is done for a good reason: to stop dishonest copywriters from sneaking into cubicles, throwing away any entries with good slogans and putting theirs at the top of the pile. However, there was nothing to stop me from entering the competitions of clients from other agencies. And that was my big money-making idea. The thinking was that since they all asked the entrant to dream up a slogan for a tie-breaker,

I'd have a huge advantage. After all, that was my speciality. I had come up with 'Great Northern Bitter. Specially imported from Manchester' as well as 'At Vallances prices you don't need to shop around'.

Plus, this was a great way to prepare for my meeting with Jeremy Sinclair. It would be like swotting before an exam. I'd be creating taglines for big national brands, which is what I'd be doing if he offered me a job in London.

I became even more convinced that fate was pointing me towards competitions as a form of income when I spotted one from Thomas Cook in that morning's *Express*. 'How to get away without paying', it said, telling me that if I booked my holiday now I could get it free by entering their £10,000 gift competition. All I had to do was pop into any one of their 175 Thomas Cook shops and pick up an entry form when I booked my – or rather Dave's – holiday. It felt exciting knowing that I could pass on the cost of Dave's undeserved trip. I paid for his holiday and picked up an entry form that lunchtime.

After that, I went on a frenzy. I bought a bottle of Croft Original just so that I could enter the 'Spot the Ghastly Blunder' competition and win a £30,000 holiday home in Spain, which would put Dave's £140 holiday to shame. The competition itself was simple, as competitions are designed to be. The tie-breaker was 'It is not a ghastly blunder to buy Croft Original because . . .', and I finished the sentence with 'it's only a blunder to buy anything else'. If in doubt, flatter the client.

Instead of sitting back and dreaming about my new Spanish residence, I decided to chase gold by entering the 'Now where did I leave the Bailey's Irish Cream £5,000 Crock of Gold?' competition. On a map, I put a cross where I thought the gold was buried and completed 'Bailey's once tasted is never forgotten . . .' by adding 'because great memories come from a bottle of Bailey's'.

Mars bars had £50,000 up for grabs in their Golden Jubilee Competition. As I ate a Mars a day, I didn't have to go out and buy any more, I already had the required three wrappers. The phrase 'The Mars bar has given fifty years of big bar value because . . .' was finished with 'it's given fifty years of working, resting and playing'.

After filling in my twentieth competition entry of the week, which had included chances to win a new wardrobe, a year's supply of bird seed and a cruise to Mexico, I finished with The Great 200g Yorkie Talkie Competition. With a three-week holiday in the US at stake, I had to invent a CB slang term for a Yorkie bar. I came up with 'Big Brick', which I was wrongly convinced I'd heard in the trucking song 'Convoy'. I sensed that this was a bit on the weak side, but after writing twenty-odd slogans I was beginning to burn out. It was time to stop.

I sat back and waited, eagerly checking the post every morning. And every night I prepared my portfolio for Jeremy Sinclair. It was hard not to get excited about showing him my work: I felt it was a lot better than the selection I'd shown his Mancunian counterpart. Apart from the Great Northern Bitter ads, we'd also done a poster for Wilson's Bitter, which showed a pint with an umbrella covering it as rain poured down from above. The line was 'It's why we put up with the weather in Manchester'. I kept the Lada campaign from my Leeds days, and added a trade ad Danny and I had done for Pritt Stick, announcing a new glue designed especially for kids. 'Prepare for the invasion of the three-foot monsters' was the headline for a picture showing a bunch of out-of-control children demanding the glue from a harassed shopkeeper. Best of all, thanks to Gordon and Great Northern Bitter, I now had a book with a video cassette in it, just like that proper adman I'd seen in reception when I went to my BDH interview.

As the day of my Jeremy Sinclair meeting drew closer, I almost forgot about the competitions. I'd already accepted that Thomas Cook wouldn't be paying for Dave's holiday in Spain, and I suspected I wouldn't be taking ownership of a crock of gold, whatever that was. I was getting increasingly nervous, and in moments of self-doubt I thought about phoning his secretary Jilly and cancelling. Was I really good enough to work for Saatchi & Saatchi? At least I was no longer embarrassed by my work. Well, not all of it.

And then something totally unexpected happened: I got home to find that the postman had left a card saying that he'd tried to deliver a package but no one was home. We drove straight to the sorting office, where a medium-sized box was handed to me. It was from Rowntree Mackintosh, who made Yorkie bars. I had won something!

I vaguely recalled that they'd mentioned runners-up prizes of a Sony video recorder. That would be perfect. I'd already got the Philips VR 20/20 so I could sell the prize for enough money to pay myself back for Dave's holiday.

When we got home, I eagerly opened the box. Inside was a cheap-looking plastic lorry, about eight inches long, with YORKIE in huge letters on the side and an aerial sticking out of the bonnet. There was also a compliments slip with the message 'Congratulations! You are one of the lucky winners in The Great 200g Yorkie Talkie Competition and we hope you enjoy your special Yorkie radio! 10-4, good buddy.'

I would have preferred the three-week holiday in the US, but at least I had something to listen to on the train down to my appointment with Jeremy Sinclair.

Or, as I had now started seeing it, my appointment with destiny.

Eighteen

As the InterCity 125 train pulled out of Manchester Piccadilly, I caught a glimpse of my reflection in the window and, like the boy in the Ready Brek 'Central heating for kids' advert, felt a warm glow all over. I thought I looked like a successful, ambitious young adman who wouldn't look out of place at Saatchi & Saatchi (as long as you ignored the large plastic Yorkie lorry pressed against my ear). I'd even bought a suit from Burton's especially for the interview. It was a black two-piece, not totally dissimilar to the one worn by Jeremy Sinclair in a recent *Campaign* article. The bulging portfolio beside me completed the picture.

Another reason for my positive mood was that I'd taken steps to ensure I didn't make the same mistake I made in my last interview. This time I wouldn't freeze when asked if I had any questions. Not only had I prepared a series of questions to impress Jeremy Sinclair, I'd also written a key word from each one on the palm of my hand.

So when I saw the word JINGLE, it would remind me to ask him why Saatchi & Saatchi never seemed to use jingles; like most other copywriters, I always resorted to them when I couldn't come up with an idea.

The word SACK would prompt me to ask if it was true that Charles Saatchi had a rule of 'Two ads a day keeps the sack away'. I'd be able to follow up by saying that I felt this was typical of my output and an entirely reasonable requirement.

P&G was a reminder that Simon Dicketts, a genius of a copywriter, had got a job there by claiming he wanted to work on P&G, the Saatchi & Saatchi account with the least potential for award-winning work. He lasted there for about ten minutes, before moving on to more promising accounts. If it worked for him, maybe it could work for me.

The flaw in my system made itself known when I looked at the word SINGLE and had no idea what the question was meant to be. I imagined a nightmare scenario of Jeremy Sinclair leaning forward and asking if I had any questions. What would be worse, looking at my palm and spluttering out the words 'So Jeremy, are you single?' or looking at my palm and requesting the name of his favourite single? Further anxiety was averted when I finally remembered – it was a question about whether it was by design that you could always pick the single-minded proposition in a Saatchi & Saatchi ad.

Another potential source of anxiety was the Yorkie radio. I was a bit worried about being taken seriously if I walked into the world's finest advertising agency with a portfolio under one arm and a blue plastic lorry under the other. Since it was too big to conceal, I decided to leave it behind on the train for some lucky cleaner.

By the time I got off at Euston, I'd rehearsed the questions for all seventeen words on my hand, including CHARIOTS, CHESS and SEYMOUR. And by the time I'd completed my deep-breathing exercises on the tube, I was ready for Jeremy Sinclair.

I have no idea how I got from Goodge Street to the Saatchi

office. I was in a daze, willing my legs to work. The receptionist was the one I'd previously imagined stepping out of a Badedas bath, and I was a bit disappointed that she didn't remember me.

'Dave Roberts for Jeremy Sinclair,' I said, while literally pinching myself.

To intimidate me further, there was a row of TV screens above the reception desk playing a selection of Saatchi adverts. For a while I stared at them unable to speak, overdosing on the genius of the thirty-second masterpieces produced for Dunlop, Schweppes, John Smith's, Penguin Biscuits and more. It was as if they were saying to me 'This is what we can do – now, what can *you* do?' The Great Northern Bitter advert suddenly seemed totally inadequate and the thought of turning round and running away was a tempting one.

'If you'd like to follow me?' said a secretary who had suddenly appeared.

She led the way up the stairs and into the inner sanctum of Saatchi & Saatchi. There was a canvas on the wall about halfway up the stairs. It was one of those where the artist had applied the paint thickly with a spatula instead of a brush. Jon had told me that one of the other art directors used to remove a little chip of paint every time he passed it, as a small act of rebellion.

I liked knowing things like this. It made me feel like an insider.

Obviously I knew which office was Jon's, but he was away on a shoot. I briefly wondered where Jeff Stark was and what he was working on. The next Dunlop campaign? Another award-winner for John Smith's?

One door was open. I looked in and saw a man with a copy of the *TV Times* on his desk – it must have been Malcolm Taylor, whose work on the account had earned him a place in *D&AD*.

I felt slightly dizzy, knowing that I was walking through the same corridor where giants of advertising strode, and briefly had to prop myself up against the award-covered wall. Charles Saatchi himself was known to visit the department once a week when he would look at the work each team had done. The ultimate accolade was when he said, 'This is researching very well in St John's Wood' (where he lived). Or, even better, he'd say, 'I tell my friends I wrote this one myself.' The knowledge that I was following in his footsteps, as well as those of people like Martyn Walsh, Fergus Fleming and Andrew Rutherford, was overwhelming. And when these are the only thoughts running through your head as you follow one of the most beautiful women you've ever seen, wearing the shortest of skirts, your single-minded devotion to Saatchi & Saatchi cannot be questioned.

She stopped at an unassuming-looking office. Just outside the door, I noticed a cupboard that was full of awards – not so much placed there as tossed in, as though it was a packing crate. The secretary knocked on the door, before opening it and ushering me in.

'Jeremy, this is Dave.'

The office was all white and smaller than I'd expected. It was also quite spartan, nothing but his desk, a couple of chairs and a huge pile of portfolios in the corner.

Jeremy Sinclair was businesslike and polite. I was a babbling wreck. My nerves had been bad from the outset, when I'd thrust my hand, with key words clearly visible, towards him and launched into an embarrassing list of ads of his that I loved. Had I then asked if he was single, I suspect I might have been escorted out of the building.

At his request, I opened my portfolio.

There's always uncertainty when you show your work. That

uncertainty is magnified a thousand times when you show your work to Jeremy Sinclair. But he was encouraging. Some of the press ads prompted a 'yup', and when I showed him the Great Northern Bitter advert, he almost seemed impressed. 'Yup, nice,' he said, and my heart soared. The only way I could have felt any more euphoric would have been if I'd actually written it myself.

If this meeting had been an advert, a stirring piece of music would have reached a climax as he stuck out his hand and said, 'You belong at Saatchi & Saatchi, Dave. Welcome aboard.' In reality there was no music as he stuck out his hand and said, 'You've done some nice work, but you're probably going to need a bit more TV on your reel.'

I thanked him for seeing me, even though the whole meeting had taken less than ten minutes.

The message, or at least my interpretation of it, couldn't have been clearer. If I could pad out my reel with a few more ads as good as Great Northern Bitter, a job at Saatchi & Saatchi (London) was mine. The only problem I could see was the complete lack of TV in my immediate future. Solvite was the agency's only high-profile client that did TV ads and Bruce was unlikely to let me work on it just to satisfy my career needs.

Reading *Campaign* on the way back to Manchester, I felt a burst of envy when I learned about all the new big-budget TV adverts about to hit the screens, the stories accompanied by posed pictures of smug creatives or, worse, stills taken in whatever exotic location they'd done the shoot. Quite a few were using celebrities. Wall's Funny Feet ice creams had just unveiled (adverts were always 'unveiled' in *Campaign*) a spot starring Kenny Everett, while Campbell's Smoked Salmon had unveiled a Pam Ayres-narrated thirty-seconder.

It seemed that everyone but me was adding to their

showreels. There was only one advert on mine, and I hadn't even written it. It suddenly felt as though I would be stuck in Manchester for ever doing trade ads and writing about, as well as living on, Chipsteaks.

The rain pounding against the window only deepened my despondency.

It was only when I reached the jobs section at the back of the magazine that I had a revelation. The only way to get more TV would be to get myself a job in a London agency. It didn't have to be Saatchi & Saatchi – that could wait. It just had to be somewhere that had a lot of TV clients.

Suddenly enthused, I started scouring the vacancies, and the one that caught my eye was a quarter-page listing from a recruitment consultant who seemed to specialize in bigger agencies. My criteria were simple: the agency had to have plenty of TV work and would preferably pay more than I was getting now – which wouldn't be hard. Several openings met these requirements, the most exciting being MDWT COPYWRITER LDN MAINLY TV, £12-15,000 PA. I put a large tick next to that. COPYWRITER MUST HAVE TV EXP FOR COVENT GARDEN AGENCY £10,000+ was another I marked, along with COPYWRITER TV/PRESS EXP FOR GROWING LDN AGENCY, SALARY NEG.

Looking through the jobs again, I realized that nearly all were suitable for my purposes. The only ones that didn't appeal were in places like Brunei, Hong Kong and New Zealand. I might be desperate for TV, but I wasn't that desperate.

The doom and gloom had been replaced by a burst of optimism. I was thrilled at the prospect of taking the next step in my journey to Charlotte Street.

I remembered Jon telling me, while trying to console me about having to work in Leeds, how Jeff Stark had spent years in the advertising wilderness before getting into Saatchi &

Saatchi. He'd been stuck in an equally unpromising job, although instead of creating Lada leaflets and rhyming-slang mailers, he'd written mail order ads for Bullworker ('build mighty muscles in forty-nine seconds a day'), Diagems ('even real jewellers are fooled'), and a forty-eight-page book about plastic pipes and guttering. A few months after joining Saatchi, he had his first ad in *D&AD*. Like Jon, it was for his work on Daffodil toilet rolls. It showed a large tear-out 4p-off coupon above a headline that said 'Save money on toilet rolls. Use this piece of paper.'

The point was that you didn't walk straight into a job at Saatchi & Saatchi. It took time. But once you were there, things moved quickly. I just needed to be patient.

When I got home, I looked again at the jobs on my shortlist. There were eight of them. Each ticked the TV box, each was in London (Caroline had said she would be happy to move again) and, encouragingly, each paid quite a bit more than I was currently earning.

Since the ad had been placed by a recruitment consultant, there was no way of knowing the names of the agencies, but that wasn't important. Wherever I ended up working would be a giant step towards being back in Jeremy Sinclair's office, this time being introduced to Charles Saatchi as his newest copywriter.

I just knew that somewhere in that list was the job that was going to change my life. As I dialled the recruitment agency's number, I wondered which one it would be . . .

End of Part Two

Ours are made to start first time.
Our comp...
Our compompo mp...
Our compompo mpompet...
Our compompo mpompetitors...

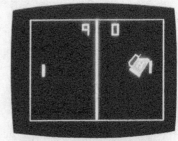

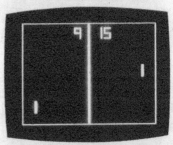

Part Three

Part Three

Nineteen

As I sat in reception on the first morning of my new job, I felt a smug sense of satisfaction. I was now creative director at one of the biggest agencies in the country, in the heart of the capital's buzzing creative scene, working on everything from Honda cars to a couple of national beer accounts.

The only slight drawback was that the country in question was New Zealand.

It hadn't been my first choice. In fact it hadn't been any of my choices. The problem was that none of the agencies on my shortlist were interested in interviewing me, let alone giving me a job. But if I was serious about a future with Saatchi & Saatchi, I had to do whatever it took to get more TV on my showreel. Even if it meant moving halfway round the world for the length of a two-year contract.

Caroline loved the idea. She'd always dreamt of moving somewhere like New Zealand and was quite happy to leave the Manchester weather behind. I could see the appeal too: the money was really good – about a tenth of a Seymour – and several of the accounts I'd be working on mirrored those I might well find myself working on at Saatchi & Saatchi, including those car and beer accounts. This would make my showreel even more relevant when I next showed it to Jeremy Sinclair.

But it was the fact that I would be creative director that really decided it for me. As well as meaning I'd be able to pick and choose what I worked on, I'd have the chance to put into practice my ideas about heading up a creative department. This was what I'd dreamt about ever since starting as a trainee copywriter and having to make tea for everyone. I'd come a long way since then, and I'd re-read my letter of appointment over and over, particularly the line 'This is to confirm your position as creative director with our agency'.

I'd given a lot of thought to my approach to the job. Inspired by Charles and Maurice Saatchi, I'd create an environment where my team worked hard and played hard. I loved how they'd taken over a funfair for their end-of-year party, with free rides and endless champagne provided. That was the sort of gesture I wanted to make as a reward. And for those times when the stick would be more effective than the carrot, there was always Charles's 'Two ads a day keeps the sack away' rule.

My intention was to make a low-key start, to assess everyone's abilities and maybe switch the teams around a bit. Obviously I'd take all the high-profile TV campaigns and do them myself, but I wanted to share the rest around evenly. It was only fair.

I also liked Dave Trott's approach. He basically saw himself as a manager. His philosophy was that he didn't want to be shown work and think 'I could've done that'. He wanted to see ideas that excited him. And so did I. I loved the thought of inspiring my teams to come up with award-winning work.

My thoughts were interrupted when the chairman, Marcus, who had interviewed Caroline and me in Manchester, came through the door and looked delighted, if a little surprised, to see me. Perhaps he wasn't convinced I'd turn up. We were both wearing suits, the international uniform of management. Mine was the one I'd worn for the Jeremy Sinclair interview, his was the one he'd worn for the interview with me.

'Let's go through to the creative department,' he said, once he'd established that we'd settled in well in our new home in Wellington. 'I'm sure you're keen to meet the team.'

And I was. They were probably going to be even more nervous than I was, wondering what their new boss was like. I'd soon put their minds at ease.

As I walked into the large room at the end of the creative department, I felt like a visiting head of state. Everyone was lined up to meet me. I wondered if I should give a speech, which would be both inspiring and reassuring. Maybe I could say something like 'I don't want you to think that I'm going to come in and change everything. Feel free to come in and see me at any time, to run ideas past me or just talk. I want you to know that my door is always open.' But before I did that, I was going to introduce myself to the troops.

The first person in the line was a greying bearded bear of a man in a plaid shirt. I shook his hand firmly, making solid eye contact. Body language was an important part of conveying authority.

'Dave Roberts,' I said, as if he didn't already know. 'Creative director.'

'Bob,' he replied, looking slightly bemused. 'Creative director.'

'Pardon me?' I asked, with a forced smile.

'Bob, creative director,' he repeated.

Why was he saying that? Was it a joke? He was definitely smiling when he said it. I felt a tiny flicker of hope when the thought came to me that he might just have an unusual surname that sounded a bit like Creative-Director, and I'd somehow misheard it due to his strong Kiwi accent. Admittedly, this wasn't very likely.

I tried to banish the incident from my mind as I moved on to a spiky-haired girl in her early twenties and repeated my introduction, with a little less confidence and eye contact than before.

'Dave Roberts, creative director. Good to meet you.'

'Chrissie, creative director. Good to meet you too.'

My heart was sinking rapidly. Apart from anything else, during my leaving do in Manchester I'd drunkenly promised at least five different people a job in my department. The best possible scenario now was that I was one of three joint creative directors – a number that could well grow, depending on how the next person in line, a handsome blond-haired arty type, introduced himself.

'G'day,' he said, thrusting out his hand. 'I'm Graham, creative director.'

I thought so. The words no longer had the capacity to shock. By the time I reached the end of the line I'd been introduced to seven creative directors and one copywriter. No idea what he'd done wrong.

To add to my misery, I noticed a large glass-fronted fridge in the corner of the room which was packed with various lagers and bitters. Did this mean everyone was a Beer Man as well?

As Marcus took me back to his office to 'iron out a few details', I felt as though I just wanted to go home and crawl under the blankets. My dreams had been shattered by a collective of creative directors. I even wondered about ringing Caroline and asking if we should just tear up the contract and go back to Manchester. It was the principle of the thing. I felt I had to make a stand. But before I had the chance to say anything, Marcus said that we needed to talk about my company car.

'Great. What will I be getting?' I asked, hoping it wouldn't be a Honda Civic.

'What do you want?'

I'd never had a company car before, but I didn't have to think about my answer. Jeremy Sinclair drove a Bristol, Jeff Stark had an Aston Martin and Paul Arden got around in a Ferrari, but there was only one car I could imagine myself getting.

'Any chance of an MGB?' I asked. 'It doesn't have to be a new one.'

He probably didn't know that I wasn't trying to save him money – there weren't any new ones. Margaret Thatcher had closed the factory down not long after I moved to Leeds.

'No worries,' he said.

Imagining myself driving along the North Island shoreline in a newish MGB, with the top down and Caroline sitting in the passenger seat, lifted the gloom considerably.

Next up he handed me my company National Bank Visa card. This was an unexpected bonus. I hadn't had a credit card since Barclaycard made me cut mine up after I went on a wild spending spree to celebrate getting it.

I remembered Jon telling me about a similar thing happening at Saatchi & Saatchi, when it was decided to issue account directors with company credit cards. They showed the same lack of restraint as me, so Tim Bell, the MD, called them into his office. 'You guys seem to think there's a big cupboard full of money somewhere in the building and we just go in there with a shovel and help ourselves,' he announced. 'You're right, of course, there is. But it's only for Maurice and Charles and me.' Suitably chastised, they adopted a more moderate approach from that moment on.

I vowed to follow the same path, using the card only when necessary. I didn't want to have it taken away. Still, being handed a credit card with no apparent limit was enough to make me abandon any thoughts of making a principled stand. If anyone could be bought off, it was me.

The chairman had one more thing for me. A small box. I opened it, and inside were a couple of hundred business cards with these words:

MACKAY KING ADVERTISING

DAVID ROBERTS

CREATIVE DIRECTOR

If that was meant to make me feel even better about the situation, it worked. I couldn't wait to hand them out or leave them casually lying around for people to find.

Perhaps things weren't quite as bad as they had seemed. The agony of finding out I was just another creative director had been cancelled out by a piece of plastic, a second-hand car and two hundred business cards. Every man has his price.

Besides, instead of doing anything rash, it seemed a lot more sensible to give it six months and see how things were working out then.

I was now ready to start my job.

My art director (and fellow creative director) was Graham, the blond arty type I'd met earlier. After sitting down, I couldn't stop myself blurting out the question that had been on my mind since being shown around.

'How come everyone here's a creative director?' I asked, trying to keep the hurt out of my voice.

'That's Marcus's idea,' he said. 'He kept promising clients that they would have the creative director working on their business, found they liked hearing that, so he promoted us all.'

At least that was cleared up.

I looked around the office we'd be sharing and was pleased to see the universal sight of a stack of old awards annuals. I was already familiar with most of them.

On our first job together, I was astonished to see Graham get a pad out and start scribbling headlines. This was almost unprecedented. Apart from Danny, I was used to art directors waiting for me to come up with something. We had to come up with a poster for Europa, a chain of service stations, promoting their range of anti-freeze products. Not exactly the sort of task that would have led to Jeff Stark relocating halfway round the world, but a nice, low-key start.

The line came to me before I'd even opened my pad.

'Cold cure for cars,' I said, confidently.

Graham stared at me. 'That's really good.'

I shrugged modestly, as though this was the kind of rapid response he should have expected.

He got to work sketching out the poster and within a few minutes had produced a layout showing the full range of products set in a small bank of snow. The headline was huge, which is the way I liked it.

As soon as he'd finished, Graham stood up. 'Come on, let's have a game of pool.'

'Are we allowed to? It's not even four yet.' I was terrified at the thought of getting into trouble on my first day. 'What if someone sees us?'

'Who's going to say anything? We're all creative directors, aren't we?'

He had a point. So we went through to the room where my dreams of leading a crack creative team, of being the Samat Busby of Mackay King, had been smashed into tiny pieces that morning, and he handed me a beer from the fridge. After I'd lost the first game and Graham had suggested we make it best-of-three, a few other creative directors drifted in and helped themselves to beers. It was, I decided, a job I was going to enjoy.

A good day was about to get even better. When I got back to my company house, there was an envelope with a Manchester postmark. Were they begging me to come back? If so, they could be in luck, depending on how I felt in six months' time.

But it wasn't a job offer. It was even better than that. The Great Northern Bitter advert had won a Silver Lion at Cannes. And my name was on the certificate.

When I finally found a way to work this into the conversation with Marcus the next day, he seemed as excited as I was and asked me to bring the tape in, which I did. A few minutes after I handed it over, a call went out for everyone in the creative department to gather in the boardroom. When everyone had arrived, Marcus produced a bottle of champagne, poured everyone a glass, and announced that we were celebrating my winning a Cannes Silver Lion. He then played the advert.

When it finished there was a huge burst of applause from my fellow creative directors. This was brilliant. By now, everyone at BDH knew that I hadn't written it. But here, they thought I had. By the same token, everyone here knew that I wasn't in sole charge of the creative department. But everyone at BDH thought I was.

These were two worlds that would never collide.

And that was when something else hit me. Because of the huge distance, I would be able to recycle ideas, even re-use headlines, from my Leeds and Manchester days and *no one would ever know*.

It didn't take me long to put this plan into practice.

Twenty

Graham announced that our first job, the 'Cold cure for cars' poster, had been approved. I felt a huge thrill. This was proof that I'd adapted easily to life in a new country – as long as you overlooked having my brother-in-law Nick send *Campaign* and the *News of the World* over every week, Jacko taking responsibility for posting Weetabix and Marmite supplies, and my friend Kevin filling videotapes with our favourite TV programmes.

'When does it go to the printers?' I asked, exhilarated by the prospect of seeing my Europa poster all over Wellington.

'It doesn't,' he said.

'What do you mean?'

'You'll find out soon enough,' he said, with an apologetic shrug. 'Things are a bit different over here.'

I didn't have time to quiz him any further, as we'd been given a brief for another job for Europa. This time it was much bigger. A TV advert.

This was perfect. I'd been there less than a week and already I was working on a TV ad. I felt vindicated. It had been the right decision, even though we were a long way from home. The sooner I could fill my showreel, the sooner we could get back.

My biggest success in selling to the car market had been the Trust Motors campaign with Jonathan, the cute little boy whose dad was too busy selling cars to write ads.

'How about we use a cute kid for this?' I said, and started to scribble down a few ideas.

'Yeah,' Graham replied. 'I don't think that's ever been done before.'

I didn't know him well enough to figure out if he was being sarcastic, so I continued in my attempt to develop a scenario that somehow linked adorable children with a national chain of service stations.

As I was pondering this, Marcus walked in, dangling a set of keys. He looked out of the window at the car park below and pointed at a white MGB with a black soft top being unloaded from a tow truck.

'If you look down there,' he said with a self-satisfied grin, 'you'll see your new company car.'

I stared at it in awe. It looked magnificent. This was the moment I'd dreamt about since first starting work at the factory in Abingdon, attaching passenger doors to MGBs. Now I was going to be driving one.

I turned to Graham. 'Fancy going for a drive?'

'Sure.'

We rushed through reception like excited children and ran down the stairs, too impatient to wait for the lift.

'Climb in, then,' I said as we reached the car.

While he tried to open his door, I got into the driver's seat, admiring the completely revamped instrument layout and control positioning that had been introduced not long after I started at the factory. Graham banged on the window to get my attention.

'What's the matter?' I shouted, desperate to get going.

'It's stuck,' he said.

'Try pulling it harder.'

'I did, and it won't open.'

I tried opening it from the inside, but he was right. It was definitely stuck. In the end I had to get out so that he could clamber over the driver's seat. I didn't mention that I was the person responsible for fitting passenger doors on this particular model and was relieved when he changed the subject.

'How about going to look at the Europa poster?' he suggested.

'But I thought you said it hadn't gone to the printers yet.'

'You'll see,' he responded enigmatically.

This was turning into a fantastic day. I'd taken delivery of the car I'd always promised myself, had an idea for a high-profile TV advert that had proved successful in the past, and I was now on my way to see the first piece of work I'd written for my new agency.

The MGB was a great car to drive. Compared to a Lada, anyway. I'd once made up an ad for it while waiting for the next doorless shell to arrive on the production line, in which I raved about its 'rapid response' acceleration (0–60 in twelve seconds), 'lightning fast' top speed (109 mph) and its impressive overhead valve gear (whatever that was). Now I was experiencing it for myself. Once we were on the open road I put the top down, even though it was early winter and the cold wind was blowing directly in our faces. Handling was perfect, thanks mainly to the thicker anti-roll bars that had been introduced, after several complaints.

Graham directed me to an entry road to a motorway and then suddenly screamed for me to stop. The front disc and rear drum brakes responded perfectly and I found myself staring at a couple of men in their late fifties, dressed in brown overalls and holding paintbrushes. They were standing on ladders in front of a gigantic blank billboard. As we got closer, I could see they were both holding a coloured-in photocopy of Graham's design and were painstakingly hand-painting it directly on to the board, which was around twenty feet wide and ten feet high.

I looked at Graham, who shrugged. 'It's the only way to do it,' he explained. 'None of the printers have presses big enough. Like I said, things are a bit different over here.'

Actually, I quite liked the idea of dedicated artists spending several days in the freezing cold just to reproduce a poster I'd written, but it also made me a bit nervous about our Europa TV advert. What would they be shooting it with? A Super 8 hand-held camera? I could just imagine playing *that* to Jeremy Sinclair.

When we got back to the office I tried not to think about it and carried on with writing the script. The scenario I'd worked out was that Jonathan, a cute little boy whose dad worked at a Europa garage, went to visit him in a home-made toy car that his dad had constructed from an old beer crate. The Jonathan character, of course, bore a few remarkable similarities to the star of the Trust Motors ads I'd written, not least his name, so in an attempt to make this one seem different I gave him a sister, Samantha. Together, they took the toy car to Dad's workplace, where Jonathan pretended to clean the windscreen, check the oil and pump petrol into it. Just like his dad would do.

At which point the viewers' hearts would melt and they would rush out to their cars and take a drive to the nearest Europa station.

I finished the script and Graham added a few touches, including Jonathan doing the voiceover, where he talked about why he came to Europa ('because everyone likes being fussed over'). The account director, Neil, thought it was excellent. He presented it to the client, who apparently felt the same way. The ad had gone through the usual channels and had been approved. This was more like agency life in Leeds and Manchester, and it raised my hopes that the old-fashioned hand-painted posters might just be a one-off.

We could now get on with the exciting part – finding a director who shared our vision (in other words, who could produce an advert that would win awards and get us a pay rise). There was also the shoot to look forward to. This would mean the chance of another cameo. Not to mention all the free food.

Just as I was about to ask Graham about local directors, he informed me that before we could move on to production the script had to go through one more stage: it had to be sent to the chief censor for approval. If he saw something in it he didn't like, the advert would never be shown. There were only two TV channels in New Zealand, and both came under his jurisdiction. There wasn't anything remotely controversial in the ad, so I wasn't particularly worried. I made three photocopies of the script, as required, and sent them to him, together with a handwritten note introducing myself. I thought this piece of sucking up could work in my favour if we ever tried to push a riskier advert through.

Graham thought that we'd hear back within a week, and there wouldn't be any harm in sounding out a few directors. The good part of this was that meetings took place over lunch, which meant that they insisted on picking up the tab. Perhaps talking to five different directors over five lunches was excessive, but we wanted to be sure.

We'd already made our choice by the time a letter from the censor arrived. I opened it, pulled out the returned script, and saw the word DECLINED stamped on it. Underneath, in a box labelled 'Reasons for denial', was typed 'Beer crate unacceptable. Unacceptable link between drinking and driving.'

The TVNZ censor seemed to like the word 'unacceptable'.

I was immediately plunged into a depression. This was meant to be the first of many adverts that would eventually fill my showreel, so that I would no longer have to rely solely on Great Northern Bitter. In fact, I had hopes that once my two years in New Zealand were up I'd be in a position to replace it with a dozen more ads that I'd actually conceived and written. This adjudication had put all that on hold.

Then Graham had an idea. 'Couldn't we just make it an apple crate?' he said.

I hadn't thought of that. I was too busy obsessing about the big picture to focus on one detail. I got the script retyped, the word BEER replaced by the word APPLES. A week later it came back. The word APPROVED was rubber-stamped on the top right corner. Our advert had been rescued! Graham immediately arranged a meeting with the director we'd chosen.

The shoot was arranged for eleven at night, when the service station closed. It went well, apart from the client changing a few of Jonathan's lines and, unbelievably, suggesting a cameo by himself. Which is why we both appeared as happy, smiling customers, shaking hands with the attendant. This never actually happened in real life, as far as I was aware, but at least I felt my performance was more natural than in the Great Northern Bitter advert. There was also a cameo for the MGB, which was being filled with petrol in the background when the kids were washing their windscreen.

As we watched the advert in the editing suite, Graham and I started to get that warm feeling you get when you can see an idea working. It was nicely shot and the acting was good, especially the brother and sister. We were both really happy with it. The client would be happy too, given the number of close-ups of the Europa logo on the attendant's woolly V-neck jumper. And the censor would be happy to see the word APPLES on the side of the cart. It felt like a job well done.

When we arrived back at work, the feeling of pride was gradually replaced by a feeling of gloom as I began to see the blatant flaw in my plan to recycle UK ideas. Jeremy Sinclair had already seen the Jonathan press ads for Trust, and there was a chance he might remember them. This meant I wouldn't be able to risk showing him the Europa ad – which was essentially the same idea – as it might just trigger a memory. There and then I made a decision. I had no choice. In future, I would have to produce original work.

As the fear began to rise at this prospect, Graham's phone rang. He picked it up, grunted something and replaced it on the cradle. 'Come on,' he said to me, getting to his feet. 'We've got to go and get a brief for a new Lion Brown ad.'

My good mood quickly returned. Straight away, a chance for redemption. This was the moment I'd been waiting for. As a Beer Man, I could now start producing the kind of ground-breaking TV advertising that would have Jeremy Sinclair reaching for the phone. As long as I didn't mention cars or driving.

'Thirty-second or sixty-second spot?' I asked Graham.

He gave me a strange look, as though he thought I might be having him on. 'You know there's no beer advertising on TV in New Zealand, right? That's why this account's such a pain to work on.'

As my head thumped against the desk, I mentally reviewed the bizarre things that had happened to me in just a couple of weeks in New Zealand. I'd been introduced to the concept of multiple creative directors, been given a company car with one working door, witnessed posters being painted by hand, had my work turned down by an all-powerful censor over a word on the side of a crate, and now discovered that in this land Beer Men were so insignificant they were probably below the likes of Roofing Tile Men in the agency pecking order.

It was probably just as well I was about to get the chance to become one. A Roofing Tile Man, that is.

Twenty-one

Everyone has a major fashion regret in their past, and mine came towards the end of 1982.

It was Dexy's Midnight Runners' fault. I was completely in love with 'Come on Eileen' and watched the video over and over again on my company-provided Sony C5 Beta Video Recorder. This meant I had an unnaturally high level of exposure to dungarees. And having been away from England for more than six months, I was convinced that their constant presence in the video was merely a reflection of what was being worn by trend-conscious young people on the streets back home and, more importantly, in advertising agencies. As a creative director at one of New Zealand's leading agencies and a huge Dexy's fan, I decided I had to have some.

Pleasingly, I couldn't find a pair anywhere in Wellington – even Hugh Wright's ('Leaders in menswear'), which distinguished itself by being open on Saturday mornings, didn't stock them. It was clearly a trend that hadn't reached New Zealand yet.

But I struck gold with the Kay's mail order catalogue, which I'd had sent over from the UK. They were prepared to send me a pair of dungarees, as long as I paid an extra £4.75 (inc. VAT) for postage. They looked perfect, even though they were from the Workwear section of the catalogue, as opposed to Men's Fashion.

When they arrived, I couldn't wait to try them on. I managed to resist the temptation to go the whole Dexy's way and team them with a red neckerchief; instead I wore them with a sleeveless shirt and rolled them up to draw full attention to my black kung fu shoes. As a final touch, when I wore the outfit to work for the first time a few days later, I'd gone without shaving for a few days. I'd been aiming for the Dexy stubble, but due to my hair colouring it looked more like the beginnings of a grey beard.

There was a reason for dressing like this instead of my usual T-shirt and jeans: I'd been asked to sit in on a new business presentation so that I could be introduced as the award-winning creative director who'd just come over from the UK, and I wanted to look the part. My first inclination had been to wear my Jeremy Sinclair-inspired suit, but I'd decided it was more important to reinforce the fact that I was a trendy adman and style leader fresh off the plane from London.

I'd been briefed about how important it was to win the Gerard Roofing account. Mackay King had been after them for a while and felt that the addition of an award-winning creative director might just tip the scales. Once the strategic part had been covered, the plan was that I'd say a few words about creative approach. I'd learned from my Stockport Tech experience and had thoroughly prepared my short speech.

When I got into work that morning, I was feeling nervous yet confident – I'd even provisionally allocated space on my showreel for the Gerard Roofing advert I would hopefully be producing. I walked into the office to find Graham already hard at work. He looked up and took in my outfit.

'You know who you look like, don't you?' he said.

'Kevin Rowland from Dexy's Midnight Runners?' I replied, with a knowing smile.

'No,' he replied, 'I was thinking Uncle Jesse from *The Dukes of Hazzard*.'

That comment was running through my head as I took my place in the boardroom, suddenly self-conscious of my dungarees. I wasn't overjoyed at being compared to a grey-bearded grandfather-figure known for saying things like 'You can't stir up a mess of trouble for other folks without spillin' some on yourself'. I wondered if the five men across the table were thinking the same thing as Graham. They were the representatives of Gerard Roofing Tiles, and had come in to hear how we at Mackay King could do a much better job than their current agency.

'This is Dave Roberts, our new creative director from the UK,' said Neil, the account director. 'He's just won a Gold Lion at Cannes and will be working on your business.'

Gold Lion? First I'd heard of it. Still, it could have been an honest mistake.

I shook hands with the men from Gerard.

'So, you're from the UK,' said the one in the middle, who had introduced himself as Don, marketing manager.

'Yup, been here a few months. Really enjoying it.'

'My wife's a big fan of the royal family, you know,' he said. 'She's just finished knitting a jumper for Princess Diana's baby.'

'That's a coincidence,' I said, sensing a chance to bond with him by finding common ground. 'I know someone who's just done the same thing.'

'Really?'

'Yes.'

I was desperately trying to remember who it was. And then it hit me. It wasn't someone I knew at all, it was a character on the last episode of *Coronation Street* I'd watched before flying out.

'Yes, woman called Mavis,' I blustered. 'Friend of mine.'

Luckily, Cheryl the receptionist/PA arrived with coffee just in time to save me from any further questions. I guessed that Cheryl had been chosen to carry out this function based more on her appearance than her coffee-making skills. She had been runner-up in the last Miss Wellington contest, a fact she managed to work into every conversation, whatever the topic.

It was nearly time for the presentation to begin and I was starting to sweat. The dungarees felt uncomfortable and I wished I'd had a shave. My chin was itching and I kept scratching it. The nerves were partially down to having never been in a client meeting before. At my previous agencies, copywriters and art directors tended to be kept away from clients so they couldn't form a relationship with them and take the business with them when they left.

Neil, who was leading the presentation, had told me that clients always loved visiting agencies, as it was the best part of their day. A huge plate of Griffin's chocolate biscuits and fresh coffee drunk from fine German china (Villeroy and Boch, Naif Collection) were just a part of the appeal. Being treated like royalty also helped. None of this helped ease my nerves.

Once the getting-to-know-you talk had finished, Neil stood up and placed a large piece of card on the board that read WHAT WE'VE DONE SINCE RECEIVING YOUR BRIEF. 'We've held focus group meetings to try and understand the perception of Gerard among the target market,' he told them. 'We found that your advert is perceived as an iconic piece of Kiwi TV, while the message of good-looking roofing had almost eighty per cent awareness. It's a highly effective spot, no doubt about that.'

The men across the table looked pleased. So was I: the chance to work on a brand described as 'iconic' should mean an easy way to produce award-winning work. What Saatchi & Saatchi managed to do with Schweppes, I would do with Gerard Roofing Tiles.

I was anxious to see what they had done to merit such a build-up. I'd never seen the ad, but the look of pride in the eyes of the Gerard team was an indication that I was about to witness something special.

Neil pressed the play button on the agency's U-Matic Video Recorder.

The opening shot was of a swarthy lothario in unbuttoned checked shirt swaggering into someone's front yard. He looked up at the roof, which inspired him to burst into song with the words 'Go for G-G-G-G-G-G-G-G-Gerard' sung à la Engelbert Humperdinck. 'Go for Gerard and your roof is looking good.'

This naturally brought the family out to see what was going on, whereupon the hero picked up a little girl who stared into the camera and also burst into song: 'Go for G-G-G-G-G-G-G-G-Gerard, go for Gerard and your roof is looking good.'

Our lothario responded in the only way he knew how, with another burst of 'Go for G-G-G-G-G-G-G-G-Gerard, go for Gerard and your roof is looking good.'

The husband then appeared out of nowhere, but his wife completely ignored him, instead turning to the (much hunkier) singer and saying breathlessly, 'John! That's a great roof!' Even though it was her own roof. He smiled, as if it had had something to do with him, and had just enough time to squeeze in one more 'Gerard'.

It was awful. I had never seen anything so bad, apart from my advert for WASS, which no one had described as 'iconic'. On the surface, however, I remained the perfect Mackay King representative – serious and appreciative. The marketing man caught my eye and I nodded.

'Nice work,' I mouthed.

But inside, I could feel laughter bubbling up. It quickly became too great to resist and my shoulders began to shake. I bit my lip hard to drag my attention away from the image of John and his obvious love for Gerard Roofing Tiles.

Neil was continuing his pitch. 'As I said, the ad has been incredibly effective. We believe it's now time to build on its success and use John to expand the market.'

I snorted.

As Neil continued to praise the worst advert in the world, I went to pour myself another coffee and tried to stop my shoulders shaking. I wrapped my hand around the cup of steaming hot coffee, trying to distract myself. But it was no good. At first, a small giggle escaped my lips. This grew into hysterical laughter as my resistance crumbled. Tears were soon streaming from my eyes.

The expressions from across the table ranged from confused to hurt. Somehow, that just made everything even funnier. I collapsed on the floor and heard myself emitting a strange high-pitched series of giggles.

Neil had been expecting a top creative director who could add credibility and gravitas to proceedings; instead he got an unshaven Uncle Jesse lookalike dressed in dungarees and kung fu shoes who was rolling around on the floor basically laughing at the very people he'd been brought in to impress. There was a look of pure panic on his face. He clearly had no idea how to handle this admittedly unusual situation.

Eventually he suggested I go away and compose myself before coming back and doing my presentation, so I went back to the office and lay down on the sofa. My ribs were in agony, eyes and throat sore from laughing so much. Breathing was difficult as I was wheezing. Graham, not unreasonably, tried to extract an explanation for what was going on, but I couldn't talk, apart from spluttering the word 'G-G-Gerard', which set off another bout of giggling.

But slowly, I began to recover.

Ten minutes later there was a knock on the door. Neil, who had aged about ten years since I last saw him, was wondering if I was ready to return. I nodded, and went back into the board-room, determined to redeem myself. The Gerard men smiled nervously, and I apologized, saying that I didn't know what had come over me and that this was my first client meeting and I'd been overcome with nerves.

I then gave my speech on the creative approach, trying to banish all thoughts of Gerard's hunky stutterer from my mind. Although it only lasted a few minutes, I managed to cover all the points I'd been told to make and was rewarded by a few nods of agreement from across the table. I sat back down, hugely relieved. As long as Neil didn't play the advert again I reckoned I'd be able to make it through to the end of the meeting.

And then marketing manager Don opened a large portfolio and took out a big cut-out of John, all teeth and hair, standing in front of a newly tiled roof. A speech bubble came out of his mouth saying 'Go for Gerard and your roof is looking good'.

'Would we still be able to use this point-of-sale material if we followed your recommendations?' Don asked.

I didn't hear Neil's answer. Seeing John had set me off again, and it wasn't long before I was being helped out of the boardroom, laughing hysterically.

According to Graham, the meeting wrapped up not long after that and they promised to get back to Neil after discussing it among themselves. The general consensus on our side was that we had no chance. But we were wrong. Despite everything, they asked that we move on to the next stage of our proposal.

I had to write the follow-up advert that had been discussed at the meeting. It was unanimously felt that I should continue to use the factors that had made them so successful in the first place. Which meant that I had to come up with an advert featuring John and his G-G-G-G-G-G-G-G-Gerard jingle.

I was pretty sure this was something I would never be showing Jeremy Sinclair.

Twenty-two

Jeremy Sinclair was looking at my showreel. His check shirt was unbuttoned to the midriff and tufts of wiry dark hair poked out. His trousers looked uncomfortably tight. He was watching my Gerard advert, which showed the hunky presenter, John, leaping from roof to roof. After it had finished, Jeremy began to laugh hysterically, unable to control himself. When he finally settled down, he turned to me and burst into song, to the tune of the original Gerard ad. 'Your G-G-G-G-G-G-G-G-Gerard ad is rubbish,' he warbled. 'Yes, it's rubbish, and your reel's not looking good.'

I crawled underneath his desk, trying to hide from the humiliation. Just then, Charles Saatchi, Jeff Stark and Andrew Rutherford burst into the office wearing identical white suits and top hats. After they'd carried out a beautifully choreographed dance routine, all four of them lifted the desk into the air and pointed their canes at me, singing, 'Yes, it's rubbish, and your reel's not looking good!'

I woke up with my heart just about bursting out of my chest, scared and sweating. Caroline was instantly awake and swiftly moved into full nurse mode.

'What's the matter? Are you all right?'

'Yeah, just a nightmare,' I said slowly, as my breathing was still laboured. 'I was showing one of my ads to Jeremy Sinclair when he started singing and then—'

She had already gone back to sleep.

I'd recently read an article in *Woman's Weekly* about the meaning of dreams (where I learned that falling apparently means your life is out of control), but in this case it was obvious: my subconscious was telling me that I needed to re-focus on why I had come to New Zealand. I came to produce ads that would make my dreams come true. Not the one I'd just had, obviously, but the one in which I finally took my place at Saatchi & Saatchi.

The only question was, how could I make that happen?

The answer took about eighteen months to come to me, by which time I'd become a father to Hazel, our first child. As well as that, Gerard had thankfully decided to stay with their existing agency and I had written a whole host of startlingly original ads for other clients, without collapsing into hysterics once. Life in New Zealand really seemed to be working out.

It was winter, and we were watching *Juliet Bravo* on TV when the words BREAKING NEWS appeared on the screen. The picture cut to Parliament, where a press conference was taking place and a very drunk-looking Prime Minister, Rob Muldoon, had just announced that a general election would be taking place in a month's time.

'That doesn't give you much time to run up to an election, Prime Minister,' said one of the journalists.

'Doesn't give my opponensh much time to run up to a 'lection, does it?' came the slurred response as he gazed at the cameras with a fixed grin, before being dragged away by a petrified aide.

I felt the adrenalin course through me as I sensed an opportunity to really get myself noticed by my heroes in Charlotte Street. An election meant election advertising, and I knew the man who was in charge of advertising for the Labour Party – Rob Muldoon and the National Party's opponensh. This was exactly the sort of work that would get Jeremy Sinclair's attention. After all, it was his work for the Conservative Party in the 1979 and 1983 UK general elections that had made him a household name. In my household, anyway.

In my file of Saatchi ads was some of his finest political work, including 'Like your manifesto, Comrade' which pointed out the similarities between the policies of the Labour and Communist parties, and a Polaroid I'd taken of a poster reading 'Cheer up, Labour can't hang on forever', which ran during the winter of discontent, perfectly capturing the mood of a country in the midst of strikes, picket-line violence and rubbish piled high in the streets. Best of all, though, was a double-page spread in the *Sun* headed 'Do this quiz to find out if you're Labour or Conservative', which somehow proved that I, a lifelong Labour voter, was in fact a Tory. More evidence of Jeremy Sinclair's genius.

I managed to suppress the feeling that I might be Conservative and rang my friend Simon, who was the one who looked after the Labour Party advertising. He told me that they'd love to have me on board and that there was going to be a meeting at 6.30 the next evening; it would be great if I could come along and meet a few people.

I hoped this didn't mean there was going to be a committee. Malcolm Reeve, who was the Conservative director of communications when Saatchi & Saatchi won the account, had publicly said that committees never worked in elections. And he should know.

I was particularly nervous as I headed to the meeting. All I'd been told by Simon was that the Labour Party had come up with the brilliant idea of calling themselves 'New Labour' as a way of distancing themselves from 'Old' Labour, who were perceived to be in the pockets of the unions. This tactic might have had more credibility if the meeting I was attending wasn't taking place in the plush offices of the country's biggest and most powerful trade union.

This was the centre of power. It was the natural habitat of people like Charles Saatchi and Jeremy Sinclair, but a new experience for me. It was something I was going to have to get used to.

I was shown into a large room with a round table. There were seven people sitting around it, eyeing me suspiciously. My worst fears were realized. This was just like Gerard Roof Tiles – advertising by committee.

'Hi Dave, take a seat,' said Simon. 'Sorry it's just us, but the others are tied up.'

The *others*? How many were there on this bloody committee?

A plate of chocolate biscuits was passed around the table. It was a silver plate, which didn't seem very Labour Party. Maybe New Labour was going to be different. I lifted a biscuit from the plate and glanced underneath. Pleasingly, it said GRIFFIN'S – superior to Arnott's, the other major brand, whose biscuits never failed to disappoint.

After everyone had been poured a coffee, the meeting began.

'Now, by way of an advertising brief,' said Simon, who seemed to be in charge, 'if the parties were cars, Labour would be a Toyota Corolla – accessible, designed for people from all walks of life, practical and hard-working, if you see what I mean?'

I nodded, as though I understood perfectly why he was comparing political parties to cars.

'Whereas National would be a Honda Accord. Elitist, divisive, style over substance—'

'Out of touch with the needs of ordinary New Zealanders?' I offered.

'Exactly. I mean, look at that advert they've got on TV,' he continued, with genuine contempt. 'Smug young bankers at a dinner party braying about the electric sunroofs and stereo cassettes that came as standard in their new Accord EXs—'

'While their overdressed women sip champagne and laugh uproariously for no apparent reason,' I added, shaking my head. 'Unbelievable rubbish, isn't it?'

Simon smiled and nodded, as did several of his colleagues. We were on the same wavelength. I made a mental note to remove the Honda Accord 'dinner party' advert I'd written from my showreel.

'This thought has to be the basis of any communications,' said Simon. 'The New Labour government, under the leadership of David Lange, will understand the needs of ordinary New Zealanders.'

I was secretly pleased that he'd used the same phrase I'd used.

Then one of the other committee members, an older woman in a full-length skirt, held up a letter. 'We've just had some very good news,' she announced, then paused for effect. 'We've been granted rights to use "Up Where We Belong" by Joe Cocker and Jennifer Warnes in all advertising throughout the campaign.'

By the enthusiastic applause and wolf whistling that broke out around the table, this was a popular turn of events. I saw it as a serious blow. The song, from the film *An Officer and a Gentleman*, was one I hated with a passion. The thought of having to use it made my heart sink. I couldn't see how eagles crying on mountains, so that love could lift us up where we belonged fitted into an election advert for David Lange, a shambling twenty-five-stone man with thick oversized glasses, but I agreed to get it in somehow.

Once the meeting had wrapped up, I went round to Graham's – he'd offered to help out on the ads. As usual, we ended up drinking and watching TV instead of working. There was a film showing that evening called *The Day After*, which had been the subject of plenty of press that week due to its subject matter: it was about what America would be like in the aftermath of a nuclear war.

'What would happen,' I said to Graham, 'if we showed a slightly exaggerated futuristic vision of what New Zealand would be like if National stayed in power for three more years?'

'How do you mean?'

'Well, we could show scenes like cars abandoned in the streets due to astronomical petrol prices, and empty supermarket shelves because deliveries couldn't be made.'

Graham sat up, suddenly alert. 'And homeless families begging outside boarded-up homes since mortgage rates were so high. We could shoot it in black and white.'

'If that isn't understanding the needs of ordinary New Zealanders, I don't know what is,' I concluded, triumphantly.

This was it. This was the big idea. It would show a dystopic vision of the future, like the latest Apple Computers '1984' advert, which had been directed by Ridley Scott. In his take on George Orwell's classic tale, an attractive blonde girl in a white tank top and tight red shorts was seen smashing Big Brother's massive TV screens with an enormous hammer. Perhaps Ridley could direct this one too?

Only one thing was more terrifying than the futuristic scenario we were painting and that was the thought of these bleak monochrome images being accompanied by Joe Cocker and Jennifer Warnes cheerfully singing 'Love lift us up where we belong'. Still, we thought we might be able to talk the party out of using it, since the idea was so dramatic.

Even more exciting than the thought of this advert winning a General Election was the prospect of it taking the place of that Honda Accord advert on my showreel. It just felt right. I tried not to get ahead of myself, but I could just imagine Jeremy Sinclair purring with satisfaction when he saw it.

Graham got straight to work on a storyboard. We decided to do the ad as though it was a live news broadcast, mainly because that was what *The Day After* had done so effectively. And that was how I wrote it.

I thought it was easily the best thing we'd ever done.

As it turned out, we needn't have bothered. The committee voted it down after deciding that it 'wasn't quite on message' and came up with some ideas of their own which looked as though they'd been decided by a committee. They simply wanted to see David Lange in a supermarket, pushing a trolley around as he talked about how he was going to bring food prices down.

I wrote the script, and after several meetings finally got the stamp of approval from everyone. Graham and I were invited along to the shoot, and if you watch the ad closely, you can see me lifting a packet of Persil from the shelf and carefully placing it into a shopping basket, stretching out my few seconds of screen time.

The advert aired and was made to look good by National's campaign, which was implausibly themed 'New Zealand, You're Winning'. On 14 July 1984, David Lange became Prime Minister by a large margin. Was it because he was a brilliant politician who'd captured the imagination of a country that was in the mood for change? Or was it because viewers saw him pushing a trolley packed with Tip Top bread, Watties Tomato Sauce and Fresh-Up Orange Juice towards the checkout while 'Up Where We Belong', the ultimate supermarket song, played in the background? Perhaps it was a bit of both. Or maybe it was simply the fact that the Labour ad was slightly less rubbish than the National ad.

The result was pleasing, but my showreel still contained nothing but the Great Northern Bitter advert. Since coming to New Zealand I'd done TV ads for Europa, with kids driving a toy car, for Honda, with rich bankers eating dinner, and now for the New Labour Party, with a huge man shopping in a supermarket. They all had one thing in common: they were rubbish. None of them would get me a job in Grimsby let alone Saatchi & Saatchi, the world's finest advertising agency. My showreel-boosting plan was backfiring in spectacular fashion, and now I was going to have to stay in New Zealand for a lot longer than the two years I'd originally allocated in my master plan before I could turn up with a fanfare in Soho again.

That night, I had a disturbing dream about falling from the top of a tall building in Charlotte Street.

Twenty-three

'Our target market,' said Neil, reading from the brief he was about to hand over, 'is families with children between the ages of two and ten, lower to mid socio-economic levels, who see doing things together as highly important.'

'No it's not,' I thought, 'the target market is Jeremy Sinclair.'

The job was to come up with a new TV advert for Cobb and Co, a chain of family restaurants. According to Neil, who was never one to squander an opportunity to state the obvious, our task was to 'encourage families to eat at Cobb and Co'.

As I skimmed through the brief, it seemed unpromising. The marketing manager wanted to demonstrate why Cobb and Co was such good value and insisted on showing the food being prepared and then enjoyed. Somehow I had to turn this into an advert that would make a massive impact on Saatchi & Saatchi. It would be a nice bonus if it also increased sales for the client.

My friend Kevin had recently sent me a video of essential UK programmes, including the first episodes of a new soap called *EastEnders*, a new comedy (to me in New Zealand, anyway) called *The Young Ones* (which I thought was totally brilliant) and, of course, some *Coronation Street*. He hadn't cut the adverts out, so I eagerly watched them to see if I could pick up on any trends. There seemed to be quite a few featuring celebrities. The Two Ronnies were advertising Hertz, Paul Daniels was promoting Midland Homes, and Griff Rhys Jones was in a really good ad for Holsten Pils (copywriter Steve Henry, for Gold Greenless Trott), weaving in old footage of a James Cagney film.

But the one that really caught my attention was for Toshiba. It was based on Alexei Sayle's hit song ''Allo John, Got a New Motor?', and showed a blueprint man on a drawing board coming to life while Ian Dury sang ''Allo Tosh, got a Toshiba?', along with lines like 'It's got a fair old bit of power' and catch-phrase-in-waiting 'We are talking quality'. The ad had been written by the genius whose book had told me how to get my first job in advertising, Dave Trott, and was a reminder of how far behind we were in New Zealand.

But it gave me an idea. A big Saatchi-pleasing monster of an idea. We would bring Alexei Sayle over to New Zealand. He was already well known thanks to his top ten single and would soon be seen in *The Young Ones* when it finally aired on this side of the world. The ad would be thirty seconds of pure slapstick, with Alexei acting as a guide to Cobb and Co, touring the kitchen and the restaurant and generally getting in everyone's way while enthusing about the quality of the food, the calibre of the chefs and the impressively low prices.

Using a celebrity had twin benefits. Firstly, you could use them to distract the viewer from an uninspired script. Secondly, they often liked to rewrite their lines, usually for the better. In this case, there was a third benefit: Alexei Sayle would be instantly recognizable to creative directors back home, one in particular. Since my political advert showing a fat bloke walking through a supermarket had failed to reach the heights of

'Labour isn't working', it was time to try the UK celebrity route to get Jeremy Sinclair's attention.

When it came time to present to Cobb and Co, I was feeling good. In my mind, I could see Alexei turning my script into a comedy masterclass. There were three Cobb and Co marketing people there, and once everyone had introduced themselves, I stood up.

'We open in a busy Cobb and Co, families enjoying their meal out,' I began, smiling confidently. 'And then the doors open and in walks . . .' I paused for dramatic effect, before the big reveal. 'Alexei Sayle. He faces the camera and says, "Good evening. I'd like to take you behind the scenes here at Cobb and Co." He then takes apple pies from the oven to show how appetizing the food is, cuts a piece of steak from the grill to demonstrate the chef's expertise, and grabs a tray of salads from a passing waitress to highlight their freshness. It's going to be a really effective spot.'

The marketing people looked at one another.

'Dave, can we just rewind a bit?' the one in the middle said. 'Who's this Alexei character?'

'Alexei Sayle. He sings "'Allo John, Got a New Motor?" It was in the top ten for ages over here. He was also recently voted best comedian in the UK TV Comedy Awards.' I didn't feel the need to mention that this was an award I'd just made up. 'And he's in *The Young Ones* – plays Mr Balowski, the landlord.'

They conferred among themselves. I could feel sweat starting to gather on my brow.

'I'm sorry, but we're not familiar with either the actor or the programme. Is it even shown in New Zealand?'

'Well, no, not yet. But I'm sure it will be. I've brought a tape of it so you can see him in action.'

I walked over to the Sharp VC-388NZ VHS Video Recorder

and tentatively pressed the play button. I wasn't just nervous about their reaction, I was also petrified of breaking such a fragile-looking piece of machinery and having to fork out the $2,499 – more than a month's salary – it would cost to replace.

A fuzzy picture appeared on screen. I'd cued up the scene earlier to show them what they'd be getting for their money. Alexei Sayle was towering over Mike, the diminutive cockney character, and subjecting him to a tirade about buying cars. I thought it was the funniest thing I'd seen on TV since the Gerard Roofing ad. It had the same effect on me every time I watched it. I laughed at just about every line, as a way of encouraging the Cobb and Co contingent to follow suit. They didn't.

As the scene finished, Alexei delivered his parting line and walked out of the door.

'What did he say?' asked the Cobb and Co man on the left.

'He said "Laugh? I nearly went to Ethiopia",' I replied, laughing hysterically myself.

The client didn't say anything. He didn't need to. There comes a time in every failed presentation when you instinctively sense things are slipping away. It was time to take the classic copywriter's fallback position.

'Obviously Alexei's just one option as our presenter,' I tried.

All three Cobb and Co representatives suddenly perked up.

'Who else have you got in mind?'

'I don't have the list on me, but I'll get it over to you in the morning, if that's OK.'

'We'll look forward to it.'

The next day, half a dozen people from the creative department sat around the same boardroom table in a panic, coming up with names from Norman Wisdom to Phil Oakey of the Human League. None of them seemed quite right.

Then Lily, the TV production assistant, had an idea: 'How about Del Boy from *Only Fools and Horses*? He'd be quite good, I reckon.'

Five creative directors all shouted 'Yes!' at the same time. It was a brilliant idea. *Only Fools and Horses* was a massive hit in New Zealand as well as in the UK. I wouldn't have been surprised if it was an integral part of Thursday nights in the Sinclair household back in London. I hoped so anyway.

'Can you see if he's available?' Graham asked Lily nervously.

It took four days for David Jason's agent to get back to Lily. By that time there were about a dozen people desperate for news. This included the Cobb and Co team – who were showing a level of enthusiasm I'd never seen from them before – Graham and me (conscious as we both were of the boost this could give our showreels), and the production company we'd lined up to shoot the ads.

When Lily broke the news that David Jason had agreed terms, we spent the rest of the day with the producer and director discussing the shoot over a lengthy lunch, which they were happy to pay for.

The only thing that remained was to get script approved by the TVNZ censor. Once I'd reassured him that it would be filmed 'responsibly' and 'in a way as to clearly show that the company do not condone the actions of Mr Jason's character', we were literally given the stamp of approval.

Five weeks later, an Air New Zealand 737 carrying the star of *Only Fools and Horses* touched down in Wellington after the short commuter flight from Auckland International airport. He spent the first few days being given guided tours of the city, meeting up with the director and producer, and being taken out to dinner by the Mackay King management and then the Cobb and Co management. The rest of us were happy to catch the occasional glimpse of a real live celebrity.

On the third day he began shooting the ads, and that night it was Caroline and me who got to take him out for dinner. It was the first outing for our elitist, divisive new Honda Accord, which we'd got after our daughter Hazel was born: the MGB wasn't really a suitable family car, especially with only one door functioning.

Since the meal would be covered by my Mackay King credit card, we had chosen one of Wellington's finest establishments, Ma Maison (or 'My Gaff' as we decided Del Boy would call it). When we arrived at the restaurant, David Jason was already there. He wasn't hard to spot, given that he was wearing a bright red jacket, bright red trousers and a pair of bright red shoes.

We'd never been to Ma Maison before – Cobb and Co was more our level, and we always had their famous Cobb Crunchies, which were basically deep-fried bits of flour that puffed up into chunky nibbles. This place was several notches above. It even had chandeliers, which reminded me of my favourite Del Boy line, one that seamlessly combined comedy with advertising: 'Asking a Trotter if he knows anything about chandeliers is like asking Mr Kipling if he knows anything about cakes.'

As everything was being paid for, Caroline and I treated ourselves to the most expensive items on the menu. David was a little more restrained. Probably because he'd been taken out every night since he arrived. I couldn't help but notice the number of people who stared at him. Someone even came up to our table and asked him to sign their napkin. This gave me a brief insight into what Charles Saatchi had to go through every time he went to a restaurant.

As the three of us were English, we talked a lot about England. It was interesting to get David's opinion on advertising. He was a fan of the Joan Collins and Leonard Rossiter Cinzano ads, and liked one that Richard Briers had done for Midland Bank. He hadn't seen the Great Northern Bitter ad. One thing he'd noticed about New Zealand was that weekends were ad-free on TV. I was able to reassure him that this was about to change and advertising would be allowed on Saturdays very soon.

Towards the end of the evening, after we'd got through a couple of bottles of Montana Chardonnay, David asked, 'What do you miss most about England?'

This wasn't something I'd given much thought to, but once I started listing the things I missed, it was hard to stop. 'Well, there's Marmite, Heinz Cucumber Spread, Walker's Cheese and Onion crisps, being able to watch adverts seven days a week, Mum and Dad, my sister, friends, Cadbury's chocolate, Marks and Spencer, Sunday papers, watching Bromley, kick-abouts in the park, football programmes, and the pubs.'

Well, he did ask. And I didn't stop there.

'I *really* miss the pubs,' I continued, wistfully. 'There was one in Manchester we used to go to every lunchtime and play Space Invaders. I even worked out a way to get three hundred extra points. You get to a new level, fire twenty-two shots and wait for that UFO to float across at the top of the screen. Then just blow it out of the sky – boosh!'

'Blimey, you really do like Space Invaders, don't you?'

'I do. They'll always remind me of the best agency I've worked for,' I added, with a depth of emotion that surprised me. I think I was more homesick than I'd realized. Or more drunk than I'd realized.

It wasn't long after that that Caroline suggested it was time to go. I think David was relieved. He'd barely had a moment to himself since arriving in the country and we were shooting the final scenes of the advert in the morning. It took Caroline and me a few minutes to find our Honda Accord in the car park, since there were about half a dozen there.

Somehow, David looked wide awake when he arrived at the location the next morning. He breezed through the first couple of scenes, which showed him being evicted from the restaurant by a couple of fed-up chefs and locked into a large freezer (this was the bit that had concerned the chief censor), and the cast and crew began preparing for the final shot, in which David would say his line 'Great food which doesn't cost the earth' as he stumbled over to the state-of-the-art computerized till. He would then tap a few random keys and the drawer would fling open, hitting him hard in the stomach and causing him to fall forward.

He only needed one take to nail it. And he added a line that wasn't in the script. As he noticed the flashing lights on the till, a look of pleasant surprise appeared on his face. He tapped the keys and said, 'Ah, Space Invaders.' A second later the director yelled 'Cut!', and David looked over at me and gave me a 'That one was for you' grin.

We had a look at the rushes the next morning and were left in no doubt that this was going to be a fantastic advert. David Jason had turned an ordinary script into a potential award winner, which would look great on my reel. I wondered if we could work together again some time. Maybe when I was back in London.

That night, his last in the country, we all went out for a farewell dinner – a dozen people from the agency and David Jason. Towards the end of the evening, one of the account directors asked him to say her favourite catchphrase from *Only Fools and Horses*. He seemed happy to oblige.

'Don't worry, Rodney,' he said, in full-on Del Boy voice. 'This time next year we'll all be millionaires.'

Everyone at the table broke out into a spontaneous round of applause.

It was a scene I'd play out in my mind over and over in the decades that followed, always asking myself the same question: 'How could he possibly have known?'

Twenty-four

While the Cobb and Co advert had done well and looked good on my showreel, it was proving harder to convince other clients to use British TV personalities to flog their product. There had been a flood of them recently, including Spike Milligan, who had become a spokesman for Supradyn vitamin pills ('For energeeeeee'), Benny Hill doing an ad for the off-licence chain Liquorland, and Penelope Keith and Paul Eddington from *The Good Life* selling Griffin's Biscuits. But since there were only a handful of British programmes on New Zealand TV, this clearly wasn't a sustainable strategy. Especially as there were a couple of other English copywriters in the country who had worked out that casting English actors in English locations was a great way to get a free trip home.

I needed to find another way to do work that would attract the attention of Jeremy Sinclair, and in the meantime the frustration seemed to be taking its toll. I'd taken a huge gamble coming to New Zealand, hoping to cram my showreel with award-winning ads, and it wasn't paying off. A feeling of list-lessness was growing, and even the Supradyn I took every day didn't seem to help, nor did the new 'Dreammaster' bed from Sleepyhead (with free quality bedspread from Lady Michelle).

Inevitably, it was Jeff Stark who came to the rescue. When he left Saatchi & Saatchi to form his own agency, Hedger, Mitchell, Stark, the shockwaves had carried all the way to Wellington. I was incapable of understanding why anyone would ever want to leave Saatchi, but literally dizzy with excitement at the thought of them needing a copywriter to replace him.

This brief burst of misguided hope (how could *anyone* think they could take the place of Jeff Stark?) turned to despondency as I realized that the only difference between the showreel Jeremy Sinclair had seen and the showreel I had now was a solitary advert for a family restaurant in Wellington. I needed to do a lot more before I could show my face in Charlotte Street again.

And that was when Jeff Stark came riding to the rescue, by casting a relatively unknown Australian called Paul Hogan in an advert for Foster's lager.

It was a thirty-second masterpiece in which Hogan, a gruff, likeable but wilfully uncultured Aussie in London, is at the ballet, watching *Swan Lake* with a gorgeous woman. 'This is just like the dances back home,' he observes, watching the all-female ensemble on stage. 'The girls used to dance with each other there too, while the blokes nipped out for a drop of the amber nectar.' His attention is then drawn to a male dancer who has suddenly appeared on stage. Hogan looks shocked. 'Struth,' he says, gripping his can of Foster's tightly, 'there's a bloke down there with no strides on.' He places a protective hand over his companion's eyes as the voiceover announces, 'Foster's. The Australian for lager.'

It was brilliant, probably one of my top ten Jeff Stark ads of all time. People loved it. It was written about in the papers and quoted everywhere from offices to school playgrounds. It was a big winner at the D&AD awards.

Best of all, it was part of the reason that the mid-eighties were a time when the British public fell in love with all things Down Under. This meant I could confidently write ads that took place in New Zealand, using local actors, safe in the knowledge that this would make me look in touch with current UK trends. A lot more in touch with current UK trends than I was with those dungarees, which I still hadn't seen on anyone outside a Dexy's video or *The Dukes of Hazzard*.

My first opportunity was an advert for Government Life, which, as the name suggests, was a government-owned life insurance company. The brief played right into my hands by asking for a 'distinctly Kiwi flavour' to the script.

There was no stopping me. I crammed every stereotype I could manage to come up with into thirty seconds, barring casting the All Blacks rugby team and filling every shot with sheep. The ad was set in a forest where rugged, well-built men in check shirts, shorts and gumboots were cutting down trees with chainsaws (one of the men was slightly less rugged than the others, with a much paler complexion and the beginnings of a beer belly, which prompted me to wonder if it was time to stop making cameo appearances). The scene was completed by a rugged old four-wheel-drive parked next to a caravan, which was being used as an office.

As anyone who was familiar with the Great Northern Bitter ad would have noted, the soft-roofed caravan and the trees being sawn down all around it gave a fairly clear indication about where this was heading.

Inside the caravan, a young Kiwi stereotype is talking on the phone as his boss (wearing hard hat, check shirt, shorts and gumboots) comes in. The young man tells his boss that the man from Government Life is on the phone, but the boss shakes his head. 'Too busy,' he says. The eager youngster gets back to enthusiastically listening to the salesman, which conveniently allows him to tick off all the benefits that had to be put in the script by saying things like 'Oh, I see. So Government Life is the only New Zealand-owned life office to return all its profits to its policy holders?' and 'You give the highest possible protection at the lowest possible cost? Yeah, yeah, that does sound good' and 'The money is government guaranteed? Really?' After this entirely natural-sounding conversation has finished, he turns to his boss with a questioning look. His boss, despite overhearing the numerous benefits, shakes his head again and says, 'Tell him I don't need life insurance.' Right on cue, a huge tree comes crashing down, just missing both men and breaking the caravan in two. The young man, still on the phone, looks at his boss, who mouths, 'Tell him three o'clock.'

Looking at the rushes the next day, I saw an enthusiasm from the Kiwi editor I hadn't seen when he was working on Cobb and Co. And he wasn't the only one. In the first couple of weeks after it had gone on air, Government Life agents reported a large increase in sales. I even heard it being discussed on a radio phone-in as I was driving to work. If I'd been at the office instead of in the Accord, I might have called in to see if they wanted to talk to the copywriter.

But before I had the chance to sit back and revel in the glory of a successful advert that people were talking about even on the radio, I was given the chance to come up with another slice of Kiwi life.

Tree International Ltd made 'casual' polo shirts, the kind you saw on sensible middle-aged Kiwi blokes with thick moustaches who liked to host barbecues. I had an idea instantly, mainly because it was one I'd been storing up since before getting into advertising. It was inspired by a Benny Hill sketch in which he tried to swap shirts with a pretty girl after playing football against her.

In my Kiwified version, a team of obnoxious townies, who arrive in elitist cars such as Honda Accords, are involved in their annual tug-of-war battle with a bunch of rugged, well-built farmer types in shorts, gumboots and, since it was integral to the plot, a variety of Tree polo shirts. 'From far and wide they came to see the annual tug-of-war,' intones the wry-voiced narrator, who then proceeds to describe the events of the day, which culminate in a not unexpected victory for the Tree-wearing country folk. As soon as it's over, the visitors offer to swap shirts – something that didn't actually stand up to close scrutiny, since their shirts were far more stylish and expensive. In any event, they are turned down. 'You keep yours and I'll keep mine,' explains a particularly wry Tree-wearer. 'Cos a man's at his best in a Tree.'

Once again it was a shoot that went really well. The actors were brilliant, particularly a grey-haired, slightly overweight member of the crowd who jumped up and down in exaggerated delight when the 'Town Tuggers' were beaten (it was reminiscent of his performance in the Great Northern Bitter advert). The rushes looked great. It was promising to be the best-looking advert on my showreel.

As a bonus, one of the lighting technicians I spoke to had worked on a Foster's advert in Sydney. It had been shot for the American market and he reckoned that the bar had been built to scale at around three quarters the size of a normal bar. This was because Paul Hogan was quite small and they wanted him to look bigger. All the extras were around five-six or less for the same reason. I loved hearing stories like this. There was a similar one going round about how the PG chimps needed extra wide doors for them to fit through. Whether or not they were true didn't matter. I just liked knowing things that made me feel like an advertising insider.

The Tree advert was a success. It even won a minor (yet prestigious) award. And around the same time Marcus proudly told me that the Government Life campaign had been the most effective one the client had ever had.

'I'm really pleased with the work you're doing,' he said with a smile. 'I might have some good news for you soon.'

I couldn't think what that might be, I just hoped that any creative directors who looked at my reel in future would be as impressed as he was with my work.

How did Government Life and Tree compare to the current crop of British advertising? Thanks to the tapes Kevin continued to send, I could see what the bigger agencies were doing. Obviously the Saatchi ads were outstanding, especially one for British Rail demonstrating that trains don't get stuck in traffic jams, and one for British Airways showing a flight steward on his way to work, dealing with a series of emergencies. The other ad that stood out was BDH's latest for Solvite. I hadn't thought much about the Manchester lads and I was pleased to see they were still doing great work. Or as pleased as I could be, considering they were doing it without me.

Apart from those three, there wasn't much of note, except one for Irn Bru that showed a kid lifting up a pavement and sweeping leaves underneath it – another idea I'd first seen on Benny Hill's show. I felt that my recent output compared quite favourably with this latest batch.

And it seemed I wasn't alone in thinking this. A few weeks after the Tree advert appeared on TV, an announcement came over the speakers at work. 'Can everyone please come to the games area,' said former Miss Wellington runner-up Cheryl in her best phone-answering voice. 'Marcus has got an announcement to make.'

We dutifully filed into the small area that was home to the agency pool table. Marcus was waving a piece of paper and looking pleased with himself.

And he was looking at me.

'I'd just like to say that Dave has been doing some excellent work recently and has become an important part of the Mackay King family,' Marcus said. 'We felt it was time to reward him. And that is why I am announcing that Dave is now a shareholder in the company.'

As the gathered crowd burst into dutiful applause, he handed me the piece of paper, which confirmed that I was indeed a shareholder. I now owned a tiny percentage of Mackay King – or at least I would when I'd found the $1,000 to pay for them. It would be worth it, though. I discovered, after several days of digging, that the shares were worth at least $10,000.

This was a perfect climax to the best six months of my life. Everything was now coming together. We'd just had a second child, a son called Billy, and Caroline and I couldn't really imagine living anywhere else. Not for the time being anyway. I was now looking at a long-term commitment. I would spend at least the next five years helping build the value of the agency and, at the same time, a really good portfolio and reel. I was taking a mature, measured view. Saatchi could wait. This was the sensible thing to do.

Having made the decision, it was time to celebrate. There were still around a dozen people left after Marcus's presentation and the drinking carried on until the early hours. The last thing I remembered was being shoved into a cab clutching on to my share certificate.

The next morning over breakfast, Caroline handed me a

glass of Supradyn that seemed to be fizzing extra loudly and asked if I was feeling any better.

'How do you mean?' I asked suspiciously.

'Well, you know you rang Saatchi in Manchester last night and begged that Arnold bloke for a job? Told him you loved Saatchi & Saatchi so much you'd fly over tomorrow if he asked. Then you said something about a "Seymour" which I couldn't make out. You were getting quite emotional. Is this ringing any bells?'

'I didn't really do that, did I?' I could feel myself turning bright red and I dropped my head into my hands. 'What did he say?'

'From what I could make out, he put the phone down on you.'

This wasn't good. It seemed as though I hadn't been 100 per cent successful in convincing myself that my long-term future lay with Mackay King. Certainly if anyone had said to me 'Dave, where do you see yourself in five years' time?', the answer would have been 'Earning a Seymour at Saatchi & Saatchi.' Especially since they now had offices in Sydney and Melbourne, both of which were only three hours away – which opened up another potential route to Charlotte Street.

But so far my reel consisted of only four adverts, two of which had things crashing through ceilings. I needed to build up a much more decent body of work. I also desperately needed to win an award or two that the people at Saatchi & Saatchi had actually heard of.

Because not only do awards impress creative directors, they also make copywriters very happy indeed.

Twenty-five

To prove that he could write great ads from any brief, Jeff Stark famously asked account directors to make them as mundane as possible.

He would have loved Mackay King.

The brief that landed on my desk for a radio commercial promoting Westpac Bank's Advantage Saver account was an object lesson in dullness. From its desire to reach 'financially sophisticated consumers' to benefits like 'up to 11% per annum interest', there was absolutely nothing to inspire.

So by the time I'd finished reading it, my heart was racing and my legs were twitching. This was the perfect brief. If I could produce original award-winning work from what I'd just read, that would show I could follow in Jeff Stark's footsteps and do it from anything. And that would be a huge boost to my career in the medium term (with Mackay King) and in the longer term (with Saatchi & Saatchi).

The brief was stapled to the outside of a 'job bag', which was a large brown envelope containing support material such as research and previous ads. I opened it and felt a wave of shock as I came face to face with my past. Inside was a magazine ad for Advantage Saver done by their Australian agency. It showed, using moody black and white photography, a watering can pouring water over a couple of banknotes in a flowerpot. The headline – and I almost knew what it was going to say before I got to it – was 'Now there's an easier way to grow your money. Westpac Advantage Saver'.

The shock turned to anger. Someone had stolen my ad. The one I'd written back in the late 1970s when I was trying to get my first job in advertising. The one Jon had art-directed, and which looked remarkably similar to the design I was now staring at.

'I don't believe this,' I said to Graham, holding it up to show him. 'Someone's only gone and ripped off my first ever ad.'

'That's rough,' he replied, looking sympathetic. 'Who was the client?'

'Bradford and Bingley Building Society.'

'Where did it appear? Would it be in any award books?'

'Well, it didn't actually appear anywhere,' I conceded. 'It was a mock-up I did for an interview.'

He nodded, and got back to doodling on his drawing pad.

Once I'd calmed down I was able to look at it a little more rationally. It wasn't entirely plausible that someone had photo-copied my ad and sent it to Australia. It was marginally more likely that someone else had come up with the same idea.

But if my first ad idea hadn't been quite as original as I'd thought, the latest one I'd just had for Advantage Saver was definitely both audacious and groundbreaking. Inspired by an article I'd read in *NME* over breakfast, I decided that I'd write the country's first ever radio commercial done entirely in rap.

Rap was a form of music that had only recently become popular. It gave a voice to disaffected young black American men in inner-city communities like Compton in Los Angeles County; the few songs I'd heard covered issues like police violence, prejudice and poverty.

An obvious vehicle, then, for a script about a flexible new savings account aimed at financially sophisticated middle-class New Zealanders.

In true Charles Saatchi mode, I grabbed my flying jacket and went on a research expedition to Colin Morris Records, the best place in Wellington for imported music, and the place I'd last visited to buy the cassingle of Cliff Richard and the Young Ones singing 'Living Doll'. Using my company credit card, I bought cassettes of *Rhyme Pays* by Ice-T and *Yo! Bum Rush the Show* by Public Enemy and ran back, eager to learn a bit more about rap.

We had a company Sony Dynapower LBT-D7 Midi System (with two-way APM speakers and compact disc player), which I took through to our office so I could play the new tapes and hopefully get inspired. I managed to get halfway through *Rhyme Pays* before Graham's increasingly insistent protests forced me to turn it off. I wished I'd bought my Sony Walkman in.

But it didn't really matter. I'd heard enough. With the words of Ice-T's '6 'n the Mornin'' still fresh in my mind, I got to work.

'Now I am here to do you a favour, and tell you about Advantage Saver,' I wrote and then sat back, satisfied. A strong beginning was essential in a radio ad. If you didn't have that, you could lose the listener.

Frustratingly, the final line wouldn't come, so I did what most rappers seemed to do and inserted a 'Yo!' That would make the rap more authentic. Also, Ice-T shouted 'Word!' before each verse throughout '6 'n the Mornin'', so I threw that in as well.

The problem was that I only had thirty seconds and there were loads of benefits to fit in. Which is why the final version ended up like this:

Word!

Now I am here to do you a favour,

And tell you about Advantage Saver.

Instant deposits, instant withdrawals,

Automatic payments of regular bills,

This savings account is sweeping the land.

Automatic tellers give you cash in hand;

Even if you use your card for living large

You won't pay no activity charge.

So if you ask me 'Where do I go?'

I'm gonna tell you: Westpac, yo!

I was pretty sure this was going to be an award winner. Not necessarily the kind of award that Jeremy Sinclair would recognize, but it would probably win an Impact Award. These were given out by Radio New Zealand every month and were seen by some as a cynical attempt to manipulate award-hungry copywriters into using radio. It worked. I was always trying to talk account directors into advertising with them.

Awards like this were meant to reward originality, but there seemed to be a strong link between winning them and the amount of money spent by the client with the station. Westpac's budget was one of the highest I'd seen for a radio campaign so I looked forward to pinning July's Impact Award certificate on the wall behind me, alongside the five I'd already won. All for big-spending clients.

At least it was an original marketing idea – appealing to the career needs of copywriters and at the same time getting agencies to rethink radio as an alternative to TV and press.

The knowledge that you could effectively buy awards with big budgets couldn't dampen the joy of winning. In advertising, any award is a good and prestigious award. That's why agencies have always gone to extraordinary lengths to win them. Often they would film at their own expense an advert that had been rejected by the client and show it once on an obscure regional channel – at, say, six in the morning – so that it would be eligible. They might even produce ads for other agencies' clients, who remained completely unaware that it had been done. One award-winning ad for the Toyota Supra (by a non-Toyota agency) compared its six cylinders with the six chambers in a gun. Which was fine, apart from the fact that Toyota only ever made a four-cylinder Supra. At least these ads were more original than the ones stolen from the pages of old annuals. Another tactic was for agencies to develop fake outrage at some local cause with good headline potential, and then pay for one insertion in the local paper. The previous year I'd missed out on a Gold Axis Award, the country's highest advertising honour, to a full-page ad protesting the council's plans to dump raw sewage off the coast of Wellington.

Despite my knowledge of the inherent flaws in the awards system, my hunger for them was as strong as ever, and the rap radio spot seemed to be a perfect opportunity to add to my collection.

When I presented the script to the Westpac client, Mark, he was surprisingly receptive to the idea, especially after I'd played him the Ice-T song. He even went so far as to suggest getting baseball caps made with the Westpac logo on the front. These would be worn back-to-front, naturally.

I suspected his enthusiasm was partly down to finally being allowed to produce something original. Most of the Westpac advertising material came from Australia and was repeated in New Zealand to save money. The bank's latest campaign from across the Tasman was built around the tagline 'We're rolling our sleeves up'. On TV, this was illustrated by a man rolling up the sleeves of his shirt, readying himself for some unspecified task, while someone sang 'Roll 'em up, roll 'em up'. It wasn't very good.

Once the 'rap' ad had been approved, I talked to Tim, the producer at my favourite recording studio, and couriered the script and Ice-T cassette over to him. Once he'd had a listen, he called me (just as I was visualizing myself sitting opposite Jeremy Sinclair, talking about my latest D&AD quadruple win) and said that he already had someone in mind to do the Westpac Rap. His name was Brett and I'd worked with him before – he'd sung the words 'Government Life, you get a lot more out of it' at the end of the log cabin advert. He wasn't really what I had in mind, but Tim explained that as far as he knew there were no rappers in the country so we agreed to go with Brett, who did a passable American accent, and arranged a time to record New Zealand's first ever rap radio ad.

Once I got there, we rolled our sleeves up and got on with the recording. Seeing a white, greying country and western singer called Brett in a denim shirt rapping lines like 'Word! Now I am here to do you a favour' and 'I'm gonna tell you: Westpac, yo!' was unusual, but I tried to ignore any doubts I was feeling. Besides, it didn't sound bad, or so I convinced myself anyway. While it was unlikely to be mistaken for a long-lost Ice-T or Public Enemy track, it would definitely stand out on radio, if only for comedy value. Was it going to win any awards apart from an Impact Award? There had to be a possibility. Radio advertising in New Zealand was desperately poor – there hadn't even been a Gold winner in the latest Axis Awards.

After we got a take everyone was happy with, Tim said, 'That's a wrap!' – a joke he'd clearly been saving up for weeks. All that was left to do was add the now embarrassingly incongruous tagline 'Westpac. We're rolling our sleeves up' (a 'voiceover artist' had to come in specially to say those six words) and the job was done.

I dropped off a cassette for Mark at Westpac and returned to the agency with another to play to Graham, who seemed happy enough.

The rap recording had begun to change my attitude to radio advertising. It was something I hadn't thought about much until I found out about the Impact Awards, although I did have a favourite radio commercial which, unsurprisingly, was written by Jeff Stark. It was for John Bull Bitter, and had a wistful 'Frank Sinatra' singing about the joys of Paris and Venice, claiming 'I've experienced such utter bliss / in Peking and Calcutta, this / is why I tell you now / of the town that beats them all.'

'Where is that?' asks 'Bing Crosby'.

'Romford,' comes the reply,

Where the dogtrack is magnifico,

The gasworks are divine,

The pubs serve John Bull Bitter

that tastes mighty fine.

They even decorate the roads

with pretty double yellow lines

down in Romford.

I couldn't help comparing Jeff Stark's taking of a musical genre and using it as the basis for something totally original to my taking a musical genre and just copying it (although, to be fair, using a rapping country and western singer to sell an Australian bank in New Zealand was probably a first). This might explain why his ad had deservedly got into *D&AD* and I would be lucky if mine won an Impact Award.

The winner was always announced on a Tuesday morning at around eleven. Although I feigned indifference, my need for awards was so overpowering that I was sweating profusely. And the feeling of euphoria when my name was announced was totally out of proportion to the achievement. This feeling lasted until Graham reminded me that Impact Awards were just a step away from coming free with a packet of cornflakes.

Still, the client was happy. Mark from Westpac was having a meeting with Neil that didn't involve us, but once it had finished he popped his head round the door. He was beaming. 'Yo, Dave,' he said. Thankfully he wasn't wearing his Westpac baseball cap. 'Great news about winning the Impact Award, isn't it?'

'Yeah, brilliant,' I agreed, relieved that he hadn't seemed to notice the row of Impact Award certificates on the wall behind me.

My enthusiasm might have been a little more genuine had I known that this was the last award I'd ever win at Mackay King.

Twenty-six

I began to sense that my enthusiasm for Mackay King was
waning early in 1988 when I realized I'd taken my entire four-
week annual leave allowance by the end of January. There were
other clues. I seemed to be constantly oversleeping, sulking
endlessly about not getting a pay rise, and coming to work in
my pyjamas as a protest against the introduction of work-in-
progress meetings at eight o'clock on Monday mornings.

The biggest sign of all came when I agreed to meet the creative director of USP Needham, a rival agency, for lunch. Part
of the reason for this was that I was broke and there had been a
clampdown on what the memo called 'credit card abuse', which
meant, distressingly, that we were having to buy our own
lunches. But I was also interested in what he had to say.

Especially any flattering things he had to say about me.

Paul was in charge of one of the more staid creative depart-
ments in Wellington, but his pitch was that he wanted that to
change, and I would have complete creative freedom if I joined
USP Needham. Warming to the theme, he insisted that my
track record meant I was just the man to turn around their
fortunes.

I nodded, as though I was told this kind of thing all the time.

His offer was that not only would I get to work on some really big accounts – bigger than anything Mackay King could offer, clients such as Ford, McDonald's, NZ Lotteries and NZ Milk – I'd also get a $130-a-week pay rise. This would address two pressing issues. Firstly, I was having major money problems – not totally unexpected when you live continuously beyond your means; the extra cash would make a huge difference. More importantly, it was fair to say that I was being overshadowed at Mackay King. Another English creative director, one of two in our Auckland office, had cottoned on to the idea of using actors from the UK. In his case, it was working out a lot better. He'd produced several adverts using British actors that I had to grudgingly admit were really good. Even my greatest moment – winning New Zealand advertising's most prestigious accolade, an Axis Award, for Cobb and Co – had been slightly overshadowed by him winning twenty Axis Awards at the same ceremony. And I hadn't won anything at all since that Impact Award for the Westpac Rap ad.

Maybe all I needed was a change.

I'd left around sixty-five jobs in my relatively short working life, usually by just not turning up the next day. But this was the grown-up world and a more mature approach was required.

If I was really thinking of leaving, there was one agency I had to try first. I rang Saatchi & Saatchi in Sydney to find out the name of the creative director, so I could arrange to see him.

'Our creative director?' said the receptionist. 'That's Ron Mather. Do you wish to speak to him?'

I was too stunned to do anything more than mumble 'No thanks' and put the phone down.

Ron Mather was working in Sydney? *The* Ron Mather? I let out a sigh. He was advertising royalty, having worked in Charlotte Street alongside Jeremy Sinclair, Jeff Stark, Martyn

Walsh and my friend Jon. His partnership with copywriter Andrew Rutherford (who had written 'Labour isn't working') had produced some of the greatest work of the twentieth century, including the infamous 'feet' ad for the Health Education Council. This simply showed the soles of four feet, the two outside feet facing upwards and the two in the middle facing downwards. The man in the middle is thinking 'I hope she's on the pill', while the girl underneath is thinking 'I hope he's careful'. It was banned by both the *Sun* and the *Daily Mirror*, but rightfully took its place in the 1979 edition of *D&AD*. It was also in my file of Saatchi classics. And now its creator had ended up working for Saatchi & Saatchi (Sydney).

It took me four days to gather up enough courage to ring him, and I was shaking when I finally got around to it. When I was put through, I explained who I was and gave a brief rundown of the agencies I'd worked for and some of the accounts I'd worked on. 'I'll be in town next week and was wondering if I could come in and show you my book?' I concluded, without explaining that the reason I'd be in town was specifically to see him.

He agreed to see me the following Friday. I'd started feeling anxious about whether my work was good enough before I even put down the phone.

Flying to Sydney was not a plan that had been well thought out, or even thought out at all. I had no leave left and since it was now only February, all I could do was simply not turn up for work. Again.

It was time to update my book, and I'd done a lot of press recently. There was an ad for Government Life showing a Bavarian castle with the headline 'If your investment is doing better than our VIP Fund, you can probably afford a nice little place in the country', which bravely challenged the Dave Trott maxim that headlines should be six words or fewer. Another, for the Department of Energy, which encouraged new car buyers to check fuel economy stickers on the windscreen, said 'Before you buy a new car, try a bit of window shopping'. I knew these weren't up to the required standard, but put them in anyway. There was always a chance Ron Mather would like them.

By the time I'd fine-tuned my book and reel, it was time to go. I flew Qantas (whose tagline 'The spirit of Australia' was nowhere near as good as Saatchi's 'The world's favourite airline' for British Airways) and spent the entire flight worrying about my work being good enough. I had a feeling it wasn't. As an adman, I had reduced nationalities to a series of stereotypes. Kiwis? Rugged outdoors types in check shirts with chainsaws in their hands. Australians? Rugged outdoors types, sleeves rolled up, wearing hats with corks dangling from the rim. Plus they had a laconic one-liner for every occasion. But it was too late to worry about that.

The excitement was palpable when I stepped out of the airport and into the blazing Sydney sun. As I looked from the window of the cab taking me to Saatchi & Saatchi, I didn't see anyone remotely matching that stereotypical description. Although the driver did say something quite laconic when I only gave him a dollar tip, thanking me for taking care of his retirement.

I arrived around an hour and a half early, but as luck would have it there was a pub directly opposite the office. I felt a bit nervous because it was an Irish pub and I hadn't been in one of those since my Dangerous Pub Friday experience, but I needn't have worried.

As I reached the bar, I had no doubt what I was going to order: 'A bottle of Castlemaine XXXX please.'

I'd recently seen a brilliant Saatchi ad for that particular beer, written by Adam Kean, which showed a bunch of sheep-shearers in the outback loading up a beaten-up old truck with crates of Castlemaine XXXX. As an afterthought, they add a couple of bottles of sweet sherry 'for the ladies'. This proves to be too much for the truck's suspension and the truck collapses. 'Looks like we've overdone it with the sherry,' says a laconic, rugged outdoors type.

After a few sips, I could see why Australians couldn't give a Castlemaine XXXX for anything else. Even an experienced Beer Man like myself still had the capacity to be impressed. And this was the finest brew I had ever tasted.

It was a boiling hot day and my first ever Castlemaine XXXX lasted a matter of minutes. I was soon back at the bar, getting a refill. Not only was it quenching my thirst, it was also helping my nerves.

An hour and a bit later I'd got through a further six glasses, and by the time it came to cross the road for my interview I was feeling a lot more relaxed. Suddenly, the thought of having to try and impress *the* Ron Mather was nowhere near as intimidating as it had been for the past week.

I was ready.

Although slightly unsteady on my feet, which I put down to being on a plane for over three hours, I made it into the building and sat and waited in the oversized reception area. I looked around and got the feeling of being in a proper advertising agency. It looked the way they were supposed to look, with stark brick walls and high ceilings. Above me I could see the old-fashioned air conditioning vents, and outside I could see the Harbour Bridge. This wouldn't be a bad place to work, I thought.

After about ten minutes I started to get restless and kept glancing at my watch and tapping my portfolio, hoping to catch the receptionist's eye. Where was Ron? Had I got the time wrong? Then I felt my face turn red as I realized I'd taken a seat as soon as I got in and had forgotten to tell the receptionist I was there. Perhaps it was the jet lag.

I ran up and told her I had an appointment with Ron Mather. She picked up the phone and a minute later I was in his office, gazing out at the sparkling blue water and the Sydney Opera House bathed in sunshine. I couldn't help but compare it to the view from my window at Mackay King, which was a usually rain-soaked car park.

Ron and I exchanged pleasantries, and I mentioned that I'd whiled away a couple of hours in the pub opposite.

'Ah, been over the Merc have you? Good pub.' He indicated my portfolio. 'OK, let's see what you've got.' It was said in a friendly but businesslike fashion – one I was determined to adopt if I was ever made sole creative director anywhere.

He skipped through my print work and looked at my reel, occasionally stopping at something he liked, such as Great Northern Bitter. My heart soared when I heard him say 'Some of this is quite good', but all the hope that was built up with that sentence was dashed by what came next: 'But we don't have anything for you right now.'

The phrase 'desired outcome' was a common one in Mackay King briefs. My desired outcome now was to get Ron Mather to agree to see me again, some time in the future.

'Can I come and see you again when I've got a bit more stuff to show you?' I asked, hopefully.

'Sure,' he said.

This was brilliant. This was the closest I'd ever got to having the words Saatchi & Saatchi on my business card. I vowed to work even harder to build up my portfolio.

Before I left I was desperate to find out why he'd left Saatchi

& Saatchi (London) – why on earth would you? I'd read in *Campaign* about Jeff Stark's ultimately unsuccessful attempt to break away when he left to form Hedger, Mitchell, Stark. He wasn't away from Charlotte Street for long. Charles Saatchi wanted him back to be joint CD with Paul Arden and got his way in typical fashion – by buying Stark's entire agency for three million quid (or thirty Seymours). Ron seemed happy to tell me why he left (he'd met an Aussie girl who lived in Sydney) and how his Saatchi colleagues reacted when he told them he was leaving (apparently Charles had threatened to make sure he didn't get a visa). There were a few more insights into working in Charlotte Street. Apparently Charles used to say 'It's poop' when shown a piece of work he didn't like. I liked that expression and decided to start using it. If it was good enough for Charles Saatchi, it was good enough for me.

On the plane back to New Zealand, I found myself thinking. Maybe a change of scene *would* do me good. A fresh range of accounts might be what was needed to give my waning creativity a boost. Especially given the fact that my Saatchi plans were temporarily on hold until I could produce work of a higher standard than my current output. Plus, I liked the sound of total creative freedom. And both Caroline and I liked the sound of an extra $130 a week.

First thing next morning, I rang Paul at USP Needham and announced that if the job was still going, I'd be happy to take it. He said that it was and asked when I'd like to start.

'How about a month from today?'

I now had to admit to Marcus that I was taking the job. In my imagination, he begged, pleaded, cajoled and bribed but I stood firm. 'Sorry, Marcus,' I said, with genuine regret, 'my mind is made up.' It went nothing like that. He seemed fine about it and wished me luck.

Later that day he came into our office waving a piece of paper. 'I need you to sign this,' he said. It was a document transferring my shares back to the company.

I was confused because I thought when I got the shares that I actually owned them. But he explained that they were only worth something if I was still employed, and even then they were only worth something if someone wanted to buy them. Given the way things were going, that was never going to happen. Which meant the shares were worth nothing and being a shareholder had been a complete waste of time.

On the plus side, I got a brilliant leaving present. The agency had recently bought a Hitachi VMC-30E camcorder (with Power Zoom lens), and someone had gone round to everyone in the agency to film them saying a few words about working with me. I knew I'd treasure this for ever – even the couple of people I didn't recognize who said, 'Good luck Dave, whoever you are.'

As I said, leaving a job was nothing new for me, but this was different. Although my head was telling me that moving made a lot of sense, my heart was saying that I was making a huge mistake. The only thing I didn't realize was just how big a mistake it was.

End of Part Three

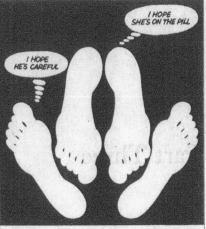

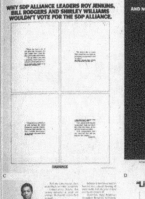

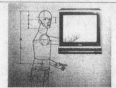

Part Four

Part Four

DAVE ROBERTS

Twenty-seven

If advertising was a young man's game, someone had forgotten to tell USP Needham. When I arrived for my first morning's work there were a couple of men who looked to be in their late fifties, with RAF moustaches and grey suits, hanging around the reception area. It looked more like the Ministry of Advertising than the relatively dynamic, thrusting atmosphere I was used to at Mackay King.

It occurred to me then that there was a lot I didn't know about the agency I'd just agreed to join. I hadn't actually visited the offices during discussions with Paul, the creative director, since negotiations had been carried out over the maximum number of lunches (five) I could squeeze out of him. And USP Needham wasn't the kind of agency people talked about in pubs or raved about in the trade journals. Charles Saatchi would have been severely disappointed with my research, which had been limited to lazily flicking through a couple of old magazines looking for ads with a USP Needham key number while I was waiting to get my hair cut.

One example I found should have set off my creative standards alarm bells, had they not been temporarily out of order due to the thought of getting that extra $130 a week. It was for Trim Milk, and was so overwritten that the copywriter must have been getting paid by the word. The headline 'Get to the source of slimness' preceded a painful, incoherent and repetitive argument which boiled down to 'drink milk because it'll make you thin'. Some of the copy was simply baffling, like 'Trim Milk is here so that you now can drink as much as you like', while other lines appeared to come straight out of a 1930s Etiquette for Young Ladies book, like this one: 'You may think you can starve yourself to achieve a snakey silhouette, but while that's one short cut to slenderness, it's also a sure way to a weak body and they are never attractive.'

I wondered if the person who wrote this had been standing at reception when I came in.

When Paul took me through to the creative department, the average age dropped a few decades and my feeling of dread started to subside. There were quite a few faces I recognized, too, people who had brought their portfolios along to Mackay King, looking for a job.

We went through to Paul's office at the end. On his wall were dozens of ads. I had a look at them, hoping to see something that would justify my decision to join the agency.

'So, have you seen any of our work before?' he asked eagerly.

I recognized quite a few of them, including a Ford ad that had the headline 'Rearing to go'. After reading the copy, it became clear that this wasn't some clever play on the words 'Raring to go'. The copywriter, it seemed, had simply got the expression wrong. I thought it best to ignore that one and instead pointed at a double-page spread that showed a slender girl drinking a glass of milk with that 'Get to the source of slimness' headline.

'I saw this one for Trim Milk in a magazine last week,' I said.

'What did you think?' he asked, beaming with pride.

'Yeah, it's great,' I enthused. 'Really well written.'

Well, there was no point getting off on the wrong foot and telling him it was poop. Especially as Paul's next act was to hand over my USP Needham Diners Club credit card and the keys to my new Ford Granada. Since Ford was the agency's biggest client, everyone drove their cars. It could've been worse. They could have handled the Lada account in New Zealand.

But even as I gratefully received the perks of the job, the Trim Milk ad was weighing heavily on my mind. It seemed to reinforce the gut feeling I'd had about the move being a terrible mistake. I was meant to be improving the quality of my work, but here I was walking into an agency that admired poop.

I decided there and then that I'd give it six months before begging Mackay King for my job back. Or pleading with Ron Mather to take another look at my showreel.

As it turned out, it took a lot less time than that to convince myself I'd made a shrewd, finely judged career move that would give a serious boost to my Saatchi & Saatchi aspirations (as opposed to a reckless gamble done for an extra $130 a week plus a credit card that could be used for lunch).

The first sign of this came towards the end of June, when several of the more senior staff members, perhaps jumping before they were pushed, decided to spend more time with their families. One of these was the general manager of the USP Needham office in Auckland. Paul decided that he fancied a move into management and was given the job. This left a vacancy for creative director in Wellington.

I was happy to take over, especially as it meant another pay rise only months after starting. There was also talk about joining the board if things worked out. I was moved to a new corner office and told to order any new furniture I wanted. There was even talk of getting a computer for my desk some time in the future.

As I was placing a row of Impact Awards on the wall, I realized that the office was bigger than Jeremy Sinclair's. And the way things were going, it wouldn't be long before I was paying him another visit, because as the only creative director rather than one of eight at Mackay King I would be able to look at all the briefs that came in and pick the most portfolio-friendly to work on.

There was also another vacancy. We needed a new general manager to replace the current one, who had also suddenly felt the need to spend time with his family. After much lobbying, the job was offered to my friend Birrell, whom I'd met when we were both at Mackay King. He had since made a name for himself as someone who specialized in bringing in new business, which the agency badly needed.

The first thing Birrell and I had to do was talk to someone else new to his job. His name was Phil, and he'd just been appointed marketing manager for the NZ Lotteries Commission. He wanted to come in for an urgent meeting.

This is rarely good news.

When he introduced himself, I thought his surname sounded vaguely familiar. And then I remembered: the little girl in the Europa shoot had the same name. And it was such an unusual name, she was probably his daughter. This was an unexpected piece of luck, especially as once he'd started talking about the Lotteries business it was clear that he'd come to fire USP Needham. And who could blame him, given some of the stuff he'd been served up with in the past?

Birrell explained that the agency was changing and that we were bringing a fresh approach to our clients. I talked Phil through some of the adverts I'd done, stressing the Europa one.

Just in case it hadn't registered, I appeared suddenly to remember something.

'I've just remembered something,' I said, in a fine piece of acting honed over several cameo roles. 'I did the casting for that advert. Wasn't your daughter in it?'

I never did find out the answer to this question, but either this reminder was as effective as I'd hoped or he'd heard something else he liked, because he decided to give us a chance and add us to the shortlist to launch their new product, Instant Kiwi. This was a new scratch card which was going to replace the old-fashioned lottery tickets and produce an instant millionaire every week.

I was bursting with ideas. The song that was impossible to get away from that summer was Kylie Minogue's 'I Should Be So Lucky', which could be a perfect soundtrack. Or we could bring David Jason back, and have him as Del Boy saying, 'Don't worry, Rodney. This time next week we'll all be millionaires.' As I scribbled these thoughts down I sat back, pondered what it would be like to be a millionaire, and vowed to buy an Instant Kiwi ticket as soon as it was launched.

Life was good again, and I only realized how lucky I was after meeting up for a long lunch with several friends from Mackay King. They told me that things were changing there, and not for the better. There were plenty of whispered conversations in the corridors and meetings behind closed doors, none of which involved them.

I felt genuinely sorry for them. Working for a multinational company which had offices in the US and Australia, I was part of the future. Maurice Saatchi had reinvented the way agencies operated when he set out on the path of globalization – operating as though the world was one big market. Maurice had had the vision to see that clients wanted to deal with one agency around the world and set about buying them up (thirty-eight at the latest count) all over the place. Bigger agency groups like USP Needham followed in their footsteps; smaller independent agencies like Mackay King were either being swallowed up or frozen out.

I took out my USP Needham Diners Club card and paid for the entire lunch, conscious of the fact that my former colleagues were no longer allowed to use theirs for eating out.

Life at USP Needham continued to improve, and the agency made rapid progress. First we picked up the lucrative Cadbury account, and then we managed to beat Mackay King in two consecutive new business pitches, part of half a dozen major deals we concluded in the first few months after I joined.

Cadbury may not have been interested in innovation, but theirs was a good name to have as part of a portfolio. My first Cadbury advert was for Cherry Ripe ('You'll fall in love with the big cherry taste'). The brief had been to appeal to people who are 'young and know what they like' and to 'tell them about new Cherry Ripe' then 'urge them to try it'. I did what any idea-bereft copywriter would have done and wrote a jingle that began 'When you're young and you know what you like, tell you something that's new, Cherry Ripe'. The rest of the words were basically a list of the ingredients that I copied off the wrapper, ending with someone shouting 'Try it!'

The visual idea wasn't really an idea either: it was to have a group of good-looking young people washing a cherry-red Ferrari (because we knew someone who knew someone who'd just bought one) while they ate Cherry Ripes. Only they didn't eat them like normal people. Being a Cadbury advert, they had to eat the chocolate sideways, at an unnatural angle, so that the front of the pack was facing the camera at all times. This was how we learned to cast good-looking young people with exceptionally large mouths.

During the shoot, I really did fall in love with the big cherry taste after sampling a couple I'd found lying around, and I mentioned this to the client. He grabbed a box he'd brought along to be used in the ad and handed it to me, saying, 'These should last you a while, then.' Inside were 144 bars of Cherry Ripe. I'd scored the occasional freebie from clients, like an economy pack of Solvite wallpaper adhesive, but nothing as desirable as this. I felt like the luckiest man alive.

Despite the fact that the advert was complete poop, and that it was impossible to keep a straight face while watching a girl twist her neck at a forty-five-degree angle so she could take a bite of a Cherry Ripe bar, the Cadbury people loved it. So much so that I was presented with a box of Pinky bars – my daughter Hazel's favourite – after a meeting to discuss the trade ad.

When Phil from Lotteries finally got back to us a few months after our initial meeting, there was more good news. For the Instant Kiwi launch it was now between us and one other agency – Mackay King, who still seemed to be going through all sorts of turmoil. By contrast, we were on a roll. The accumulation of discarded Cherry Ripe wrappers in the bin was a daily reminder of my good fortune.

Everything had fallen into place. I'd taken a courageous risk (as I now saw it) joining an old-fashioned agency that had been going nowhere, but it had paid off. I was now creative director of one of Wellington's biggest agencies, and on a hot new business streak, which could only help to get me nearer my Saatchi & Saatchi dream. Even though some of the stuff I was doing was poop, I was also doing some of the best work of my life. An ad for Mobil Oil, which showed the Space Shuttle and carried the headline '2,364,000 miles without an oil change', won a Gold at the prestigious London International Advertising Awards.

For the first time in my career, I felt I was in the right place at the right time.

But it was a feeling that wouldn't last.

One morning in the middle of September my luck ran out in the most spectacular manner imaginable.

I was enjoying a leisurely cup of PG Tips (our client) with Trim Milk (also our client) and reading the morning paper when I saw a small article that sent shivers of shock running down my spine. I began to shake uncontrollably, spilling tea all over the newspaper. I felt dizzy and slumped forward. I tried to ring Caroline, but I was physically incapable of picking up the phone. It wouldn't have mattered anyway since I'd lost the power of speech.

As I banged my head gently against the desk, I experienced a small burst of hope. Maybe I'd misread it. Or even imagined it. Surely no one could be that unlucky? But when I looked again, the headline was still there. And it still said the same thing: SAATCHI BUYS MACKAY KING.

Twenty-eight

Although the words were swimming in front of my eyes, a few sentences managed to get through to my brain: 'New Zealand advertising agency Mackay King has been sold to London-based giant Saatchi & Saatchi for $25 million' and 'billings for the combined company would be between $95 million and $100 million in 1988'.

The numbers were meaningless. All I could think was that if I hadn't walked out a few months back, my business card would now say DAVE ROBERTS, CREATIVE DIRECTOR, SAATCHI & SAATCHI. That was all I'd wanted since the moment I first set foot in an advertising agency.

I was trembling with shock and feeling empty. Why did I ever leave? If I hadn't, I would now have a direct route to Charlotte Street. I'd be able to meet Jeremy Sinclair at Saatchi's renowned creative director conferences.

Just then, a breathless Birrell burst through the door and interrupted my thoughts.

'Have you heard? Mackay King sold to Saatchi.'

I nodded, wearily.

He paused before adding a fresh piece of information that felt like a sledgehammer on my already shattered heart:

'Apparently all the shareholders are instant millionaires.' He paused again, as though suddenly remembering something. 'Weren't you a shareholder?'

I couldn't bring myself to respond. Instead, I just let out a pitiful little whimper. There is only so much a man can take before the body's natural defences kick in, bringing a welcome feeling of numbness.

A million dollars. Even Geoff Seymour would have had to work a few years to earn that much. I'd never had more than a couple of thousand in the bank. A million would have set me up for life.

And I'd left for an extra $130 a week.

As I sat there, staring into the distance, my mind went back to the last day of the Cobb and Co shoot, when five shareholders from Mackay King sat and listened to David Jason telling us not to worry because this time next year we'd all be millionaires.

And now four of them were. And one wasn't.

The mature way to deal with this would have been to accept that I had been the architect of my own misfortune and to work even harder to achieve my professional goals. In other words, to turn a setback into an opportunity. The immature way would have been to drive home, go to bed and pull the blankets over my head, hoping that it would all go away.

When I finally resurfaced three days later, it was only because Birrell had summonsed me for an important meeting. Somehow, despite the crushing disappointments of recent days, I had to present a new campaign for Peter Jackson cigarettes. Luckily, my art director Steve and I had worked on the ads before the devastating Saatchi news so all I had to do was stand up and talk about what we'd come up with.

Cigarettes were one of the harder products to advertise,

because of all the restrictions. There was a huge list of things you couldn't do, including showing someone smoking. I felt that the only people who had ever got it completely right were Saatchi & Saatchi (London) with their work for Silk Cut.

I remembered Jon telling me that it had been Charles Saatchi's idea. Among his collection of paintings was one by an Italian artist, Lucio Fontana, that basically depicted slashes in a canvas being sewn up. Charles had decided that this would be the next Silk Cut campaign – a picture of a large sheet of purple silk with a slash in it.

Over the next few months, the art director, Paul Arden, hired five of the world's leading still-life photographers at great expense to interpret Charles's vision. These photos were then blown up to poster size and pasted on to a specially constructed hoarding on the roof of the Charlotte Street office, so that the most effective picture could be chosen. The budget was several hundred thousand pounds and the result was one poster, although the campaign had been running ever since. The latest *D&AD* annual contained a Paul Arden advert that showed slices of white bread falling from a purple silk wrapper. Somehow, this had managed to sell a lot of cigarettes.

We had $5,000 to come up with a couple of black and white press ads, so we were slightly more limited in what we could do. I took one last look through the work, which had been mounted on black cardboard as this tended to make ads stand out more, and wondered how on earth we were going to sell these ideas. I was also trying desperately to banish the words 'Saatchi' and 'millionaire' from my mind. At least for the duration of the meeting. Bursting into tears was unlikely to make a good impression.

Before we started, I got out my cigarettes, Carlton Long Size, and carefully transferred them to an empty packet of

Peter Jackson. It was important for the client – an ambitious young Englishman called David, whose favourite expression was 'go for it' – to see that I was loyal to his product.

As we sat down in the boardroom, I removed a cigarette from the Peter Jackson packet and lit it, hoping that it would help me concentrate on the presentation.

'We have a few ideas floating around which I'd like to talk you through today,' I began, exhaling a cloud of smoke.

'Go for it,' said David, encouragingly.

I cleared my throat. 'The first is built around the name Peter Jackson. As you know, we already have a well-known Peter Jackson in New Zealand. We were thinking of having a split page, half taken up with a picture of him in full table tennis gear and the other half showing a pack of Peter Jackson cigarettes with a line like "Peter Jackson. The name on everyone's lips".'

It had seemed a perfect fit. Although it was a bit of a stretch calling him a 'name on everyone's lips', Jackson had recently competed at the Seoul Olympics. He hadn't won any medals, but he had quite a high profile in the country. Unfortunately he was the only famous Peter Jackson we could think of. There was another man with that name, a short scruffy bloke who made photographic plates for our local paper and horror films in his spare time, but he was hardly known outside Wellington.

'This is a campaign you could also run in Australia,' I added, 'using Peter Jackson the international rugby league legend.'

As David thought about this, he took a cigarette (or 'stick' as he called them) from the packet in front of him and lit it with a silver lighter. I looked at the packet he'd put back on the table and felt a jolt of cold fear. At first I thought it was some kind of delayed reaction to the Saatchi trauma, but quickly realized it was something far worse. His packet was nearly empty. He only had two sticks left. Once he'd got through them I'd have to offer him one of mine and he'd discover the deception.

How much more could go wrong for me? What had I done to upset the advertising gods so much?

There was only one thing for it: get the meeting over with as quickly as possible.

'Our other idea is a campaign built around the pack in unusual situations,' I continued, hoping that I wasn't talking too fast. 'We want to give Peter Jackson a personality, like Silk Cut have in the UK.'

I hurriedly picked up the sheet of black cardboard and propped it up on the easel. There were six ads stuck on to it. One showed a pack of Peter Jackson on its side; the headline read 'This packet of Peter Jackson has had a hard day'. Another showed a packet upside down and said 'This packet of Peter Jackson is trying yoga'. Possibly the oddest one showed nothing but black space (not unlike an ad I'd seen that had nothing but a purple silk sheet) and said 'This packet of Peter Jackson has gone missing'.

It was one of those campaigns you come up with unsure if they're good or a load of poop. It could win awards, or it could be the kind you claim was done by someone else. But currently, that was the least of my worries.

As I finished my abbreviated pitch, David took another stick out of the rapidly emptying packet and lit up. There was now only one left. We needed to wrap up the meeting fast.

Eventually he spoke. 'I like it – that second idea,' he said. 'Let's go for it.'

I felt the familiar glow of pride. It's always a great feeling when a client says yes. I would have sat back happy and relaxed had it not been for the client-running-out-of-sticks situation and the Saatchi/Mackay King monster lurking beneath the surface of my consciousness.

It was now the turn of Bob, our media manager, to present his plan, and he seemed to drone on for ever about demographics and circulation versus total readership figures, all of which was inevitably followed by his theories on the importance of pass-on rates for magazines versus newspapers. Didn't he realize the urgency here? I felt myself starting to sweat and wished I'd put on more Old Spice anti-perspirant ('The mark of a man') that morning.

As Bob moved on to the justification for choosing one Christchurch publication over another, David reached into his packet and took out his last stick. He lit it and managed to look interested as Bob continued to speak passionately about something nobody else in the room cared about.

The next few minutes were agony as I stared at David's last cigarette, perched on the edge of the ashtray, slowly burning down. Eventually he picked it up, took a drag and stubbed it out. I knew that in precisely fourteen minutes he'd be ready for another one. I knew this because I'd been timing him.

I watched the boardroom clock slowly tick away the minutes. The meeting was still dragging on, now embroiled in a seemingly endless discussion about a possible increase in media spend.

Finally, David reached for his briefcase. Was he getting ready to leave? Had I got away with it? He opened it, then looked at me, as though he'd suddenly had an idea.

'How many sticks have you got left, Dave?' he asked, in his typically enthusiastic way.

I paused, panic-stricken. I felt trapped. I briefly considered pretending I hadn't heard him, but quickly abandoned that ruse.

'Just a couple,' I replied, in an attempt at a cheerful, relaxed voice.

I waited for him to ask me for one, but he didn't. Instead he reached into his briefcase, took out three packets of Peter Jackson and threw them across the table to me. I thanked him a little more profusely than was strictly necessary, more out of relief than gratitude.

All in all, the meeting worked out pretty well. The fact that we'd sold a campaign was good, and avoiding a humiliating episode with a client was also pleasing, although these minor triumphs didn't compensate for missing out on my lifelong dream as well as a million dollars. The wound remained raw; all I could think about was how life would have been so much better had I not left Mackay King.

The only way I was going to get over that, or at least learn to live with it, was to face up to reality and accept that it had happened. I picked up the phone and dialled Mackay King's number (I couldn't bring myself to use their new name) so I could speak to Graham. We arranged to meet for lunch the next day to talk about the takeover. I assured him that he would be paying and chose a restaurant ('Wellington's leading fine dining establishment') I'd always wanted to eat at but had never been able to afford.

I sensed that my resentment hadn't quite evaporated yet.

Over a filet mignon ($47.50) and a bottle of Limestone Ridge ($28.50), I learned that apart from a few impulse purchases, most of the newly rich hadn't embarked on the sort of spending spree I would have launched myself into, like trying to buy my favourite football team, Bromley. There was talk of one person buying a vineyard, but that was about it. It was an enjoyable lunch, which was finished off nicely with a glass of Courvoisier ($15.75) and a Carillo cigar ($12.50). Any pleasure

I derived from these was soon cancelled out by the knowledge that Graham was heading to Saatchi & Saatchi afterwards, and I was not.

The only thing that had gone right since I'd read the terrible, heartbreaking news about the takeover was getting the go-ahead for the Peter Jackson campaign. The only piece of 'fine tuning' David wanted to make was the addition of a tagline. At the bottom of each ad it now said 'Peter Jackson. Go for it'.

There was a further blow to my already fragile state of mind when I got back to the office. I was reading my copy of *B&T*, the weekly magazine of the Australian advertising industry, when I saw a face next to one of the lead stories that looked familiar. As it should have done: it had only been a few months since I'd sat in his office overlooking the Sydney Opera House. The headline said SAATCHI TO LOSE CREATIVE DIRECTOR. Ron Mather was leaving the agency to set up his own TV production company, which meant he would be unlikely to have any interest in taking another look at my portfolio.

All the Saatchi doors seemed to be slamming in my face at once.

Twenty-nine

Nothing could ease the pain of missing out on a million dollars. It seemed that every day brought fresh reports on how the new millionaires were spending their cash. One of them had bought a house on the best street in Wellington. A couple had splashed out on the sort of exotic European cars (not Ladas) that Jeff Stark, Jeremy Sinclair and Geoff Seymour used to park outside the Charlotte Street office. Another, who was in the middle of a divorce, would have to spend hundreds of thousands of dollars on the extra alimony demands that came with his windfall, but I could take no solace from that.

Nothing could stop the questions that assailed my brain at random moments throughout the day and night. 'How much had my seemingly worthless shares actually been worth?' I'd ask myself while trying to read my daughter a story about a hungry caterpillar. 'Who got my shares, and did they have to pay for them?' was running through my mind as I sat in the doctor's office, telling him about my recent problem of over-sleeping. 'What would it feel like to have a million dollars in the bank instead of an overdraft?' once distracted me when I was trying to get out of a speeding ticket I couldn't afford.

In the meantime, USP Needham underwent a change of

name, to DDB Needham, one benefit of which was that it gave us instant respectability. This was because DDB Needham's London office just happened to be one of the world's best agencies. Previously known as BMP, they had recently become the somewhat less receptionist-friendly BMP DDB Needham Worldwide Limited. This was an agency so good that they'd survived Dave Trott leaving after nine years and still managed to make some of the greatest non-Saatchi adverts of the era. Our London office (as I now called them) were responsible for Smash's giggling Martians ('For mash, get Smash'), the Cresta bear with his 'It's frothy, man' catchphrase, and Rowan Atkinson's classic slapstick advert for Barclaycard. Not to mention the best beer advert I'd ever seen, the Dave Trott and John Webster 'Gertcha' masterpiece for Courage Best.

And BMP DDB Needham Worldwide Limited weren't just about past glories. At the latest D&AD they'd picked up the thirty-second TV Gold Award. This was for an ad showing nothing but a solitary pea on a white plate while a stirring piece of cello music plays underneath the dramatic voiceover 'Oh pea, oh perfect viridian orb, what mighty table will one day thy splendour grace? Friend to the fish. Brother to the banger. Chum to the chicken. Oh pea. How could one improve on one so perfect as thee?' This question is answered when a fork enters the frame from the right and carefully mushes the pea. They then cut away to a can of Batchelor's Mushy Peas.

This was an ad so good it could have come from the typewriter of Jeff Stark or the fountain pen of the debonair Jeremy Sinclair. Instead, it had been written by someone who worked for the same agency I did. Technically, at least.

This thought gave me a new lease of life, helped by the fact that we were doing good work and were putting on plenty of new business – including beating Mackay King (or whatever they called themselves now) for the highly prized Sealink account.

Part of the brief for that was to conjure up a new name for the ferry connecting the North and South Islands of New Zealand. We came up with five options and put them all on large boards. We then sent a junior team on to the ferry, armed with boards and the agency's video camera, to ask passengers which they preferred. They filmed people's responses, and when they got back we edited out all the ones that didn't say 'Interislander', which was our favourite, and showed it to the client. He was impressed by the unanimous approval of our name and gave us the business.

Because of the growth spurt, I was beginning to discover there was a bit more to being a creative director than simply having CREATIVE DIRECTOR on your business card. On the plus side, I was able to farm out all the jobs I couldn't see any award potential in. And talking of awards, thanks to the merger there was yet another one on offer, the prestigious Pinnacle Award. This was given out every month for the best piece of work done by any agency within the DDB network.

As I was reading about this, I had one of those moments you see in cartoons, when a bulb lights up above a character's head. 'Hang on,' I thought, 'if I can win one of these, I'll get the attention of the creative director of BMP DDB Needham Worldwide Limited, one of the best agencies in the UK, and maybe get a job there.' This was followed a few seconds later by another bulb flickering to life. 'Wait a minute. If I was working for BMP DDB Needham Worldwide Limited, one of the best agencies in the UK, it would be much easier to get a job with Saatchi & Saatchi, their greatest rivals.'

I closed my eyes and pictured myself at BMP DDB Needham Worldwide Limited's Bishop's Bridge Road office, reclining in my Mario Bellini 'Imago' leather desk chair and taking a phone call from Jeremy Sinclair himself. What one merger had cruelly snatched away, another merger had handed to me on a plate – a clear route to Saatchi & Saatchi in London.

Suddenly, winning a Pinnacle Award became my number one priority. And the chance came sooner than I'd anticipated.

When a brief came in for a Mobil Oil mailer, I was about to hand it over to a junior team when I had yet another light-bulb moment. Sensing Pinnacle potential, I snatched it back and scribbled a few lines down. Admittedly the idea needed a bit of fine-tuning since it called for small amounts of Mobil 1 SAE 5W-30 synthetic engine oil to be put into thirty thousand little cellophane packets and then sent to motorists. I'd get back to it later.

Another side effect of becoming an agency on a roll was getting daily phone calls from art directors and copywriters who wanted to show me their work. One young copywriter, who was currently freelancing, made a big impression. I'd seen quite a few of the ads in his portfolio, and one in particular, a double-page spread for IHC, a charity helping the intellectually handicapped, stood out.

'I love this headline,' I said, then read it out loud: 'Ten years ago, Murray couldn't walk into a shop. Today he manages one.'

He beamed at the compliment. 'Thanks. I'm quite pleased with it.'

I read through the copy slowly, nodding with satisfaction at the final paragraph: 'Today, Murray has a mind of his own and a life of his own. And perhaps one day, with a little help, he'll have a shop of his own.'

I rested the book on the desk in front of me. 'Nice ending. Very nice.'

'Cheers.'

'Where did you get the idea from?'

'Dunno really. Just came to me, I guess.' He paused, gathering his thoughts. 'Charity work is something I do as often as I can. It's good to give something back.'

I nodded. Admen have always loved doing charity ads. Not because they are kind, compassionate human beings, but because it's an easy way to win awards.

'I've known Murray for ages,' the young copywriter continued. 'He's a friend of the family. So when the IHC came to me asking for an ad, I suggested using his story. He's always been a real inspiration and they thought it was a great idea.'

I looked at him. 'You do know that I wrote this ad, don't you?'

'Seriously?' he said, turning pale.

'Yep, did it at my last agency. You cut it out of *More* magazine, didn't you?'

'Oh shit,' he replied, as his head slumped. 'Sorry.'

I actually felt quite flattered that he'd chosen one of mine to pass off as his own. But I wasn't about to tell him that.

'I hate to ask this, but are *any* of these ads yours?'

'Yeah, of course,' he said, looking affronted. 'Most of them.'

'Well, that's something.'

I followed this with an outbreak of silence. My mind had gone blank, which was a dangerous thing. It meant I started thinking about missing out on working for Saatchi & Saatchi, missing out on a million dollars, as well as missing out on those creative director conferences with Jeremy Sinclair and maybe even Charles Saatchi himself. I needed to focus, so I scanned my memory bank for things I'd been asked in interviews.

'So, where do you see yourself in five years' time?'

He shrugged his shoulders. 'No idea.'

That was it. I'd run out of questions and the interview was over. As he was putting his scarf on, he asked if I had any advice apart from sticking to showing his own work in future.

I thought for a moment. 'Always remember,' I said sagely, 'the magic is in the product.'

He looked at me as though I'd just given him the key to unlocking the mysteries of life. 'Wow. That's great. Thanks.'

After he'd left, I reflected on the fact that he hadn't been the only one to borrow someone else's ideas. I'd got my quote from the *Little Grey Book of Bill Bernbach*, which had been given to everyone at DDB Needham. Bernbach was the 'B' in DDB and was like a 1960s American version of Charles Saatchi, someone who had revolutionized the industry through work for clients such as VW Beetle ('Think small') and Avis ('We try harder'). Ads like these gave our small agency in Wellington instant credibility. It meant we could suddenly claim credit for great work done decades earlier on a different continent.

The *Little Grey Book* wasn't the only thing we got out of the merger. A memo arrived announcing that we would be having a four-day 'creative workshop' with Bill Wells, who was the 'Dean of DDB Needham University'. It was a timely reminder that we were now under American ownership.

And, of course, there was the Pinnacle Award. I couldn't help feeling that Mobil Oil mailer was a good way of going about it, even if it did involve sending out those thirty thousand see-through sachets of synthetic oil stuck to a piece of white card that had just two lines on it: 'Mobil 1 SAE 5W-30 lasts so long, you've probably forgotten what it looks like. So here's a reminder.' To my mind, this mailer was exactly what Bernbach was talking about when he said 'Rules are what the artist breaks; the memorable never emerged from a formula.' This was breaking several rules. The rule of cost-effective advertising, for one.

I somehow managed to convince the client that this mailer was going to lead to a significant increase in sales and left my art director, Steve, to sort out the minor details, like getting someone to put tiny amounts of oil into tens of thousands of cellophane sachets, then stick them to sheets of white cardboard. The rule-breaking artist does not concern himself with detail. Besides, I was really enjoying work for the first time in a long time.

Steve and I had come up with an idea for an advert for Diamond Pasta that was reminiscent of the work on Courage Best done by our London office. It had a very similar Chas and Dave-type soundtrack, but I didn't feel as though I was ripping it off. I preferred to think I was maintaining consistency with the house style. The script was probably the best thing I'd ever written and I couldn't wait for the shoot. Even Birrell was impressed, simply saying 'I'd buy it' after looking at the story-board. This was his mark of approval.

I was also particularly pleased with an ad for AMP, announcing their sponsorship of the Festival of the Arts. The first line of copy read 'Do you know the difference between Shostakovich and Rostropovich? Do you know vich is vich?'

Well, I thought it was quite good.

All I needed now was for my work to be noticed by the creative director of the London office. As Bill Bernbach said, 'If your advertising goes unnoticed, everything else is academic.' He was right. Which is why I entered pretty much everything Steve and I produced for the Pinnacle Awards.

What made me feel even better about the work we were doing was that most of the portfolios I looked at contained a fair proportion of poop. There were ads with no ideas, others with great ideas stolen from awards books, and one that stumped me completely. It was a mock-up done by a junior copywriter for an account I was very familiar with – G-G-G-G-G-G-G-G-Gerard Roofing Tiles. It showed a kitten walking across a range of roofing tiles, with the line 'Cat on a hot thin roof'. What did it even mean? I had no idea, and didn't really want to ask him, since he was bigger than me.

I wondered if Jeremy Sinclair felt similar bewilderment

when he looked at people's books. Had any of my ads caused the same kind of reaction when he'd looked at them all those years ago?

One morning, when I was still trying to work out what the G-G-G-G-G-G-G-G-Gerard ad meant, I got into work to find unusually high levels of excitement around the place. A fax had arrived overnight from DDB Needham's New York office, announcing that the Mobil mailer had won the latest Pinnacle Award. It was officially the best ad of the month in the entire global network. Including London.

This was the break I'd been waiting for, ever since first hearing the news about the Saatchi merger. And things were about to get even better. Not long after winning my first Pinnacle, I was made the youngest board director in the agency's history. Admittedly that history only stretched back a couple of years, but that wasn't the point.

I was also happy. Caroline had recently given birth to our third child, a son we named Frank, and I couldn't wait to get home and see him every day. On the work front, I was thinking less and less about the lost million and more and more about what was really important, for me and my family – my future with Saatchi & Saatchi. Because when you're on a mission, you can't afford to be distracted. And for the first time in a long, long time, I was completely focused. I was doing work I could happily put in front of Jeremy Sinclair; I was getting creative recognition from some of New York's leading admen; and I was creative director of a hot agency in a big global network. I finally felt I had a real shot at landing my dream job in Charlotte Street, even if it was via the offices of BMP DDB Needham Worldwide Limited.

And the shoot for the advert that could take me there was just around the corner.

Thirty

I was just taking a mouthful of Diamond Pasta when I heard an almighty crash coming from above. Looking up, I saw a James Bond lookalike in a tuxedo crash through the ceiling, parachute trailing behind him, as he landed in a chair at the table. 'Just thought I'd drop in,' he announced in an almost perfect Timothy Daltonesque deadpan delivery. He then casually picked up a spoon and fork and began to expertly wind spaghetti around the fork, striking up a conversation with the postman sitting beside him.

'Cut!' screamed Lee, a slightly built man in his thirties, with hair as grey as mine. This was one of his first directing jobs, but you wouldn't have known it.

Everyone immediately put their cutlery down and stopped eating. Not that there was anything wrong with the pasta, but this was the eighth take and it was starting to lose its appeal.

'I never want to see another plate of this stuff in my life,' said the vicar sitting next to me.

The idea behind the advert was that Diamond Pasta was so irresistible that whenever it was being cooked, people would drop round, inviting themselves to dinner. That's why I was sitting at a table with what appeared to be a family of models

253

who had been joined by milkmen, clergymen, various trades-men plus a couple of chefs. And, of course, James Bond.

While the ceiling debris was being swept up, I walked over to Lee, who was sitting in his director's chair watching a video playback of the scene he'd just shot. He was replaying the moment the impeccably dressed guest smashed through the ceiling and fell perfectly into his seat at the table.

'I never thought I'd be directing James Bond,' he said, watching the scene over and over again.

He smiled. We were both happy. The shoot, in which yet another ceiling had been destroyed – the third of my career, following Great Northern Bitter and Government Life – had gone well.

After running through the six-second clip a few more times, we went outside and joined the queue at the catering van. I was trying not to get carried away but was definitely starting to think that this was turning into an ad that could lead to my second Pinnacle Award in two months. And who knew where *that* could lead?

But just because I thought it was a good ad didn't mean anything. As Bill Bernbach said, 'There is no such thing as a good or bad ad. What is good at one moment is bad at another.' To be honest, I wasn't sure what he meant with that one. Was he saying that sometimes poop wasn't poop? Was that possible? This could put a whole new light on my adverts for WASS and Westpac Advantage Saver in particular.

I removed my Stone Roses 'I Wanna Be Adored' sweatshirt as, despite this being my eighth summer in New Zealand, I still wasn't used to boiling hot weather in December. Underneath I was wearing a Diamond Pasta athletic singlet, which was basically a string vest with DIAMOND printed on it. This would normally have cost $6 plus two empty pasta packets, had I not stolen it from Birrell's office.

I was glad I'd worn it. It wouldn't do any harm for the client to see my immense loyalty to his brand.

When I reached the counter, I opted for the Greek penne pasta salad.

'You're the first one to ask for this today,' the girl who was serving said, looking faintly puzzled.

I'd only chosen it because I had decided to get healthy. I knew pasta was really good for you because I'd written a magazine ad saying exactly that. It showed a square-jawed male model jogging in his Diamond Pasta athletic singlet with the scientifically contentious line 'You'll go faster with Diamond Pasta'.

After years of never even thinking about my health, I'd noticed a few changes over the last few months and they'd started to worry me. I felt permanently exhausted, which led to frequent oversleeping, and not in the ten-minutes-late-for-work kind of way. Sometimes I wouldn't wake up until two or three in the afternoon. I'd missed most of the first day of the Diamond Pasta shoot because I was too tired to get out of bed.

In Adworld, when there's something wrong you take a pill and by the end of the advert you're back to your old self. Real life was apparently a little more complicated and all the doctor could come up with was that I should adopt a healthier lifestyle. This was why I had decided not only to change my diet, but also to take the unthinkable step of giving up smoking, starting on New Year's Day. It was something I'd been thinking of doing for about eleven years, ever since I first saw an ad that said 'Next time you feel like a packet of cigarettes, choose a tobacconist five minutes away. Run there. And then see how you feel.' Being impressionable, and since it had been produced by Saatchi & Saatchi, I did as the ad asked. And as the ad predicted, I was coughing, breathless and feeling a bit sick. It had been enough to convince me to fill in the coupon and send off for my free copy of *The Smoker's Guide to Non-Smoking*.

Once I'd read that, I decided that giving up sounded far too hard and thought about switching to a tobacco substitute instead. But Saatchi & Saatchi were far too clever to let me get away with that. The next ad in the series showed a man falling from a tall building, much like a dream I'd once had. But it was the headline that really got my attention: 'Switching to a cigarette with tobacco substitute is like jumping from the 36th floor instead of the 39th'. I got the message. I was going to have to cut them out completely. As Andrew Rutherford said in the copy, 'the only safe substitute for tobacco is no tobacco'. There was, in the words of Margaret Thatcher, the Saatchi brothers' most famous client, no alternative. I was going to have to do it now.

It was going to be especially hard since I wasn't having to pay for my sticks – David's seemingly bottomless briefcase always held a few packs of Peter Jackson which he passed over to me and Steve. They weren't my brand of choice, but they were free. And since I was one of the few non-millionaires in Wellington advertising, free was a major benefit.

I decided to get through the packets I had stored up in the top drawer of my desk and then just stop. There was no point waiting until New Year's Day. It seemed unlikely that David would ever encourage anyone to give up sticks, but if he did he would probably say, 'Just go for it.'

The last cigarette I ever smoked was at the agency Christmas party, which was held at a local Mexican restaurant. This paled in comparison with Saatchi & Saatchi (London), who hired out Alexandra Palace and recreated the whole of the Charlotte

Street offices inside. They were no strangers to excess by now: a couple of years back they'd tried to buy the Midland Bank.

This confirmed what I'd known since I was a teenager: Saatchi & Saatchi were my kind of agency. And their latest work was still as good as anything that was on my 'Saatchi Gallery' wall at work. They'd just done a brilliant advert for Real Coal fires that featured a dog, cat and mouse bonding in front of a fire while 'Will You Still Love Me Tomorrow?' played in the background.

And the standards being set in London were being followed in Wellington, where the latest Saatchi office had got off to a good start. Their best work had been for NZ Telecom, and we were about to go head-to-head with them for the NZ Lotteries account. We were quietly confident, especially since *Admedia* magazine had said that 'the chances of Saatchi's winning the account appear slim'.

I sat at my desk just before the Christmas break, chewing Nicotinell ('It needn't be hell with Nicotinell') and trying to come up with Instant Kiwi ideas, but only one thought came to mind. I remembered a scene from the film *Airplane* where the captain, forced to deal with yet another life-or-death crisis on the flight, says, 'Looks like I picked the wrong week to quit smoking.'

When he was briefing us, Phil the Lotteries marketing manager had talked a lot about 'attitude'; he wanted to see it in his ads. This was a new word that had started creeping into client meetings, and I wasn't entirely sure what it meant. Usually ads that were cited had people shouting in them. As I tried to inject a bit of 'attitude' into my idea based on Kylie singing 'I Should Be So Lucky', I stared longingly at an unopened packet of Dunhill cigarettes lying on Steve's desk. I managed to resist, telling myself that the only thing worse than giving up smoking would be having to do it twice. But I was really struggling.

Usually I had no trouble coming up with ideas, even if they were poop. Now my brain was giving me nothing. How did people like Jeremy Sinclair, Jeff Stark and Ron Mather manage to come up with brilliant ads so consistently? I hadn't really developed anything since the initial chat with Phil, when I'd had the vague idea of using that Kylie song as a soundtrack. But if you're ever in doubt about what to show, the general rule is to show the product as much as possible. And that was exactly what we presented – a series of quick cuts showing people scratching their Instant Kiwi tickets, winning, and then doing a celebratory dance (with attitude) to the music.

That was it. That was my big idea.

We'd re-recorded 'I Should Be So Lucky' with a singer who did a passable Kylie impression and it did sound good blasting out of the boardroom Bang and Olufsen speakers. I usually used music soundtracks to disguise a mediocre idea. This was no exception. I just hoped Bill Bernbach was right about there being no such thing as a good or bad ad.

Phil's response was better than I'd hoped, in that he appeared to take it seriously and didn't fire us on the spot. As he was leaving he thanked us for an excellent presentation. We analysed his words for hours afterwards, looking for some hidden meaning.

That night, as I was drifting off to sleep, I finally had the idea I'd been waiting for. I sat upright, grabbed the writing pad from beside the bed and, careful not to wake Caroline, began drawing a matchstick figure walking down a busy street. He was reading a paper and was unaware that he was continually narrowly avoiding danger – by just stepping over an open manhole, by bending down to avoid a swinging girder, and by walking out of a building just as a meteor (inevitably) crashed through the ceiling. At the end, the words 'Feeling lucky?' would appear on screen, followed by a close-up of an Instant Kiwi ticket being scratched.

It was too late, of course. And possibly not totally original: I had a feeling this was yet another scenario I'd seen on Benny Hill's show. But at least I'd proved to myself that I could still come up with ideas.

I put the pad down and dropped off to sleep. The day had worn me out so much that I wondered if I'd ever be able to get out of bed again.

My usual strategy of dealing with illness was just to do nothing and hope it would go away. Caroline, who was a little more practical, took me back to the doctor and insisted he do something to find out what was wrong.

On the day NZ Lotteries sent Birrell a letter informing us that Saatchi & Saatchi (Wellington) would be handling the Instant Kiwi launch, I was in hospital having a series of tests. They couldn't find anything, but by that point I knew there was something seriously wrong. I'd put on a lot of weight and was sleeping until the early afternoon. As if that wasn't bad enough, I was in a crowded supermarket one day when I suddenly felt a huge wave of heart-thumping panic descend on me and had to run outside.

My absences from work went from being hours at a time to days, then weeks. In the end, it wasn't a hard decision for the national CEO to make. In February 1990, at the dawn of a new decade, I was given a month's notice.

And it wasn't just my job I'd be losing. One of the secretaries came up to fetch the Ford Falcon, my company car. One of the accounts people was sent round for my company credit card.

And the TV rental company took back the company TV (Sharp 21-inch with Teletext) and company VHS (Panasonic GD48 Digital 4-head). The only person to come round and give me something instead of take something away was Steve, who turned up one afternoon and gave me a large white envelope.

'Thought you might want this,' he said.

I opened it. Inside was a certificate from DDB Needham saying that the Diamond Pasta advert had won March's Pinnacle Award.

It was a final reminder of what might have been. Would it have been enough to give me a foot in the door of BMP DDB Needham Worldwide Limited in London? I would never know.

Still, I did have one consolation. While I hadn't exactly gone out in a blaze of glory, at least there had been a flicker.

Thirty-one

I'd always known how to treat myself when I went down with something. If I had a tense, nervous headache, I knew that nothing acted faster than Anadin. For a bunged-up nose, it was common knowledge that Tunes helped you breathe more easily. On the few occasions I was hoarse, I'd go suck a Zube. And whenever I had a cold or flu, I took comfort in the knowledge that Lucozade would aid recovery.

But this illness was different. This was something that didn't appear to have a ready-made over-the-counter solution. Which was why I threw myself into researching my symptoms with the same levels of commitment I'd shown with washing machines and A. E. Arthur dress forms. Half an hour after waking (which was still usually around three in the afternoon) I'd be in the near-empty library, poring over medical textbooks and making notes.

Sleeping up to sixteen hours a day? That could well be Idiopathic Hypersomnia. And how about the inability to concentrate or remember things? Cognitive Dysfunction couldn't be ruled out. The feelings of panic sounded like anxiety attacks. As for the carbohydrate cravings, that was quite possibly Cushings Syndrome, and the sudden weight gain probably had something to do with the two packets of Griffin's Digestives ('Always fresh, always good') I was getting through every day.

When I shared my new-found knowledge with the doctor on his next visit, he said he felt it was stress and suggested I take the next three months off and just rest.

This was brilliant news. Three months was nothing. I'd taken that long to write the Great Northern Bitter script and it hadn't even been my idea. Who knows how long it would have taken if I'd had to do it on my own?

The thought of an imminent return to advertising was all the motivation I needed to take his medical advice and do absolutely nothing. This meant sleeping until I woke up instead of getting Caroline to wake me at 2.30 in the afternoon. Even though I was still exhausted, I would spend the remaining waking hours in bed reading medical textbooks from the library. As an *EastEnders* fan, I was delighted to find Dorothy Cotton's recently released *Stress Management – an Integrated Approach to Therapy*, but apparently this was written by a different Dorothy Cotton, not the chain-smoking laundrette assistant from Walford.

I also read *Campaign* from cover to cover, circling ads for copywriters in the back section as I daydreamed of making a comeback that would put me back on track to Charlotte Street.

I usually had the TV on in the background, often as a way of staying awake. I always stopped reading during the ad breaks so I could keep up with who was doing what. And it was during one of these breaks that I saw something that wiped out much of the optimism I'd been feeling and replaced it with fear.

A pair of fairly serious middle-aged men are fly-fishing in a stream. Suddenly, their peace is disturbed by a slice of white bread landing in the water with a splash. They look up and see a check-shirted Kiwi stereotype standing on a bridge throwing several slices into the stream. As he does this, the words 'The Attitude' appear on screen.

By this point I had a fairly good idea who the client was.

The man then sees a trout take his bait and dives off the bridge, a bungee cord attached to his ankle, grabs the fish from the water with both hands and rebounds to the bridge. The ad then cuts to the words 'Have you got it?' over an Instant Kiwi logo.

It was so perfect that I just put *Stress Management – an Integrated Approach to Therapy* down and sighed. The ad had been produced by Saatchi & Saatchi (Wellington) but it could just as easily have come from Saatchi & Saatchi (London).

My first thought when it finished was 'I'd buy it'. My second thought was to put that into practice by clambering out of bed and heading to Dilip's Corner Shop, where I could spend the last of our money on Instant Kiwi scratch cards. Not only had the former Mackay King come up with a fantastically inventive scenario, they'd also built the whole thing around attitude. Everything the client had asked for, and they hadn't even shown anyone shouting.

No wonder we hadn't won the account. This was so much better than my idea that I felt totally crushed, and turned off the TV so I could go back to sleep. That's the thing about being a copywriter. It can only take thirty seconds to ruin your entire day.

Despite this further blow to my self-esteem, or perhaps because of it, I spent much of the following weeks planning my comeback with new levels of determination. In three months, I'd be ready. And that bungee-jumping fisherman was the main reason I needed to get back out there. It had set a new benchmark in New Zealand advertising.

Did I have the attitude? Without a doubt. I was so desperate to rejoin the world of advertising that I started going through some weird sort of withdrawal, scribbling down ideas for ads and taglines for anything I could think of. The line 'You can't say no to Sanyo' was inspired by staring at the infra-red remote control of our Sanyo X888 Rack System. The simple act of picking up the evening paper from the lawn once had me excitedly rushing back to my notepad to write out a scenario for a TV advert. It would show a dog going out and fetching his owner's paper. As he delivers it, he is rewarded with a Bonio ('The nation's favourite dog biscuit'). He then goes back out and comes back with dozens of newspapers from all the neighbours' front gardens. This would be perfect if I ever got to work on the Bonio account. I'd read in *Campaign* that they'd recently changed agencies, but couldn't remember who had won the account. I promised myself I'd find out when I got better.

But as my notepad filled up and the weeks dragged by it became obvious that the three-month estimate had been as realistic as a copywriter promising that a job would be finished on time. If anything I was feeling worse, with even less energy; I felt panicky even going for a short walk. Some days I couldn't get out of bed at all.

By the time a year had passed, I was getting seriously worried. There was no sign of improvement and the doctor, by now a frequent visitor, had tried a variety of drugs. None of these had had any effect at all. I'd even offered him a few more possible causes that my research had uncovered, including a new thing called Yuppie Flu, but he didn't seem that interested.

Another year passed with no progress, then another. And at about that point everything rapidly fell apart. In the space of a few months the freelance work I'd been getting completely dried up, and I'd fallen so far behind with the mortgage that I was scared to open letters from the United Building Society. On top of that, I was barely able to leave the house. But far worse was to come: Caroline left me, after one too many arguments. She'd just had enough of my moods. As she said while packing her bags, 'You keep telling me this is what you want. Now you've got it.' We agreed that the children would divide their time between us and that we'd sell the house and split the proceeds.

If 1992 had been the Queen's annus horribilis, 1993 was mine.

I moved into a small airless flat directly above someone who seemed to be playing Boyz II Men every time I woke up. It felt as though I'd reached rock bottom. Missing out on a million dollars and a Saatchi career was a positive highlight in comparison.

It's hard to try and get over a loved one when you constantly hear songs of heartbreak and pain coming from somewhere beneath the floorboards. There was one song that seemed to be on constant repeat. It was about reaching the end of the road, and lines like 'Girl you know we belong together' and 'Yes baby, my heart is lonely' didn't help my state of mind. I was beginning to suspect that the young man downstairs had also experienced some form of rejection.

When I did force myself to pick up the notepad and start writing ads again, they seemed to have a common theme. I came up with a scenario for Kleenex tissues in which a couple had evidently just broken up after a massive row. Both were alone in different bedrooms, looking through old photos to the sound of Boyz II Men singing 'End of the Road'. Another idea, this time for the Polaroid Instamatic, at least didn't have a maudlin Boyz II Men soundtrack. It featured another couple who had just broken up and were looking through old Polaroid photos of happier times, accompanied by Crowded House's 'Don't Dream It's Over'.

Even the adverts I watched on tapes sent from the UK seemed to follow the same path. There was one for VW Golf that I found particularly upsetting, since it showed a woman walking out on someone who was possibly her husband and throwing away everything he'd given her, apart from the car. 'If only everything in life was as reliable as a Volkswagen' read the tagline. To make things worse, it had been done by BMP DDB Needham Worldwide Limited, my old London office. I had little doubt it had won them a Pinnacle Award.

As I was desperately trying to come to terms with life on my own, and with no sign of getting my health back, a new advert from Saatchi & Saatchi (Wellington) appeared during an episode of *Not the Nine O'Clock News*. This time it was an advert selling themselves – two minutes of clips from various award-winning ads they'd created, with the backing tune of 'Accentuate The Positive'. It was as if they'd put together a mini showreel just to torment me and make me once again wish I'd never left Mackay King.

The really upsetting thing, apart from the fact that all the ads were brilliant, was that I couldn't think of one positive thing to accentuate, let alone negatives to eliminate.

I had become Mr Inbetween. My life had turned into a version of *Groundhog Day*, without the happy ending. It had become an endless cycle of waking up in the afternoon, picking the children up from school (the solitary highlight) and lying in bed, exhausted and anxious, reflecting on better times. With no choice but to listen to my daily dose of 'I'll Make Love to You', 'End of the Road' and 'I Swear' (I knew the complete lyrics to all three) coming from beneath me.

Around eighteen months after Caroline left, I heard she'd

found someone new. Luckily, by then the CD player downstairs had died of overuse – either that or its owner had moved out – and there was no music to make it worse.

It really did feel like the end of the road. I was even beginning to doubt whether life would ever improve. Much of the 1990s flew by before it did.

Then one day, as I was optimistically reminding myself that 'the darkest hour is just before dawn', once again finding comfort in a cliché – albeit in my case this hour had stretched into several years – my luck suddenly and unexpectedly turned. Because just as I was getting used to the feeling of complete helplessness, I experienced a Gold Blend moment. Which is what happens when there's a knock on the front door and you open it to find a beautiful woman standing there. In the Gold Blend advert it was a brunette trying to borrow some coffee for her dinner party guests; in my case, I found myself face to face with a stunning, long-legged blonde who was even better looking than the would-be coffee borrower.

'Hi Dave,' she said, showing a set of Colgate-perfect teeth. 'I'm Bernie – I rang you last night.'

'Come in,' I said.

Thirty-two

As Bernie brushed past me, I caught the scent of a fresh summer meadow coming from her long blonde hair. My brain scanned through the shampoo section of adverts I'd seen throughout my life and told me that she used Timotei.

She had come round to give me a brochure. Bernie was a friend of Steve from DDB Needham and had asked him if he knew anyone who might want to buy her old computer. He'd immediately thought of me.

As she opened her handbag to get out the brochure, I thought I caught a glimpse of a packet of Peter Jackson. It was comforting to think that I had probably played a small part in her decision to buy them through the highly persuasive ads I'd written years before. This illusion was soon shattered when she mentioned that Steve had given them to her, as he still got them free at work but preferred Dunhill.

She handed the Apple Macintosh Performa 6310CD brochure over and I eagerly flicked through it. The nearest I'd come to owning a computer was my Atari 2600 Video Game Console ('The number one video game'), which I'd got so I could play Space Invaders (high score: 12,875) in bed. And while that was brilliant (the console, not the rubbish high score), this sounded even better. I told her I'd let her know as soon as I'd had a proper read-through. For once I wasn't broke, as I still had a bit of money left from the sale of the house.

As soon as I started perusing the brochure that night I felt the familiar thumping of my heart, but this time it was excitement, not anxiety. I was hooked. Just like she knew I would be. 'The Performa 6310CD will meet your needs well into the future,' it promised, before boasting of 'a 1.2 gigabyte hard drive – large enough to store applications and information for years to come'. I just couldn't imagine how years' worth of information could fit into one small box. My mind was already made up by the time I got to the part saying 'you can access World Wide Web sites and internet electronic mail with a high-speed (28.8 kilobytes per second) modem'.

It all sounded incredibly exciting. I mentally gave the brochure copywriter a pat on the back. I had no idea what any of it meant, but I knew I had to have the Performa 6310CD.

I'd heard of several copywriters at London agencies having their own computers and I needed to know how to use one for when I got back into advertising full time. It would give me a huge advantage. I'd have to learn to type with more than one finger, but there was even a touch-typing tutor software program ('Mavis Beacon Teaches Typing') that came free with the computer.

I rang Bernie, and within two hours was listening to the ear-shattering ba-doom-ba-doom-ba-DOOM of the 28.8 kps modem warming up. Within a matter of a few short days, the computer – *my* computer – was online.

My day was now divided between sleep, spending time with the kids after school and getting to know my Performa 6310CD after they'd left. The latter was easy. All I had to do was move the mouse and click on the picture that said PERFORMA

TUTORIAL. Electronic mail took a while to get the hang of, and to begin with I sent myself several job applications. But the main thing I was using the computer for was research. This machine was the gateway to a whole new world of information. I wondered how people like me and Charles Saatchi ever managed without it.

I couldn't believe how easy it was to find medical information. I just had to go to a website called Alta Vista, type in my symptoms, and it would then give me hundreds of websites to visit. My life had gone from *Groundhog Day* to *Lorenzo's Oil*, the film about a desperate race to find a cure for an obscure illness.

One of the most consistent recommendations was cutting out wheat and dairy. I had already been through the latest coupon book from New World Supermarket ('First in food') and torn out coupons for Tararua Mild Cheese ($4.99 with coupon) and, to go with it, Huntley & Palmers cream crackers ($1.29 with coupon), when I made the decision. 'Looks like I picked the wrong week to quit wheat and dairy,' I thought, but I was so desperate I was prepared to try anything.

Having to do without my cheese and crackers was going to be hard enough, but then the full repercussions of the diet hit home: it would mean no more Griffin's Digestives. This was particularly upsetting as I had an entire cupboard dedicated to my favourite biscuits. There would also be no more Diamond Pasta, which I'd switched to ever since seeing the James-Bond-crashing-through-the-ceiling advert at home on TV. In other words, I'd actually persuaded myself to buy it.

Since there was nothing in the coupon book that would be allowed on my new diet apart from Growers Dark Plums ($2.25 with coupon), I went down to New World and filled my basket with possibly the healthiest food I'd ever bought. At the same time I started taking huge amounts of minerals and vitamins. Because that's what the internet told me to do.

After five days of this diet, when I was on the verge of giving up, something odd happened. I woke up around 10.30 in the morning feeling unusually relaxed. This was four and a half hours earlier than usual. It was the first time since leaving work seven years earlier that I'd managed this. Also odd was the fact that I didn't just lie in bed feeling sorry for myself, I actually found the energy to get up and made myself my first breakfast in ages. That's if you count a couple of Healtheries Smokey Bacon rice cakes as breakfast.

It was a small step forward, but it was exciting to think that if things continued to improve at this rate I would soon be back on track in terms of resuming my advertising career.

It wasn't just the possibilities for medical research that made the Performa 6310CD so invaluable. In the middle of 1998 I started talking to an American woman, an art director, whom I'd met on an advertising forum. Her name was Liz and we soon bonded over a shared experience of working on lottery accounts, hatred of 'Barbie Girl' by Aqua and love of Mars bars (she understood my pain in having to go on a Mars bar-free diet). Eventually, conversation spread to other subjects like music, TV and where we lived.

'I've always wanted to visit New Zealand,' she said, after we'd been chatting for a couple of months.

I was going to say something bland like 'Yes, it's lovely here' when I thought of a Bill Bernbach quote. I often thought of Bill Bernbach quotes, but this one seemed more relevant than usual: 'Playing it safe can be the most dangerous thing you do.' So even though I hadn't known Liz for long, and we'd only spoken a couple of times on the phone, I invited her to come over. Unexpectedly, she agreed, saying that she'd already thought about doing just that. I suspected this was more down to the '100% Pure New Zealand' tourism campaign running in the US than my charms, but to be honest I was just glad I'd get the chance to meet her.

I warned her that I was on a slightly unconventional diet. She seemed fine with that, and asked if there were any more surprises in store. 'None whatsoever,' I replied, failing to mention that my claim of being 'quite athletic' might not be entirely consistent with the twenty stone four pounds (down from a pre-diet weight of twenty-five stone) my Salter scales had shown that morning. I did, however, tell her about my health problems, including the whole not-waking-up-until-late-morning thing. This can't have been a huge problem for her as she set a date for her arrival – 16 November 1998.

Liz booked herself into a small hotel on the outskirts of the city and on the 'Stopwatch' application program on my computer I started counting down the months, weeks and then days until she came.

By the time she arrived my sleeping pattern had improved even more and I managed to get out of bed before nine. I spent a nervous morning eating Smokey Bacon rice cakes and playing chess on the computer (I was practising just in case Jeremy Sinclair fancied a game at some stage). And then I heard the knock I'd been waiting for ever since Liz had told me she was coming to visit me.

When I answered the door and found myself face to face with a willowy blonde with pale blue eyes, it felt as though I'd stepped into yet another Gold Blend advert. She'd sent me a scan of her driving licence photo, but she was even more beautiful in the flesh, wearing a stunning 1940s-style floral print dress.

I learned two things during our first day together. Firstly, you can't disguise an excess six and a half stone by holding your stomach in, and secondly, I'd somehow managed to find my perfect woman.

Over the fortnight she was in Wellington we cooked for each other, watched ads together, and she even supported me in my diet by polishing off all the Griffin's Digestives, thus kindly removing the temptation. We got on brilliantly, the kids seemed to like her, and when she moved over permanently less than six months later I felt like getting in touch with Apple with an idea for using our story in an ad. It would show me and Liz in moody black and white with the headline 'How the Performa 6310CD helped me win the lottery'.

To celebrate her moving in I'd mail–ordered a present that I'd found in a magazine. It was a packet of biscuits. But this was no ordinary packet of biscuits, it was 'Griffin's Collectors' Edition Millennium Biscuits, in a specially signed, limited edition tube'. 'But be quick,' the ad had warned, 'we won't be doing another batch until the year 3000!' I couldn't wait for her to open the box containing the tube so I could see who had signed it. I was particularly thrilled when I saw the signature of the recipe creator, Christine Philip of Dunedin.

My computer had helped me improve my health and found me Liz, but there was one more thing I needed it to do for me – help me take the first step back on the ladder that led to Saatchi & Saatchi.

Thirty-three

I decided to start on the bottom rung, which was trying to get freelance work from small, local design agencies that occasionally needed copywriters. The thinking behind this was that (a) it would be much easier to get work that way, (b) their standards would be lower, and (c) I'd be able to work my way up to writing for a top agency.

I was confident that I was now well enough to work. Liz and I had been to a few restaurants and supermarkets and I'd managed not to run away. I felt ready. So I went to Yellow Pages online and wrote down the names of all the design agencies in town. I then rang each one to get the name and email of the creative director.

Once I'd done that, I spent the next day writing personalized emails to all forty-three of them. This was hugely enjoyable. I was basically writing an ad about how brilliant I was and how many awards I'd won ('including around a dozen national awards and two Pinnacles' sounded a lot better than 'seven Radio New Zealand Impact Awards and a couple of Axis Awards, mainly in minor categories'). Once I'd settled on the copy and run it past Liz, it was ready to go. I pressed send, and sat back and waited.

And waited and waited and waited.

I'd deliberately sent my mass email at ten in the morning because that was when I used to finish the morning paper and start work. By mid-afternoon I was slumped in front of the computer, staring at the screen, willing just one creative director to reply. Eventually I gave up and dragged myself through to join Liz and break the news to her.

It was then that I heard the 'ping' sound which notified me that an email had arrived. I rushed back to the Macintosh Performa 6310CD and saw a reply to my mass mailing. Bevan from Press Play Design had written 'Sure, drop in any time. Always on the look out for copywriters!'

I waited a few hours before emailing Bevan back and saying that I'd drop by in the next day or so. I wanted to appear keen, but not too keen. Besides, this gave me time to take a look at their website. I was relieved to see that they had no national accounts and much of their work was for the local city council, designing brochures and leaflets. It was all fairly standard stuff. The sort of work I'd had to do when first starting out in Leeds. I even began to think of alternative headlines for one of their less impressive efforts.

The website was also helpful for finding out a few things I could ask Bevan about in the interview, when he asked me if I had any questions. I'd ask about Press Play Design's creative philosophy, even though it appeared to be exactly the same as everyone else's creative philosophy.

The other thing I needed to prepare was my portfolio. It had been a long time since I'd shown it to anyone. I spent the rest of the day going through my life's work in agonizing detail. Should I keep the Mobil Space Shuttle ad at the back or promote it to the front in place of the Westpac Advantage Saver rap ad, which looked a bit dated? Would it be better to show just the 'Murray' IHC ad (hopefully he hadn't already seen it in another copywriter's portfolio) or the whole series? And what about the Trust Motors ad starring Jonathan? It was now a couple of decades old, but I was still pleased with the copy.

The showreel was next. Thanks to my cameo performances I was able to watch myself age over the years I'd spent in advertising, from the enthusiastic twenty-something pub regular jumping up and down with delight in the Great Northern Bitter advert, on to the more middle-aged motorist at the Europa petrol pump, and finishing with the pale, bloated, grey-haired dinner guest in the Diamond Pasta ad. My entire career was here.

It was an unpleasant reminder of how old I'd grown, but I reassured myself by thinking that it shouldn't matter. After all, no one knows the age of a copywriter when they're looking at an ad. Plus, I felt proud of a lot of the work I'd done – the Mobil mailer that won a Pinnacle award, the Cobb and Co shoot with David Jason, and, of course, the Cannes Silver Lion advert. This ought to be enough to get me work writing brochures about rubbish collections and library hours.

We were on the verge of a new millennium – what better time to make a fresh start? I'd only had one response to my mass email, but sometimes one response is all you need. I just hoped Bevan wasn't going to ask me where I saw myself in five years' time. In five years' time I'd be fifty. And that was something I really didn't want to think about.

The next morning I emailed Bevan and said I'd pop in that afternoon, if it was OK with him. 'Sure' came the reply a few minutes later, which was a welcome sign of enthusiasm. Perhaps they had some urgent work for me. 'Any time after 2.30' he added.

Liz was concerned that I looked the part, making sure my

hair, now fully grey, looked properly styled. We'd picked out a tweed jacket with T-shirt and jeans – smart, yet casual.

After re-jigging the portfolio one last time (switching around a couple of AMP ads to give them a more logical sequence), I was ready. Liz took one last look through it and, as I looked to her for reassurance, said, 'Don't worry, these are good. They've won awards. You'll be fine.'

It was what I needed to hear. This was my chance to start over and build a reputation. Once I'd eased my way back into advertising, I could start approaching bigger agencies. My heart began racing at the prospect.

Just as we were about to leave, Liz handed me a bright yellow Philips Xenium mobile phone that she'd bought me, saying, 'If you're going to be a proper freelance writer, you'll need one of these.'

We got into town twenty minutes early and there was a bus stop right outside the building. I had to fight hard to keep down feelings of panic. I just wanted to turn around and go home, but I reminded myself that this was my last chance. If I didn't take it, I'd be finished. Liz made a final adjustment to my hair and then, taking a deep breath, I forced myself to walk into the offices of Press Play Design.

I was immediately struck by how different things looked since I had last set foot in an agency. I had to remind myself that the world was now a different place. The Soviet Union had broken up, the Channel Tunnel had been built and, shockingly, Jeremy Sinclair and the Saatchi brothers had broken away to form a new agency, M&C Saatchi, taking British Airways, Silk Cut, Dixons and the Mirror Group with them. Their Auckland office had come up with the '100% Pure New Zealand' campaign.

But while a lot of things had changed, others hadn't. The

agency atmosphere was exactly the same as it had always been. I looked around, taking in the sights and sounds. I hadn't realized how much I missed the busy excitement. Everyone seemed to be either rushing around or screaming into phones. I immediately felt at home. It was good to be back.

'Hi,' I said to a young woman whose desk was nearest to the door. 'Dave Roberts. I'm here to see Bevan.'

She picked up her phone, and seconds later a short, energetic man in his mid-twenties came bounding over. He had a look of slight confusion on his face, which was quickly replaced by a smile.

'Dave,' he said, 'I'm Bevan, great to meet you. Let's sit down.'

I was aware that I was nearly twice his age and felt a bit self-conscious about wearing similar trainers, although his probably cost about ten times the price of mine. He started leafing through the portfolio, spending no more than a couple of seconds on each ad. I noticed that he wasn't reading any of the copy, just skimming over it. The other slight concern was that he wasn't reacting at all – no smiles, no laughs, no sounds of admiration.

He closed the portfolio and looked at me with a distinctly underwhelmed expression. 'Great. So, Dave, I was wondering if you had anything more recent? Any viral ads, that kind of thing?'

I wasn't sure what 'viral' meant. I explained that I'd been ill for a few years, but I was now back and ready to carry on where I'd left off.

Just then, a flustered arty-looking type came over. 'Sorry Bevan,' he said, 'but can I grab you for a sec? Something's come up.'

Bevan looked at me. 'Do you mind?'

'No worries,' I said. I understood the pressures of his job. I'd been in his shoes.

I sat there taking in the atmosphere, imagining myself at one of the spare desks, knocking out a brochure for the council. When it became apparent that Bevan was going to be detained for a while, I stood up and had a look at some of their work on the wall. I knew I could do better – all I needed to do was convince Bevan.

He was still talking to a couple of people. It didn't seem that serious – they were laughing – and occasionally he glanced over at me. Eventually he came over, looking apologetic and slightly embarrassed. He didn't need to say anything.

'If you need me to get off now . . .' I said, standing up.

'Yeah, sorry about that. You know how it is. Look, I've seen what I need to see and I'll call you if we need your services.'

I knew he wouldn't. He hadn't even asked for my phone number. As I walked out, I knew I was finished. If I couldn't get work at a tiny design agency, I wouldn't be able to get work anywhere.

When I got home I slumped into the armchair while Liz wandered off to do some gardening. The day had taken me from excitement and anticipation to disappointment and despair. I even briefly wondered if life might have turned out better if I hadn't pursued what turned out to be a stupid, impossible dream.

On the coffee table was a tape that Danny, my old art director in Manchester, had recently sent me. On it was a Channel 4 programme that had just been on in the UK called *The 100 Greatest TV Adverts*. I wasn't entirely sure I'd be able to scrape up any passion for advertising after what had just happened, but thought that watching this would be the perfect way to find out.

Graham Norton, in trademark understated purple suit and bright green shirt, started by saying that by the time we reach the age of thirty-five we've seen 150,000 commercials. Or, in my case, at least triple that.

As the countdown unfolded, I learned several fascinating things, from the Milky Bar Kid not liking Milky Bars to the fact that the girl in Coke's 'I'd Like to Teach the World to Sing' advert couldn't actually sing. I was also reminded about the huge part advertising had played in my life. The next two and a half hours (including adverts) took me on a journey that started when I was three years old.

The PG Tips chimps advert was ranked a healthy 24th in the Top 100, while the advert featuring the first slogan I committed to memory, Rowntree's 'Don't forget the fruit gums, Mum', came in at number 81.

The Milky Bar Kid (27th) was who I pretended to be in the playground, while the claim that a million housewives said Beanz Meanz Heinz (49th) every day was the first slogan I actively questioned. A few years later, when I wasn't dreaming about being the James Bond-like hero in the Milk Tray 'avalanche' advert (43rd), I was dreaming about successfully proposing to the Flake girl (26th).

The Cinzano advert with Leonard Rossiter and Joan Collins (11th) took me back to Leeds and my date with Margaret, while Shake 'n' Vac (18th) reminded me of my efforts to get my bedroom ready for her. Seeing Dave Trott's 'Gertcha' ad for Courage Best (85th) and the John Smith's dog-doing-tricks-for-cloth-capped-northerners piece (33rd) took me back to my Manchester days as a Beer Man.

The Mars bar 'Work, rest and play' ad (71st) was responsible for me eating a Mars bar a day for fifteen years, while the Yorkie bar ad (63rd) reminded me of winning a large plastic radio, which I left on a train. "Allo Tosh, got a Toshiba?' (66th) was an uncomfortable reminder of my failed attempt to bring

Alexei Sayle over to New Zealand for the Cobb and Co ad, but Paul Hogan's 'ballet' ad for Foster's (39th) was a happier reminder of the most productive period of my career.

The countdown reached its climax with Guinness's 'Horses and Surfers' (the only ad ever to win two D&AD Gold Awards in the same year), which pipped the Smash Martians to the top spot. The only flaw I could see was having just two ads by Saatchi & Saatchi in the entire programme, Real Coal fires and Castlemaine XXXX (although Jeff Stark had directed two more, for Boddington's 'ice cream' and Impulse).

The sheer excitement I'd felt sitting through the programme proved to me that even if I couldn't be a part of advertising any more, it was always going to be a big part of me.

As the credits scrolled, I got up, walked to the bay window, which looked like a giant TV screen, and gazed out at a perfect Wellington day. Where the trees broke, I caught sight of the harbour glistening in the distance. An overweight wood pigeon sat contentedly in the branches of a pine tree directly outside. Someone, somewhere nearby, was listening to 'Wonderwall' on their radio.

My sons Billy and Frank, now thirteen and nine, were playing cricket with an old tennis ball, my old bat and a wicket chalked on to the fence. It looked like New Zealand were setting England a huge total to chase on the final day. Their older sister, Hazel, was sitting on a blanket, ignoring her brothers while she read a piece on Blink 182 in her *Smash Hits* magazine.

I looked over to see Liz reaching over a rosebush with a pair of McGregor's pruning shears. She was wearing an oversized sunhat and her face was scrunched up the way it always was when she was concentrating.

'If this was an advert for my life,' I thought, all the disappointments of the day forgotten, 'I'd buy it.'

End of Part Four

Now you know what people see in a Real Fire.

GOOD THINGS COME TO THOSE WHO

GUINNESS

Ode to a pea.

Hi! Can I borrow some coffee?
I have guests and I ran out

2,364,000
kilometres without
an oil change.

Epilogue – Present Day

I had just sat down at my MacBook Pro and embarked on a six-hour *EastEnders* marathon when Liz poked her head round the door.

'Don't forget your deadline,' she reminded me.

The hand holding a McVities Chocolate Digestive that I was about to dip into my cup of PG Tips hovered in mid-air as I froze. She was right. This was far more important than what was going on in Albert Square. I dipped the biscuit, thankful that I no longer needed to go without wheat and dairy, and paused the on screen action.

I then opened a Word document and got on with what I was meant to be doing – writing about prawns. How lucky can one man get?

'At Royal Greenland, quality is more important than speed. That's why we let them grow for five to six years in the icy cold, unpolluted waters of the Arctic.' I savoured every word as I typed. 'Only then do they reach the sort of texture, colour and size which set them apart.'

I sat back, satisfied. This was back to doing what I loved most, writing ads. When I was doing this, it was easy to forget that we were living with Liz's parents in a blue-collar part of

Hartford in Connecticut, just until we got on our feet again, after having to leave New Zealand when the money ran out.

As I tried to come up with a killer final line, I thought about how our luck had started to change with that out-of-the-blue phone call from Andy, the junior art director from my Manchester days, the one I worked with on Indesit. I asked him what he'd been doing since I last saw him and almost immediately wished I hadn't. After BDH, he'd done something I'd never managed to do – worked for Saatchi & Saatchi. Arnold, the Manchester office MD, had given him a job and he spent several years there doing ads for Cold Shield windows and Moben Kitchens until the agency managed to lose both accounts in quick succession, and Andy was left wondering what to do next.

That was when he decided to open his own agency in Macclesfield with an account director colleague. And that was why he was ringing. Would I like to be their copywriter? He could email me layouts, which meant I could do it from home in the USA. It would only mean an ad every couple of weeks since most of their clients needed only design work, but that could change if they put on some new business.

When you've done nothing for years, there is no feeling that compares with being asked to do some gainful work. Even if it is just an ad for a prawn recipe that's going to appear in *Sandwich and Snack News*.

The headline I settled on was 'Mojito-style prawns. Preparation time – 5 to 6 years'. It had taken me only marginally less time than that to come up with it. The copy needed to stress the slow growing time that made them so tasty and I was confident I knew enough about the subject to write what was needed.

This was because the one useful thing I'd learned from my

Saatchi obsession was to place as much value on research as Charles did. And now, thanks to the internet, I didn't even have to go to the library any more. I spent literally hours online reading up about prawns ('a suborder of decapod crustaceans', according to Wikipedia) and now knew more about them than any man should ever know (biologists are in two minds as to whether prawns feel pain). When thousands of red prawns were washed up on a beach in southern Chile, I knew about it within minutes, thanks to Google Alerts.

And it hasn't just been decapod crustaceans I've written about. A major benefit to working for a small Macclesfield agency (as every adman knows, there's always a benefit if you look hard enough) was that my work was appearing in places it had never appeared before. *Caterer and Hotelkeeper* magazine carried my ad for Interface 'Flor' Flooring ('Try something new in the bedroom'), while the back page of the *RIBA Journal* was home to a Perspex Tables ad ('Perspex bring something different to the table'). Page nine of the *Bradford Telegraph and Argus* featured my ad for the Royal Armouries Museum ('In 1066 the Vikings invaded Yorkshire. Next week, they're back'), and my brochure selling sound-absorbing panels to offices ('Business has never been quieter') was distributed at the 100% Design Exhibition in London.

I made sure I got copies of every one of these sent over. And although Andy's agency hasn't actually done a TV advert in its short history, I make sure I keep up with the latest UK trends just in case. When friends send over DVDs, I always ask them not to cut out the ads, which are often the best part. For me, anyway.

On a recent DVD, one advert in particular caught my eye. It was for Covent Garden Soup, and opened with a group of chefs preparing soup in their kitchen. It was then that things took a familiar turn: they went outside to a giant catapult, launched the carton of soup into the air, and it landed in the outstretched hand of a Mrs Jones. I'd like to think a young copywriter somewhere saw the Great Northern Bitter ad while leafing through an old awards annual. I know that was how I got plenty of my ideas.

But there were other, more original ads, especially one from Matt Skolar at Saatchi & Saatchi. It opens in a classroom, where all the boys are dressed like Hank Marvin from The Shadows. We follow one of them home, where his mum gets a packet of Mattessons Fridge Raiders from the fridge and hands them to her heavily bespectacled, guitar-carrying son. As he starts eating them, the cockney voiceover says, 'Mattessons Fridge Raiders. For when you're Hank Marvin.' I'd waited my entire career for someone to use authentic rhyming slang in an ad. The wait was finally over. Perhaps he'd seen my Trust Motors leaflet – although strangely that had never appeared in an awards annual.

I always looked forward to getting a fresh batch of British ads, because the general standard of American ones has slipped a bit since *Mad Men* days. There are still some thirty-second bursts of brilliance, like the campaign for Dos Equis created by the Beer Men at Euro RSCG. In these ads we meet 'the most interesting man in the world' and discover that 'his business card simply says "I'll call you"', that 'he is fluent in all languages, including three that only he speaks', and 'if he were to punch you in the face, you would have to fight off the urge to thank him'. Each of the ads ends with him saying, 'I don't always drink beer, but when I do, I prefer Dos Equis.'

But for every 'most interesting man in the world', there are dozens of ads selling cures for ailments that sound as though they've been invented by copywriters. Low T Syndrome?

Smother yourself in Androgel. RLS or Restless Leg Syndrome? Ask your doctor about Requip. Erectile dysfunction? Pop a couple of Cialis pills.

It's medical products that seem to bring out the worst in American copywriters. One ad in particular, for Phillips Colon Health, has the distinction of being the worst I've seen since a certain WASS ad from 1979. It is set at a local council meeting. The chairman asks if there are any questions. This prompts a woman wearing a shirt bearing the words DON'T WORRY, BE REGULAR to stand up. She is holding a packet of Phillips Colon Health and shouts out, 'Anyone have occasional constipation, diarrhoea, gas, bloating?' One of the council members acknowledges that yes, he does. This is her cue to tell him, and the assembled crowd, that 'One Phillips Colon Health probiotic cap each day helps defend against these digestive issues, with three strains of good bacteria.'

'Approved!' says the woman running the meeting.

How this ad was ever approved is beyond me.

Whenever I think about advertising, which I do far too often, I think of the people and places that played a part in my story, and what became of them.

Fred, the man who gave me my first job in advertising and taught me how to keep my sentences short, went from Leeds to Frankfurt to London to Leeds (again) to Washington DC and finally to Málaga in Spain, where he now works as a freelance writer and takes really good photos, especially of dogs.

Jacko (aka Leszec Jakubowski) became Lee, because he got fed up with being the only person in Leeds in the 1980s with a Polish name. He now has his own marketing business and also designs book covers. I met up with him last year. He looked about thirty and must use Camay Soap (1960s advertising joke there).

Failure has had a highly successful life which has included designing fluffy toys, illustrating greeting cards, drawing cartoon strips which have appeared in the *Dandy* and the *Beano*, and co-producing a series of books that sell an envy-inducing number of copies. He recently celebrated his sixtieth birthday. The first things he got in the post the next day were an NHS bowel testing kit and a SAGA 'cruises for the mature traveller' brochure.

Saatchi & Saatchi (Wellington) didn't just become the best agency in New Zealand, they were also named as one of the top ten agencies in the world by *Campaign*.

Bevan's Press Play Design agency in Wellington sadly appears to have gone out of business.

Birrell left DDB Needham to go and work for Saatchi & Saatchi, but despite this we remained friends. His job took him around the world, including managing the global advertising account for Toyota and Lexus. He is now chairman of an IT company operating in Japan and Singapore, which I am a lot happier about.

The short, scruffy Peter Jackson went on to make some of the highest-grossing films of all time. He has, at the time of writing, won three Oscars – the film world equivalent of getting into *D&AD*.

Jeff Stark moved to Saatchi New York, before leaving to sail round the world with Mrs Stark as crew. They got as far as Tonga before getting bored and returning to London, where he directed TV ads for the next twenty years. He still directs but is easing into retirement and doing a bit of stand-up.

Jeremy Sinclair is chairman of M&C Saatchi, the world's fastest-growing independent agency.

Bruce from BDH went on to become executive creative director of the similar-sounding (but much more impressive)

BBH in London, taking over from the legendary Sir John Hegarty. He has made the pages of *D&AD* four times. As he predicted back in 1981, his son Peter Crouch grew up (and up and up and up) to play for England, scoring twenty-two goals in forty-two appearances to date.

Lee Tamahori, who directed the 007 lookalike in the Diamond Pasta advert, went on to direct a real James Bond film, *Die Another Day*, with Pierce Brosnan.

As for me, I'm better now. My health problems have just about gone, though I still take mineral and vitamin supplements.

My life in advertising has been more than I ever could have imagined when I started out on that cold morning in Leeds. I've seen the business go from hundreds of independent agencies with names like BDH, BBH and BHB to a handful of corporations called things like Publicis, Omnicom and Interpublic.

I've seen media options go from a TV ad, radio ad, press ad and trade ad to a list that includes social media, email blasts, product placement, mobile devices and digital TV, where you can buy a thirty-second spot for around £15. Very popular, I would imagine, with agencies needing to air fake adverts that they want to enter for some award or other.

I've sat in a studio with one of Herman's Hermits and recorded a rap song with a Kiwi cowboy. I've listened to a woman talking for hours about tailor's dummies and talked to a room full of students about Jeff Stark. I've heard a client describe the Honda Accord as 'the Rolls-Royce of cars' and fallen in love with an Indesit 101, the Rolls-Royce of automatic washing machines. I've destroyed ceilings in three different adverts and demolished 144 bars of chocolate in a week.

But nothing lasts for ever (except a DeBeers diamond ring, obviously) and, apart from a couple of prawn, Perspex or sound-absorbing panel ads every month, my advertising life is over. It's always been said (even by me once) that advertising is a young man's game, and I'm fifty-eight. It's time to finally give up on my dream and move on to the next adventure.

Unless Charles, Maurice or Jeremy happen to be reading this.

The End

About the Author

Dave Roberts has been one of those annoying bike couriers, a security guard, a civil servant, a KFC chef who was fired for trying to steal a sample of the secret recipe, and a train driver – all before reaching the age of twenty. After that, he settled for a career in advertising, which was eventually cut short by illness, but not before accidentally winning a Silver Lion at Cannes. He now writes books, which all seem to have a theme in common: obsession . . .

If you'd like to get in touch with Dave, write to him at dave@daverobertsbooks.com, follow him on Twitter @thebromleyboys or visit his website, www.daverobertsbooks.com. And once you've read this one, go to www.sadmen.co.uk as well.

Acknowledgements

Thanks to Giles Elliott, a terrific hands-on editor and occasional companion on the terraces at Hayes Lane; David Birrell, who sometimes seems like more of a co-writer than reader; Tom Bromley for all the expert advice as well as coming up with the title; Lisa Horton for yet another great cover design; Kate Hordern, my agent; Dan Balado – a seriously good copy editor; the great Jeff Stark for filling in a lot of the blanks; everyone at D&AD for their help; Ron Mather for sharing his memories; Steve Garthwaite for some excellent ideas; Mike Coulter for being a loyal pal; Fred Shively for giving me my first job in advertising (and not firing me); Pat Buza and the Nolis for giving me somewhere to write this book; and Liz for her support and for making me Sausage Surprise to celebrate finishing it.

32 Programmes

Dave Roberts

Shortlisted for the William Hill Sports Book of the Year

> 'Very funny in wry, Nick Hornby-esque fashion . . .
> This memoir will gain a lot of fans.'
> *INDEPENDENT ON SUNDAY*

When Dave Roberts and his wife move to the USA, he naturally assumes that his treasured collection of 1,134 football programmes will accompany him on the plane. Wrong. Dave is informed that space is at a premium and he will have to whittle his precious hoard down to what will fit in a Tupperware box.

As Dave relates the story behind each of the 31 (yes, 31) programmes he selects, they stir memories of times gone by, evoking bitter-sweet reminders of how far he's travelled. And Dave would never have predicted the chain of events that would lead to the final, 32nd programme and a homecoming that would bring a lump to the throat of even the most hardened midfield destroyer.

32 Programmes is a brilliant, funny, charming and heart-warming tale of an obsession. But it also a story about the passage of time and the true meaning of family, friends . . . and football.

> 'A brilliant idea nicely executed.'
> *INDEPENDENT*

> 'A book that every woman should study, for the unique insight it offers into the impenetrable enigma of the male mind.'
> *DAILY MAIL*